THE WHO'S WHO OF
BRITISH CRIME

THE WHO'S WHO OF
BRITISH CRIME

IN THE TWENTIETH CENTURY

Jim Morris

AMBERLEY

This edition published 2017

Amberley Publishing
The Hill, Stroud
Gloucestershire, GL5 4EP

www.amberley-books.com

Copyright © Jim Morris, 2015, 2017

The right of Jim Morris to be identified as
the Author of this work has been asserted in
accordance with the Copyrights, Designs and
Patents Act 1988.

ISBN 978 1 4456 7202 1 (paperback)
ISBN 978 1 4456 3935 2 (ebook)

British Library Cataloguing in Publication Data.
A catalogue record for this book is available
from the British Library.

Typesetting and Origination by Amberley
Publishing
Printed in the UK.

CONTENTS

Introduction		7
Who's Who?		9
A	Adams, Dr John Bodkin; Allitt, Beverly; Aram, Colette; Archer, Jeffrey; Armstrong, Katherine; Armstrong, Terence	9
B	Backhouse, Graham; Bamber, Jeremy; Bank of America, Mayfair; Barlow, Elizabeth; Beck, Adolf; Bible John Mystery; Bindon, John; Birkett, Norman; Bridgewater, Carl; Brighton Trunk Murders; Brown, Martin and Howe, Brian; Black, Edgar; Black, Robert; Blake, George; Brinkley, Richard; Brinks-Mat Robbery; Browne, Derek; Bryant, Frederick; Bulger, James	24
C	Cameo Cinema Murder; Camps, Francis; Cannan, John; Carruthers, Glenis; Chapman, David; Chester, Peter; Childs, John; Cochrane, Kelso; Confait, Maxwell; Cook, Peter; Cooper, John; Crimewatch; Crippen, Hawley; Cummins, Gordon	64
D	Dando, Jill; Delaney, Robert; Denning, Alfred; Dickman, John; Dix, Glyn; Dobkin, Rachel; Dryden, Albert; Dunblane	92
E	East Anglia; Edmund-Davies, Herbert; Ellis, Peter; Ellis, Ruth	107
F	Fabb, April; Fairley, Malcolm; Flannelfoot; Fletcher, Yvonne	117
G	Gadd, Paul; Goddard, Rayner; Goozee, Albert; Gray, Gilbert; Great Train Robbery; Gutteridge, George	124
H	Haigh, John; Hall, Anthony; Hall, Archibald; Hall, John; Hanratty, James; Harsent, Rose; Hart, Michael; Heath, Neville; Hewart, Gordon; Hill, Billy; Hogan, Terry; Hoskins, Percival; Hindley, Myra and Brady, Ian; Humphries, Christmas; Hungerford	137

I	Ireland, Colin	173
J	Jeffreys, Alec; Jenkins, Billie-Jo; Jones, Harold; Joyce, William	176
K	Kiszko, Stefan; Kray Twins	187
L	Lamplugh, Suzy; Lawrence, Stephen; Leeson, Nick; Lloyds Bank, Baker Street; Lockerbie; Lord, Alan; Lord Lucan	192
M	Manningham-Buller, Reginald; Manuel, Peter; Mark, Robert; Markov, Georgi; Mayes, Roderick; Miles, Sydney; Mnilk, Heidi; Moonlighting Mums; Morris, Raymond	210
N	Neilson, Donald; Nelson, James	231
O	Olive, Clive; O'Nione, Paddy; Operation Eagle; Operation Julie; Otterburn	236
P	Paisnel, Edward; Poulson, John; Prison Escape	245
R	Railway Rapists; Randall, Amanda; Regan, Florence; Reprieves; Reyn-Bardt, Malika; Richardson, Gerry; Richardson Gang; Rosenthal, Daniel; Ruxton, Buck	252
S	Saunders, Ernest; Saville, Derek; Seston, Jackie; Sheffield Pub Massacre; Shipman, Harold; Silverman, Sydney; Sims, Edwin; Spilsbury. Bernard; Spriggs, John; Stonehouse, John; Straffen, John; Sutcliffe, Peter	275
T	Thirkettle, George	294
W	Waddington, Yolande; Wallace, Julia; Ward, Stephen; West, Rosemary and Fred; White, Alice; Whybrow, Christopher; Williams, Ivy	297
Y	Young, Graham	309
Index		313

INTRODUCTION

Just over three weeks into the timeframe of this book the country was plunged into mourning at the death of Queen Victoria. By the end of the century, 31 December 1999, her great-great-granddaughter was our queen. There have been a few changes to the world in this time.

Two World Wars claimed a lot of lives. In the Great War, something like 16 million lives were lost, but in the Second World War the figure was anything from three to four times that total – some were killed by an enemy bullet, some died in bombing raids, some were swept away by water from a breached dam and some were washed away with falsified records. 'One death is a tragedy; one million is a statistic,' said one man – Joseph Stalin – who saw several million off in the general direction of the Pearly Gates.

But this book is not about mass-slaughter or war crimes. It's about the ordinary crimes, the ones the bloke round the corner or the lady one nods at politely in the supermarket are guilty of. Some are well known and some are not, but they are all tragic in their own right; it's only coincidence that the first two cases accuse a doctor and then a nurse of murder!

One would need a number of volumes to completely cover the

twentieth century, and as such, this book intends to discuss only a selection of them.

In the text I have headed each separate piece with a title: sometimes this is the name of the prominent character – the criminal, the lawyer or the victim – or what the case was known as. The index provides a more exhaustive guide to all cases and people mentioned in this book.

Who's Who?

Adams, Dr John Bodkin
Cleared of the murder of Edith Morrell
Not prosecuted for the murder of Gertrude Hullitt

In the spring of 1957, Dr John Bodkin Adams, an Eastbourne GP, was tried at the Old Bailey for the murder of a patient in November 1950. He was acquitted, but there were some odd elements to the case: the prosecution didn't pursue an alternative, stronger case, and nor did they do so following the acquittal of the first case. The Lord Chief Justice (Rayner Goddard) was seen in the company of two of Dr Adams' closest friends. Some nursing notes that the police didn't find at his surgery actually were there, and were the deciding factor in his acquittal. And a Fleet Street journalist who had the most amazing network of contacts pronounced Dr Adams innocent long before the jury.

John Bodkin Adams was born in 1899 in Randalstown, twenty-odd miles from Belfast. He went to Eastbourne to practice medicine after graduating from Belfast in 1921. He wasn't a brilliant doctor, but his patients thought he was kind and gentle and his practice grew with mainly elderly residents.

Private patients usually paid their GP on visiting, but Dr Adams said he paid too much tax so was keen to be remembered in the wills of his patients. This led to questions about his ethics, and gossip became rife; that gossip grew so loud that the police started an investigation. Initially there were two suspicious deaths of patients: Gertrude (Bobby) Hullett and Edith Morrell. Both left him gifts of considerable value in their wills; in fact, over a hundred of his patients left him something in their will.

So did he help his patients to the next life, or did he send them there? His trial for the murder of Mrs Edith Morrell at the Old Bailey was before Mr Justice Devlin. The main witnesses for the prosecution were nurses who'd looked after Mrs Morrell during her final illness.

These nurses were Nurse Stranoch, Sister Mason-Ellis and Nurse Randall. They lived in Eastbourne so travelled to and from the Old Bailey each day, discussing the case on the train. This came to the attention of the defence counsel, Mr Geoffrey Lawrence QC, at a point in the proceedings that proved to be a disaster for the prosecution: Nurse Stranoch had given her evidence, Sister Mason-Ellis was in the process of giving evidence and Nurse Randall was yet to give evidence. And it became clear that what they said to the police in the investigation was different to what they'd recorded contemporaneously.

The defence got hold of the notes the nurses had made on Mrs Morrell, which recorded the administration of drugs, doctors' visits, the patient's demeanour (alert, drowsy, confused, etc.), elimination and diet taken, among other things.

When the notebooks were produced the nurses said they were an accurate, factual account of the nursing. The notes were found in Dr Adams surgery and Mr Justice Devlin wondered why Dr Adams had kept them – but they chronicled the routine nursing and medical management of a dying patient, not a murder.

During the police investigation the nurses said Dr Adams often didn't tell them what drugs he gave and that he'd given so many injections it would have made Mrs Morrell drowsy, if not comatose, and unable to perform basic functions like eating.

Mr Lawrence for the defence asked Nurse Stranoch, 'You told me that everything of importance, including the doctor's visit … would have been put down by you, as a trained nurse, in your contemporary record made at the time, didn't you?'

She replied, 'Yes.'

Mr Lawrence continued, 'Now will you pay close attention to … your writing on 12 October: "7.30 p.m. Visited by Dr Adams. Hypodermic injection morphia gr. ¼, heroin gr. ⅓, omnopon gr. ⅓". Is it here in your writing?'

Nurse Stranoch: 'It is'.

Mr Lawrence: 'You have there recorded the exact nature and the exact quantities of the injection which was given to Mrs Morrell when the doctor visited, have you not?'

Nurse Stranoch: 'Yes, I have.'

Mr Lawrence: 'So it is quite clear that on that occasion at any rate you knew what the injection was, isn't it?'

Nurse Stranoch: 'Yes, it certainly is.'

On another occasion Nurse Stronach claimed that Mrs Morrell was 'almost semi-conscious … and rambling'.

But the contemporaneous entry, not what her memory told her, was, '6.45. Seems very bright this a.m. and not confused. Breakfast. Boiled egg, bread and butter, bramble jelly, 2 cups of tea. 11.00. Hot milk with soda water and brandy. 1.00. Lunch. Partridge, celery, pudding and brandy and soda …'

Mr Lawrence asked, 'Consumed by this semi-conscious woman?'

Nurse Stronach replied, 'I have nothing to say.'

Sister Mason-Ellis didn't fare any better, but Mr Lawrence had established that there was no evidence of high doses of medicines. He asked Sister Mason-Ellis, '… what you wrote and signed was everything of significance that happened … when you were there?'

Sister Mason-Ellis: 'Exactly.'

Mr Lawrence: 'You wouldn't have left anything out any more than you would have put anything that was wrong?'

Sister Mason-Ellis: 'No.'

Sister Mason-Ellis's recorded notes gave no evidence of excessive doses.

It was roughly here that the conversation between the three nurses on the train, which was overheard, was something Mr Lawrence wished the court to consider. The nurses discussed what they should and shouldn't say, and one nurse said, 'Don't say that or you'll get me in trouble.'

Mr Lawrence elicited the details, and it was enough to

demonstrate to the jury that the nurses' evidence was not only wrong, as the notebooks had shown, but also unreliable, as their evidence was rehearsed.

Medical evidence was called, too. Dr Arthur Douthwaite maintained the doses Dr Adams prescribed were intended to kill Mrs Morrell and Mr Lawrence tried to ascertain when this process commenced – Dr Douthwaite changed his mind, and therefore impressed neither the jury nor the judge.

Dr Michael Ashby was indecisive in his evidence, but did say that if Mrs Morrell was given what it was claimed she was given it would have led to her death.

So the question was: what was she given in the way of medication? The nurses' notes didn't suggest foul play.

But Dr Adams' own records were poor; there were legal requirements for the storage of drugs and he was heavily criticised by the British Medical Association.

Sir Reginald Mannigham-Buller was Attorney General and would prosecute in cases of poisoning. He was deflated by the note-books and sunk when Mr Lawrence decided against putting Dr Adams into the witness box. He'd be crushed by Sir Reginald – he was called Sir Reginald Bullying-Manner, and for good reason.

Professor Francis Camps, a pathologist at the Home Office, thought Dr Adams bumped off over a hundred elderly patients. Lord Devlin was later to say that he wouldn't be at all surprised if Dr Adams had assisted in 'Easing the Passing'.

Dr Adams died in 1984.

Allitt, Beverly

Attacked and murdered small, vulnerable children in hospital cots

Many illnesses have a path, and where along that path the illness is picked up may influence its outcome. Most of the time, folk take the initiative themselves and will take a couple of days off work and rest to let mother nature do her work; a trip to the GP may result in treatment, or perhaps only reassurance is needed. But sometimes a more intense medical and allied professional input is needed, and hospital is the place with the resources for a speedy recovery. Relatives may need reassurance, and these days they may even be part of the treatment plan. This is particularly important when children are ill, and mum and dad will need to be with them for longer periods. Even when the illness might be terminal, the doctors and nurses can support the family for the final few days.

When something out of the ordinary happens it's often been discussed beforehand and plans are in place: natural disasters, major transport incidents and even gunmen on the loose are a few examples. But there have been occasions when the whole situation is baffling and it might take a while for the realisation to come that something is seriously wrong. In 1991, staff at Grantham Hospital's special children's unit were witness to a series of unexplained and unexpected deaths.

The worse fear of all is that there is a killer on the staff. It started on 23 February. Liam Taylor, who was eight weeks old, had a chest infection. A purely routine job, but he died and it seemed to be an undiagnosed heart condition, which may have simply been what the press were told, because the experts would have picked this up. So what was happening?

Cerebral Palsy had been with Timothy Hardwick since birth: he was eleven, and he would have seen a lot of health professionals. He'd had a seizure, but two days later he suddenly had a heart attack and died.

Then another unexpected heart attack was diagnosed in Kayley Desmond, who was just past her first birthday. She'd come in, again with a chest infection, which again was a routine job with a rapid recovery expected. But suddenly there was a call for the crash team – these are in all hospitals and are called when there is a medical emergency. It was Nurse Allitt who called for them. Kayley survived.

In late March five-month-old Paul Crampton went down the same path, but when resuscitated went to another hospital, as did five-year-old Bradley Gibson.

It might be said that staff were baffled, but they would have known something very abnormal was happening. Paul Crampton's blood sugar levels had shown such a severe fluctuation that text books and experience were all confounded. Things seemed to improve, but then, just before he left hospital, he went down again – when it happened a third time he was sent to Nottingham Hospital, where his 'illness' progressed as expected and he recovered.

It was later discovered that large doses of insulin had been injected. This wasn't to treat an illness; it was likely to cause an illness – it could have caused a death. Two-year-old Yik Hung Chan, known as Henry, came into hospital after a fall and unexpected symptoms prompted his transfer to Nottingham, where his recovery, again, progressed as expected.

Becky Phillips was admitted and Nurse Allitt thought she looked ill, but another nurse didn't agree, so she checked her vitals – temperature, pulse, respirations and blood pressure – and all were in normal limits. General observation by the nurse reinforced her view. She was discharged, but that night had a seizure and died.

Katie was Becky's twin sister and when the parents brought her to the hospital they wanted Katie checked over. About ten minutes after Nurse Allitt had started to look after Katie she turned blue and collapsed. The crash team were summoned and, although she was resuscitated, her brain was deprived of oxygen for a long period so she suffered permanent brain damage.

Then the inexplicable incidents accelerated. Michael Davidson, a seven-year-old, suddenly had a heart attack. Nine-month-old

Christopher King had a stomach problem and eight-month-old Christopher Peasgood had a seizure. Seven-week-old Patrick Elstone was suddenly found unconscious – with an ear infection!

Claire Peck had an asthma attack and the staff thought her recovery would be straightforward, but her breathing stopped and her face turned blue. She died. It was discovered she'd been injected with the drug lignocaine which is a local anaesthetic.

Questions then became loud. Doctors and nurses expect that a certain number of patients will die, but not this many and not for such inexplicable reasons. The police were called in; senior managers and Detective Superintendent Stuart Clifton read all the reports and listened to the concerns of the staff. DSupt Clifton knew if there was evidence that one of the incidents was a criminal act, the rest probably were too.

Paul Crampton's post-mortem showed his body contained a huge amount of insulin; in fact, one report suggested it was the highest level on record.

DSupt Clifton and his team started to investigate the murders – that was the description given to account for some of the deaths. And they found the common denominator was Beverly Allitt. Some vital documentation had vanished, and after Ms Allitt's arrest the documents were found at her home.

She was charged with four murders and twenty-two incidents of attempted murder or grievous bodily harm, the worst tally of such crimes ever committed against children. At Nottingham Crown Court in 1993 she was convicted, but psychiatrists suggested she had Munchausen Syndrome by Proxy, a mental illness where caregivers injure those in their care to derive attention or other benefit. The term itself is misleading, and on both sides of the Atlantic other terms, such as Fabricated or Induced Illness by Carers, are used.

Ms Allitt was found guilty and is currently in Rampton Special Hospital. In 2007 it was publicised that her minimum tariff was thirty years, but she is also detained under the Mental Health Act. At any rate, the parole board will have to be satisfied she poses no danger to the public, though the real question may be how much of a danger the public will be to her.

Aram, Colette
Murdered by Paul Hutchinson

It must have made the police officer blink when he found that the DNA testing of a twenty-year-old involved in a road traffic accident matched a suspect in a twenty-four-year old murder. But this wasn't the only 'first' in this case.

The media were always keen to help the police but at times the police were a little reticent. That changed a bit in the 1960s; when *Police Five* with Shaw Taylor debuted in 1962 it had a moderate success for a programme that ran for five minutes, featuring Shaw presenting and the occasional picture. But television was developing and when high-tech features and reconstructions became possible, with the police realising the power of television, the BBC embarked on a series of programmes with the well-known catch-phrase, 'Don't have nightmares.' This was very serious stuff, and in June 1984 two frontline presenters, Nick Ross and Sue Cook, set the ball rolling. The very first case featured the abduction, rape and murder of a sixteen-year-old girl in Nottinghamshire the previous autumn.

Colette Aram was born in February 1967 and had grown up in Keyworth, Nottinghamshire. By the second half of 1983, Collette had left school and was training to be a hairdresser. She had a nice boyfriend, Russell, and after spending some time baking at home she kissed her mother goodbye and left for Russell's – his car was off the road. She didn't want to inconvenience her mum and reassured her that she would 'be fine' – it was a one and a half mile walk, which would take her twenty minutes or so.

That afternoon and evening a twenty-five-year-old man had watched a number of girls, looking for one to abduct. Colette met a group of friends on her way to Russell's – they were to be the last people to see her alive, apart from her murderer. Shortly after this a scream was heard and a car was seen driving at speed. By 10.30 p.m. the police were alerted and searches began. Although Colette was recovered at 9.00 a.m. the following morning, her family, the police and the rest of us had to wait twenty-six years for a conviction. Collette was raped before she was murdered and every last piece of dignity was robbed from her.

A murder investigation was launched at once, but it was difficult; although science had helped to accelerate police investigation success, it still relied on witnesses to kick-start it or give it that momentum. The killer was able to cover his tracks – interestingly, that phrase is only 'cover'. But the investigation was soon beginning to stall, and some police officers would lose a lot of sleep with the worry of another rape and murder.

The first episode of *Crimewatch*, which featured Colette's case was to prove how television was now a highly powerful tool.

The programme brought in several hundred fresh pieces of information, but the police could only use the information and the leads it gave them to whittle down the list of suspects. It has been said that the list of suspects in Colette's murder fell by fifteen hundred, so one shudders at the thought of how big their list was to start with. Cases like this are never closed and the more the police learn the more likely it is the investigation will succeed.

The killer taunted the police with at least one anonymous letter – 'You'll never catch me' was one of his taunts – but the paper he wrote on carried his DNA, and a fingerprint. The police were able to take the letter as a further clue and a help to catch the killer, but the effect on Colette's family took its toll.

The killer remained at large. When *Crimewatch* reached its

twentieth anniversary the murder was featured again. DNA technology was there but the police still needed a match.

Then, quite unrelated, there was a twenty-first birthday party arranged for June 2008 to which the twenty-year-old Jean-Paul Hutchinson was on his way to when an accident occurred – he was arrested for a traffic offence and had no problem providing a DNA swab, which had become routine in policing. His DNA was a near identical match to that left at the scene of Collette's murder and found on the taunting letter – his age would clear him of suspicion.

In April 2009 there was finally a charge for the murder of Colette. Paul Stewart Hutchinson was Jean-Paul's father, but he tried to blame his brother Gerhard, who'd died and was cremated, so no DNA would be available. Would it? When the police told him his brother's DNA wasn't a match, he confessed.

It came to court in December 2009, over twenty-five years after Colette's passing. He pleaded guilty and on 25 January 2010 Mr Justice Sweeney sentenced him to life imprisonment. He said, 'The terror and degradation that this poor girl must have suffered in her last few moments are unimaginable.'

When he wrote the taunting letter, he said, 'No-one knows what I look like … You will never get me.'

Detective Chief Superintendent Kevin Flint saw the close of the case and commented that it was unusual for someone to commit 'so grave a crime and then blend back into society'.

Professor David Canter, a criminal psychologist, doubted his clean record, suggesting for other attacks, 'He may simply have got away with them or been very lucky.' However, the police would have thoroughly investigated whether or not he was involved in other crimes, as far as they could, and put innocent families' minds at rest.

Just about nine months after his sentencing he was found unconscious in his cell in Nottingham Prison. He was taken to hospital but was dead on arrival. One suggestion was that he had taken an overdose of medication, which should be detectable, but the post-mortem was claimed to be inconclusive.

Archer, Baron Jeffrey of Weston-super-Mare
Perjury

Jeffrey Howard Archer has sold 250 million books worldwide and has been involved in charity work virtually since his teen years. He was a politician in the early 1970s for Louth in Lincolnshire, and in the mid 1980s was deputy chairman of the Conservative Party. He became a life peer in 1992.

An article in the Sunday newspaper *News of the World* suggested he'd paid a prostitute, Monica Coghlan, £2,000 'to go abroad'. This was done through a third party so it's uncertain as to why this money changed hands, but the *Daily Star* then decided he'd had some kind of paid for sexual liaison with Ms Coghlan. So the *Daily Star* was taken to court for libel because, his lawyers argued, it was an act of philanthropy and no more. The outcome was that the *Daily Star* paid him £500,000, which could well have been helped by Mr Justice Caulfield's remarks about him having a happy and successful life and happy marriage and so, 'Is he in need of cold, unloving, rubber-insulated sex in a seedy hotel ...?'

Lloyd Turner was sacked by the *Daily Star*. Journalist Adam Raphael found proof of perjury, but that's as far as things went at that time.

Together with his family, Baron Archer put the whole thing (sort of) behind him, but in 2000 his long-time friend blew the whistle. The friend faced charges of perverting the course of justice, as did Baron Archer. The friend had given him a false alibi on the night he was supposed to have met Ms Coghlan, though he thought it was another lady.

Sadly, Ms Coghlan had died in the meantime and during the trial Baron Archer's mother passed away too. The libel case was civil but this was criminal law, so in his summing-up Mr Justice Humphrey Potts gave it to the jury straight. He was convicted of perjury during the 1987 trial and given a prison sentence of four years.

However, the 1987 libel trial had resulted in the *Daily Star* paying damages of £500,000, so he had to repay that sum but was also faced with a legal bill from the time.

Armstrong, Katherine

Murdered by her husband, Herbert Rowse Armstrong

It was in February 1921 that the small market town of Hay-on-Wye in Breconshire (now Powys) made the headlines. For the first and only time in the United Kingdom, a solicitor was convicted of murder and hanged. The town itself has never had a population that couldn't be counted in the low thousands, and these days it is more notable for rare books.

Katherine Armstrong, or Kitty as she was known, had a history of ill health and was even admitted to a mental hospital for a while, when she was reported as delusional. Her symptoms on other occasions were more akin to a physical malady – vomiting and diarrhoea, with acute pain and loss of some sensation in her extremities (mainly in her hands). This might have been brought about by poison, but this was the last thing on any doctor's mind; a full-time nurse was brought in but still the mysterious illness couldn't be abated. Finally, Kitty died. It was no secret that her marriage wasn't made in heaven and that Major Armstrong (he had seen inaction on the south coast in the Great War) was fond of the ladies.

It was said that Mrs Armstrong was fond of ridicule and seemed to enjoy publicly embarrassing him, but she was a 'popular lady' in the town; however, few turned up for her funeral, and the 'heart-broken' widower was soon away on holiday for a few weeks! On his return he was on the lookout for a second wife and commenced his proposals shortly after.

But from elsewhere in the major's sphere of activity, a violently ill contemporary under the care of the same doctor had given urine and vomit samples. The samples contained arsenic.

Major Armstrong was eventually interviewed and charged with attempted murder, but investigations also focussed on Kitty. He was eventually charged with her murder, and an exhumation order was requested for Kitty's remains.

At his trial at Hereford Assizes, opened before Mr Justice Charles Darling on 3 April 1922, he was defended by Sir Henry Curtis Bennett KC, who had to try and convince the jury of his innocence despite several facts that didn't help. Major Armstrong had purchased arsenic, and at the post-mortem Kitty's body was said to contain a large amount; she'd ingested it shortly before her death. Dr Bernard Spilsbury had examined Kitty's body after she was exhumed and recorded the cause of death as arsenical poisoning.

Kitty had made a will in which she left everything to their children, though Major Armstrong produced a will after her death which said she left control of her estate to him – this was thought to be a forgery.

After a ten-day trial, the jury found him guilty. He was sentenced to death.

There was also now strong suspicion that Kitty wasn't his only victim. Oswald Martin, discussed above, was a local solicitor who'd had a dinner party where his brother's wife had become violently ill after eating chocolates. And Mr Martin himself went to tea with Major Armstrong and ate a scone – the major had actually handled it. Mr Martin became very ill.

Herbert Rowse Armstrong appealed to the Court of Appeal but

it was rejected. Hereford prison was closed so he was lodged at Gloucester prison, where he was hanged by John Ellis, assisted by Edward Taylor, on 31 May 1922.

Armstrong, Terence
Murdered by his father, John

John and Janet Armstrong had the worst tragedy one can imagine when their son Philip Stephen died in February 1954, but Janet soon fell pregnant again and, about a year after the tragedy, Terence was born. But when he too died, at only a few months old, suspicions were aroused.

At the post-mortem Dr Harold Miller recovered some red 'skins', which at first were thought to be from red berries, but closer analysis suggested they were the gelatine sleeves of the drug seconol, which is a barbiturate and used for sleeping. A police officer who called at the parents' house on the night of the tragedy found them sitting watching the television. When the officer was later asked if the parents were distressed at the events of the day, he said, 'Not in the least.' Bizarre seems an inadequate description.

Two exhumations and post-mortem examinations were made on both the little boys by Professor Keith Simpson, but the cause of Philip's death couldn't be ascertained. However, when the coroner's court was held, the parents were either unable or unwilling to answer questions about the two incidents.

John Armstrong worked in Hasler Hospital in Hampshire, which is for Naval personnel, and he'd taken some seconol tablets to help him sleep when he was on night duty. After the second death, he told his wife to get rid of them, which she did, but later she made a statement and told Police Inspector Gordon Gates of the dumping of the drugs.

They were jointly charged with Terence's murder and appeared at Winchester Assizes in November 1956. They both pleaded 'not guilty' to murder, and the prosecution, led by Sir Reginald Manningham-Buller, said, 'I shall call evidence to show that one of them must have put the fatal capsule in the baby's mouth.'

In his opening address, Sir Reginald claimed Dr Lewis Nichols of the Metropolitan Police Forensic Laboratory had said that Terence could have swallowed three to five of the capsules.

'I submit,' continued Sir Reginald, 'that they were in it together.'

It came out that Mr Armstrong had the opportunity to administer Terence the drug when he'd come home at lunchtime on the day his son died, but Mrs Armstrong had been home with the child too. In the witness box each said that if they hadn't done it then the spouse did, as nobody else had any access to the capsules. It came down to the timing of the administration, and Professor Simpson had given an erroneous opinion based on the old ingredients in the capsule's manufacture. When he could review his assessment and allow for the differing times with the newer capsule's sleeve, which was made of methylcellulose, it prompted the court to conclude that Mr Armstrong could have given the fatal dose as his wife was preparing his lunch, but it was a very close thing.

Mr Justice Pilcher, in his summing-up, told the jury that they could find guilt in both or one or the other or neither. He knew it would be difficult for the jury as there was no evidence of motive, and the police officer who'd attended the house on the night of Terence's death had found them watching the television!

The jury didn't think that both were in on it, and convicted Mr Armstrong of murder but acquitted Mrs Armstrong. On went the black cap as he reeled in the dock. He had to be helped by two warders. 'I am innocent,' he protested.

Rab Butler was Home Secretary and he commuted Mr Armstrong's death sentence to life in prison. He also arranged for the trial transcript to be available to MPs who were uncomfortable with the verdict.

Wormwood Scrubs was to be his new home as his MP Dr Donald Johnson launched a campaign to get Mr Armstrong's conviction reviewed. This was given more vigour when Mrs Armstrong actually admitted she gave Terence the fatal dose – even as far as going on television to declare her guilt. Terence had been in a bad way on the fateful day and she wondered if the drug would help him sleep. Rab Butler responded to Dr Johnson by letter, explaining that he had reviewed all of the new evidence given by Mrs Armstrong but that her husband's life sentence would stand.

This was a dilemma and makes the case worthy of further study. In law, an acquitted (until recently, and then only in certain circumstances) individual couldn't be retried for the same crime, so the law was stuck. Mr Armstrong couldn't have a retrial unless it was ordered, and Rab Butler was having nothing of it. The answer might be found in the fact that Mrs Armstrong was later interviewed by the police and made a statement; one wonders at the content of that statement. Whether the matter was referred back to the Director of Public Prosecutions or not is unclear.

The records at the National Archives probably won't tell us either – they are closed until at least 2032 and they will only take us up to the verdict. The papers of Rab Butler are archived at Oxford University Bodleian Library, but it is likely to be usual politicians' fodder when discussing a court's verdict: '... there seems no reason to interfere with the due course of the law.'

Backhouse, Graham

Attempted murder of Margaret Backhouse and murder of Colyn Bedale-Taylor

Creating a web of deceit and intrigue is a once-in-a-lifetime exercise for most murderers, but solving it and clearing it up is routine for the police aided by the experts. In April 1984, one man, who was evil, cunning and ruthless, tried to kill his wife with a car-bomb and then frame a neighbour, whom he later murdered too. His motive was money – he was nearly £70,000 in debt – and this former London hairstylist turned Cotswold farmer had insured his wife's life for £100,000.

Graham Backhouse had been married to Margaret for ten years and they had a young son and a daughter. The family lived in a small hamlet in the Cotswolds, where Mr Backhouse struggled to succeed as a farmer. He'd inherited the 390-acre farm a few years before and the previous three years had been dreadful for the business.

He came up with a plan to murder his wife and then frame a neighbour, and nearly succeeded. In the first instance, his plan was to create a nasty vendetta against himself, which involved the receipt of threatening letters. It started with him 'finding' a sheep's head on a stake with a note saying he'd be next. He claimed there were threatening phone calls. Eventually, his wife's car was on the blink, so Mr Backhouse suggested she take his.

When she turned the ignition the bomb planted under the driver's seat exploded, but miraculously – and thanks to Volvo's robust manufacture – the bomb didn't kill her. Off she went to Frenchay Hospital in Bristol for extensive surgery. The police who'd been active in investigating this 'hate campaign' stepped up their activity. On a neighbours garden they found some piping which matched the piping the 4,500 shotgun pellets had be put in with the detonator, and planted under the driver's seat.

The neighbour was at once under suspicion, but apart from the piping there was nothing else to link him with the crime. Mr Backhouse called him to the farm – Colyn Bedale-Taylor was a handyman and it was on this pretext he was called.

Later, when the police went to the farm following Mr Backhouse's phone call, they found a scene of carnage. Colyn had been blasted with both barrels of Mr Backhouse's shotgun, and lay dead – he had a carpenter's knife in his hand. Mr Backhouse had a long cut on his face. The story was Colyn attacked him and he ran to the front door where his shotgun was. Just in time, he managed to point the gun up at Colyn and discharge both barrels to defend himself from further attacks. It seemed convincing.

Then the experts started to look. They were unhappy about the size of the wound on Mr Backhouse's face as he would have needed to stand still for it to be inflicted in the way he described. The alleged attack by Colyn was followed by Mr Backhouse racing to escape but the blood had just dripped onto the floor – no sign of movement or 'tails' on the blood spatter so it didn't suggest the blood had come from one trying desperately to escape. On his route to the front door he hadn't spilt any blood, nor was there any blood on the shotgun which he'd just about managed to point up at Colyn after his vicious attack.

It then became clear his finances were a mess, and – as if by magic – two insurance policies emerged. A threatening letter that Mr Backhouse claimed he had received had some fibres on it from his own cardigan; when the sheep's head was left with the note 'you next', the police found a doodle on the paper which exactly matched a doodle imprinted on a pad in Mr Backhouse's study.

Those are the bare facts the jury were asked to consider.

But Mr Backhouse wasn't beaten yet. He boasted of a string of sexual relationships with local women and suggested a partner had found out and he was to suffer as a consequence. He even said he'd had a relationship with his best man's wife; after the bombing the police interviewed the man for three days before he established his innocence.

Before the jury retired to consider the case, the prosecution suggested he was a 'devious, dangerous, and determined man'.

The jury of eight men and four women were out for over five

hours, which is always a nerve-racking time for the police. But the experts were sure. They found him guilty by a 10–2 majority of trying to blow up his wife with a car bomb and murdering Colyn Dedale-Taylor in an elaborate cover-up plot.

Jailing him for life for both crimes, the sentences to run concurrently, Mr Justice Stuart-Smith told him, 'You are a devious and wicked man. The enormity of your crimes is very rare. Not content with trying to kill your wife, who according to your evidence loved you and had done you no wrong, you then set about cold-bloodedly to plot and kill your neighbour who had done you no harm and who you barely knew. In your defence you slandered his name and memory with an allegation that he was a homicidal maniac who had tried to kill your wife.'

The judge hedged away from making any recommendation as to length of sentence, preferring to leave it to the Home Secretary.

It was suggested that his wife, Margaret, had sat through the full seventeen days of the trial because at first she simply couldn't believe it to be true. After the verdict and sentence one of her relatives was quoted to have said, 'The news that he had other women hurt Margaret more than the realisation that he had tried to kill her.'

Detective Superintendent Tom Evans, who led the investigation defended his officers who were at first taken in by the story, saying, 'It was a very complicated case.'

It was the second blow for Colyn's family, as their nineteen-year-old son was killed in a car crash some while before events started to unfold – even this fact was used when Mr Backhouse suggested Colyn had blamed him for it. The guilty verdict cleared his name and his daughter Carey said, 'I'm glad it's finally over. It's been a long ordeal but I am pleased my father's name has been cleared.'

Just ten years into his double-life sentence Graham Backhouse suffered a heart attack and died.

Bamber, Jeremy Nevill

Father, mother, sister, two nephews murdered

Within a few days of what could be called the Whitehouse Farm Massacre the police revised their conclusion of what had happened.

This is a brief resume of the known facts. Mr Bamber and his sister Sheila had been adopted at a few weeks old and had had quite a pleasant up-bringing on a farm in Essex. Nevill and June Bamber had given them everything they could, but things didn't turn out too well for either child. Sheila had a developing modelling career but then was struck with mental health problems. Mr Bamber grew to dislike his adoptive parents and he started to think about what life could be like without the family. He'd inherit the estate worth an estimated £500,000 if they died.

He hatched a plan to kill them. Sheila had married, but by the late summer of 1985 was back at the farm with her parents, together with her six-year-old twin sons. The jury decided Mr Bamber, who lived nearby, had got into the house and shot the five of them – he knew of a way in and out which was away from the main doors – and had driven back to his home where he called the police. The police surrounded the farm and eventually armed officers got into the farmhouse and found the carnage. Mr Bamber said his father telephoned him to say his sister had gone 'berserk and had a gun'.

He was given a life sentence in October 1986. From that time on he has protested his innocence and that the original idea the police had, that Sheila was responsible, was the true version. But one of the main arguments was that Sheila couldn't have shot herself because she couldn't have reached the trigger if the gun was turned towards her, though there was a lot of conjecture as to whether a silencer was used or not. There is also some talk about the original positioning of various things around the house which differed from the police photographs. Controversy also exists of the original log of radio conversations between the police.

After his conviction, Mr Bamber appealed, but the Court of Appeal rejected it. The Home Secretary, Michael Howard, put him on a 'whole life tariff' but this was overturned. He could appeal to the parole board but they are unlikely to suggest his release; they are concerned with the guilty who admit their crimes and want to start afresh. With the gravity of what he was convicted for, it's doubtful he'd receive much from them anyway.

He'd appealed to the Criminal Cases Review Commission (CCRC) twice before he lodged a third appeal in 2012.

If the CCRC refer the case back to the Court of Appeal it's highly unlikely that even if they do quash the conviction he'll be a free man; if there are grounds, they'll almost certainly order a retrial. If that happens then apart from some of the old evidence, there is new and compelling evidence from ballistics experts about the gun and silencers which may or may not sway the jury. But as Bob Woffinden suggested, some evidence which was ruled inadmissible at the original trial would be admissible now – Nevill Bamber told the farm secretary that he feared what his son might be capable of doing and said he feared for his life. The original trial judge also told the jury that they could convict Mr Bamber on his ex-girlfriend Julie Mugford's evidence alone – Mr Bamber told her he intended to kill them.

There is another possible problem, and that's a jury. The case has received a lot of publicity, most of which has come from Mr Bamber. It is therefore possible that one or more of the jurors will have some idea before they are sworn in.

The Bank of America, Mayfair
London

One of the key aims of any crime, in the eyes of the robber, is to get away with it and enjoy what life will bring through the ill-gotten gains. This has led to terms like 'master-criminal' and 'professional thieves'; what this means is that plenty of planning has been put into the job. This was certainly the case when the Bank of America in Mayfair was turned over in April 1975.

Like many other jobs there was inside information – in this case it was a weak link who turned Queen's Evidence – but the gang had detailed information about the layout of the bank and how they could disarm the alarm system. Just as importantly, when they got into the bank they searched for any unforeseen problems – there were three employees still on the premises who were tied up.

Their haul was reportedly £8 million, of which only about £500,000 was ever recovered. Detective Chief Inspector John Peal was quoted to have said: 'This was certainly not a matter of luck. It was a well-planned professional job. They had really gone into the bank beforehand and cased it well.'

There were four raiders altogether and one was able to hide in the bank after it closed. When he thought the coast was clear and that all staff had left the bank, he knew exactly where to go to find the alarm, to put it out of service. They'd also discovered an underground passage through which they could get in and out of the bank – it led to a side door and set of gates – and this is where the other three gang members got in. As part of their intelligence, they knew that their inside man could hide himself in the ceiling above the vault door where he'd seen the combination tapped in by staff.

Only two hours later the robbery was over and they were on their way out through their underground passage, which was then discovered shortly after. However, only two of the men used a mask and at least one of their hostages were able to identify them.

The bank had about 600 safety deposit boxes, so started to notify the owners. Within a few months, and with the help of the inside informant, three of the robbers were jailed for over twenty years each. It was thought the gang leader had travelled to Morocco from where extradition wasn't possible.

Barlow, Elizabeth
Murdered by her husband, Kenneth

The term 'A Perfect Murder' is a contradiction: what this phrase generally means is that a murder is so clever that it can fool the police, the forensic scientists and the courts. An individual who has hatched the plot is up against people who have dedicated years to solving crime – and as students they learn how others before them solved crimes.

One case is that of Elizabeth Barlow. She'd been married to Kenneth for just under a year and was about two months pregnant. The couple had a son from his previous marriage – his first wife had died on 9 May 1956. Elizabeth died on 3 May 1957.

It was at about 2.00 a.m. on the morning of 4 May that Dr David Price, a Home Office Pathologist, went to the house in Bradford in Yorkshire where Elizabeth had died – she'd fallen either unconscious or asleep in the bath. Mr Barlow knew his wife was dead – he was what in those days was called a state registered nurse and he said he'd tried to resuscitate her when he discovered her at about 11.20 p.m. The family GP attended and pronounced Elizabeth dead. It was then that Dr Price received his summons.

The day hadn't been unusual and they'd had their tea at about 5.00 p.m. Elizabeth went to bed early but when Mr Barlow came up to bed at about 9.30 p.m. he noted she'd vomited, and she'd been sweating profusely. Eventually she went to the bathroom and ran a bath; Mr Barlow explained that he'd lain on the bed reading and fell asleep.

He said he awoke at about 11.20 p.m. and went into the bathroom where he found his wife under the water. He wasn't able to lift her out of the bath but allowed the water to drain. After he'd tried resuscitation he ran to his neighbours, who had a phone; the doctor was called, and arrived within a few minutes. The GP was quite baffled by the sudden death so notified the police, who called out Dr Price.

Dr Price wasn't happy; death from drowning in a bath at home was rare in a woman only in her early thirties and quite healthy. But when he heard Mr Barlow's story that he'd vigorously tried resuscitation, Dr Price wondered how a small amount of bath water remained in the crook of her arm. He also noted her pupils were dilated but couldn't think why.

The police had a good look around the house and found some hypodermic syringes in the kitchen, but there was no evidence drugs had been administered – that is to say, there were no empty vials around.

The post-mortem examination was carried out with the minimum of delay but the findings confirmed the story that Elizabeth had drowned. The central question for the forensic staff and Dr Price was *why*. Acting on a hunch, Dr Price took blood samples from various parts of her body as well as urine, considering poisoning. Dr Price was able to link up with Dr Alan Curry, who was the leading forensic toxicologist of his generation, but he could find nothing in the samples to support Dr Price's feelings. The police, however, were also uncomfortable about the case.

The dilated pupils also played on his mind – it would be expected but not to the extent he'd found. There was also the vomiting and the police found sweat-soaked pyjamas. This pointed, if she was unconscious when she drowned, to insulin. Dr Price re-examined the body and had the use of a magnifying glass and brighter lights: on each of Elizabeth's buttocks were two tiny needle marks. He took samples of tissue from the two sites and stored them in a refrigerator. The expertise in those days was waiting to be gained and Dr Price racked his brain to think of how he could find a scientist and a laboratory to test the samples. He wanted the samples tested for insulin.

There were a few places he could try, and Boots Chemist laboratories, one of the small number of insulin manufacturers in the country in those days, agreed to help. They found small traces of insulin in the samples Dr Price had sent; he'd also sent specimens from other tissues of other corpses which showed no evidence of insulin. The insulin, therefore, was the big clue and was highly suspicious: Elizabeth wasn't a diabetic and had never been prescribed insulin. And it's difficult to self-inject in the buttocks.

It was time for the police to act. Mr Barlow said he'd injected Elizabeth, but not with insulin; he'd injected her with a drug called ergometrine, a drug given to deliver the placenta and other mechanics after childbirth, but it was also given illegally in those days to induce abortions. However, Dr Curry had already investigated this and concluded ergometrine hadn't been injected. It was also not evident on the hypodermic needles found in the house. Kenneth Barlow was arrested and charged with murder.

He vehemently denied the charge. At his trial at Leeds Assizes in December 1957 he was unable to explain how insulin was found in Elizabeth's tissue samples – he suggested she'd administered the drug herself. He was then asked where the empty vials were. This, together with the lack of plausibility that Elizabeth had injected herself didn't go down well with the jury.

He almost got away with it. The amount of insulin found on the tissues at Boots Labs was considerable, enough to keep two insulin-dependent diabetic patients going for a day. Elizabeth had vomited and sweated excessively – both signs of an insulin overdose – but as she wasn't prescribed the drug it wasn't going to be the most obvious conclusion. If Elizabeth hadn't had a bath and drowned then her body would have metabolised the insulin and there would have been no trace at all.

As a charge nurse he did have a good knowledge-base for

insulin, and he had discussed with two of his colleagues previously, albeit years before, about murder with insulin.

It was the hunch of Dr Price and his and others' dedication and hard work that cracked the case – a fact that Mr Justice Diplock wanted to emphasise as he jailed Mr Barlow for life. The crime was a 'cold, cruel, carefully premeditated murder which, but for a high degree of detective ability, would not have been found out'.

The motive can only be guessed at, and wasn't an issue in the trial.

He was released from prison twenty-six years later, in 1984, still maintaining his innocence.

Other nurses have been convicted of using insulin to kill, such as Jessie McTavish in Glasgow in the 1970s – her conviction was quashed on appeal. Colin Norris was convicted in the new millennium, as was Benjamin Geen; both are controversial, with big questions over the convictions. Things have moved on from Dr Price's time. A nurse in the Netherlands was also exonerated on appeal, so we'll have to watch this space.

Beck, Adolf
Identification evidence and the problems it can engender

Adolph Beck originally hailed from Norway and was aged twenty-four when he came to England – he'd trained as a chemist but didn't pursue a career in that area. Rather, he became a shipping clerk and at one time was a professional singer. He'd left England as he liked the idea of making his fortune in South America – he left in 1868 and returned with some considerable wealth in 1885. He settled back in England and bought a mine in Norway, but this swallowed up most of his money and even where he lived, in a Covent Garden hotel, he couldn't pay his bills.

It came to light in 1895 that one Mme Meissonier had fallen for a con trick and had lost her jewellery. She'd been stopped on the street and asked if she was a Lady Everton. She replied that she wasn't but found the gentleman quite engaging and he introduced himself as Lord Willoughby. After a little more preamble over afternoon tea at her home he invited her to visit the French Riviera on his yacht. She was taken with Lord Willoughby and he gave her the gift of a cheque for £40 to purchase a suitable wardrobe. He also advised her he should meantime buy her a few bits of jewellery, so took rings and a watch to match the size.

The cheque was worthless and he never returned with her jewellery. As luck would have it she saw Adolph in Victoria Street and claimed to know him. He scarpered, but was caught by a police officer.

The publicity of this brought a number of ladies forward, all with similar tales, and Mr Beck was charged with a number of offences. But was it Mr Beck? He pleaded not guilty, but one police officer recognised him from 1877, when he was convicted at the Old Bailey, in the name of John Smith, of stealing a lady's earrings. Mme Meissonier was certain Mr Beck was the man who'd come to her house for tea and had taken her jewellery. A considerable number of Lord Willoughby's other lady victims identified Adolph Beck as the culprit.

On 5 March 1896 he was found guilty and sentenced to seven years. He denied the charge and also denied any knowledge of John Smith, but he was given Mr Smith's old prison number with a 'W' added to signify it wasn't his first conviction. He was released after five years, but Thomas Dutton, his solicitor, hadn't been idle. On numerous occasions the lawyer asked for the case to be re-examined, and Mr Dutton also discovered John Smith was really one Wilhelm Mayer, who was almost a twin of Adolf – when first seen one might think it was him, with a few more years and a little more weight. And, of course, Adolph had been in South America when John Smith had served the earlier prison sentence.

In June 1904, Adolf was at the Old Bailey again on a similar charge. Five women identified him and the jury convicted, but Sir William Grantham deferred sentence as he had his doubts. And then, while Adolf was on remand – which gave him a pretty reliable alibi – Wilhelm Mayer/John Smith struck again, and in September 1904 he pleaded guilty. Adolf Beck was released with a free pardon and given compensation (equivalent today of about £320,000). A committee was set up to look into the case to see how these two miscarriages had come about. This case established that eye-witness evidence wasn't reliable. The case was highly influential inasmuch as England didn't have any formal way of appeal; the Criminal Appeal Act of 1907 was passed into statute and the Court of Criminal Appeal was created.

As for Adolf Beck, it had all taken its toll and he passed away in hospital with pleurisy and bronchitis on 7 December 1909.

The Bible John Mystery

The Barrowland Ballroom, often called Barrowlands, is also a concert venue that opened in Glasgow in 1934. It became infamous in the late 1960s when three girls – one in 1968 and two in 1969 – attended a dance there and were found shortly after, murdered. The name associated with the killings is Bible John. It has led to much speculation and there is a major suspect, but it would be as well if I described the three crimes first.

On the evening of Thursday 22 February 1968, Pat Docker was going out for the evening. She told her parents she was going to a local dance hall, which in the event she did attend, but later went on to Barrowlands. Pat, who was twenty-five, was found naked and dead only a short distance from her home on the following morning: she'd been raped and strangled.

The police concentrated the early part of the investigation on the local venue, which didn't help the investigation. Her handbag and clothes were never found, and neither, sadly, was her killer.

It wasn't until 15 August 1969 that he struck again. Thirty-two-year-old Jemima McDonald had gone the Barrowland Ballroom on the Thursday evening. Over the weekend local children were talking about a body in a disused tenement block, and Jemima's sister heard about it and went to investigate. She hadn't been seen since she left her three children to go out on the previous Thursday night. She found Jemima, who'd again been raped and strangled; although she'd been left fully clothed, her handbag was missing.

This time, though, the police felt more confident of a successful outcome because Jemima had been seen leaving Barrowlands at about midnight with a man. He was described as tall and slim with red hair. The police undertook door-to-door enquiries but little materialised except one lady who'd heard a scream but couldn't be sure of the time. The investigation petered out.

It was only two months before he struck again, and this time even more information was gleaned in the investigation, following the murder of Helen Puttock, who was again raped and strangled.

Helen was found on Friday 31 October 1969: she'd been to the Barrowland Ballroom the previous evening with her sister, Jean. They both met and got chatty with two men named John, one of whom wasn't quite so chatty and didn't say which part of Glasgow he was from. It was with this John that Helen and Jean had left Barrowlands and shared a taxi. Jean lived over on the western part of the city and was dropped off first. Helen was found in the back garden of the block of flats where she lived; as with Pat Docker and Jemima McDonald, she'd been raped and strangled. Again, the handbag was missing but the contents had been emptied out. Helen had a vicious bite mark on her leg.

Jean could tell detectives that he was quite a well-spoken man who'd quoted from the Bible – this led to the press calling him

Bible John. He was tall and slim, well-dressed, with reddish or fair hair, aged mid to late twenties and about 5' 10" in height.

However, other witnesses said he was short with jet-black hair, but as this came from the doormen at Barrowlands they may have mistaken her companion with someone else close. On the other hand, Jean told the police she was drunk.

The police had no doubts that the victims were all murdered by the same man. Barrowlands was the common factor, their handbags were missing and they were all raped and strangled and all found close to their homes. They were also menstruating and their sanitary wear was close by.

A new venture for the police was to create a 'photofit', and later his hair was coloured reddish. About a thousand suspects names were put forward and all eliminated.

No further victims were associated with Bible John but the police didn't make any arrests, despite one of Scotland's biggest investigations, with over a hundred detectives and nearly 50,000 statements taken. Part of the investigation was police officers attending Barrowlands, particularly on Thursday evenings.

The story remained newsworthy down the years, and people came forward to say they knew the suspect, had been to school with him and so on. None gave the police any solid leads.

One of the original suspects had a cousin who committed suicide and his body was exhumed for DNA tests. Semen had been found on some of the girls' clothing, but the tests were inconclusive. However, in the new millennium an 80 per cent match was found at a crime site, which might show the killer's family, but that's about all.

There has been some speculation that jailed serial killer Peter Tobin was Bible John. But as the police have his DNA and a semen sample from one of the girls' clothes then charges would surely have been brought. So far they haven't, so all that can be done is to wait and see.

Bindon, John
TV Hardman accused of murder

It has been said that actor John Bindon – known to play violent villains and uncompromising policemen on television – was heavily involved in the London underworld and ran protection rackets, but just where the truth lies we'll never know. However, there was a huge brawl in the Ranalagh Yacht Club in Fulham in late 1978, where it was alleged two gangs clashed, and right in the middle of it was John. It was to lead to his decline as an actor – he'd been declared bankrupt two years or so before.

He grew up in Fulham and twice went to borstal as a teenager, but was invited to consider a role in a film; this could well have saved his later difficulties, but didn't.

However, it was at the Ranalagh Club where he hit the headlines. Mr Roy Dennis was later to say John had pulled a man away from him as he was being stabbed – the cause of the affray was unknown, but it led to another stabbing, of which Mr John Darke, who'd been Mr Dennis' assailant, died of stab wounds.

John Bindon was injured in the brawl and fled the club. He was bleeding badly due to stab wounds, but flew to Dublin and was later treated at St Vincent's Hospital. When the police tracked him down there he was put under An Garda Síochána guard, as reprisals from London were feared. One of the two gangs who were feuding in the background were said to have paid John £10,000 to kill Mr Darke. When he'd recovered sufficiently he was flown back to London and would stand trial for Mr Darke's murder. Mr Darke was also well known in criminal circles.

When the trial opened at the Old Bailey in October 1979 it was suggested that Mr Darke was an underworld 'grass' – a police informant – and his recent activities had led to two men being arrested for armed robbery. He was also said to be a blackmailer and had a 'string of convictions': John was hired as a hitman. He denied murder and affray and said the injuries Mr Darke sustained had been made in self-defence.

Detective Sergeant John Ross, of Scotland Yard's Flying Squad, gave evidence to say Mr Darke had recently been paid a sum for information that led to the arrest of armed robbers. He could also tell the court that Mr Darke's other convictions had been for armed robbery and unlawful wounding.

A Mr William Murphy, who'd known John when the two men were in Brixton Prison on remand, said John had admitted the murder of Mr Darke. But the jury acquitted him of Mr Darke's murder – though they were out for thirty hours considering their verdict.

John Bindon's career went into decline and he became almost a recluse. He died in October 1993.

Birkett, Baron Norman KC

(William) Norman Birkett was born in 1883 and was a barrister, judge, politician and preacher. He was also involved in the Nuremburg Trials.

His father was a draper and he joined the business before going to Cambridge in 1907, where he read theology, history and law. He was called to the bar in 1913 and took silk just over ten years later. He couldn't serve in the Great War as he'd had tuberculosis. He was an MP for Nottingham East in the 1920s.

He was a Methodist preacher for most of his life. He worked for a while as George Cadbury's secretary and met Ruth 'Billy' Nilsson, whom he later married – they had a daughter, Linnea, and a son, Michael.

Because of his affiliation to the Cadbury family he moved to Birmingham, where he found work in the chambers of John Hurst. He became a first-class defence brief, and a local magistrate suggested a move to London, which he was initially nervous of. However, he went, and was junior to Attorney General Gordon Hewart in the 'Green Bicycle Case'. Edward Marshall Hall, defending in that case, was very impressed and so Norman was offered a place in his chambers, where the clerk found a way of promoting his status to instructing solicitors.

At the end of the Second World War, there was a trial of war criminals, and in August 1945 he was asked to serve as the British judge at the Nuremberg Trials of German War Criminals.

He plodded through his life on the bench, but had found work as a barrister far more challenging. He had a reputation as a great speaker since his Cambridge days, and the BBC even invited him to give radio broadcasts on some of his more distinguished colleagues; not surprisingly, Edward Marshall Hall topped a distinguished list.

He went to the House of Lords in 1958 as a Lord of Appeal in Ordinary and was present for his final speech in early February 1962, where he defended the environment; Manchester City Council had wanted to drain a dam, but they were defeated. However, he wasn't well, and the following morning he complained of heart symptoms – in the early afternoon he collapsed. In hospital he was operated on for a rupture in a major blood vessel but passed away on 10 February 1962.

Bridgewater, Carl
An unsolved murder

Carl was murdered in September 1978. It was a senseless killing and various theories have been put forward to suggest why it happened. Carl was thirteen and on his evening paper round. He was about three miles north-east of Stourbridge, at Yew Tree Farm – the door was open. Suddenly, he was grabbed and bundled into the sitting room and on to the sofa, where he was shot in the head at point blank range. His death was instantaneous.

He'd been busy that afternoon, and had a dentist's appointment, so in break time at school he cycled round to the newsagents and said he might be late. In the event he only had a check up and was soon on his way, commencing his delivery at about 4 p.m. His round was along Lawnswood Drive and by the time he got to the farm, he only had two more stops to make.

Mary Poole was one of the occupants and her consultant from hospital decided to call in on her on his way home. He discovered the break-in, took the bull by the horns and ventured inside. The scene was one of carnage; he went to his own home to phone as he didn't want to touch anything.

Carl was rarely late home, so when he didn't show up his parents knew something was wrong. The family lived just off the Lawnswood Road, he had a brother and a sister: his mother and father described Carl as a 'happy and caring' soul. He was a member of the boy scouts.

The murder of Carl Bridgewater is officially unsolved, but a lot has happened since that fateful afternoon.

Detective Superintendent Bob Stewart led the hunt with a team of fifty detectives – one theory was that Carl was silenced because he recognised someone, but that petered out. But police method sometimes takes a while where the murder motive isn't obvious. In November 1978 a small-time crook called Vincent Hickey from nearby Birmingham had been talking to police – he was helping them with their enquiries about another robbery at a farm which involved four men and was only about half an hour's drive away. He'd been the getaway driver. He had a cousin, Michael, who'd been on an armed robbery at a Tesco store with Jim Robinson. But it was Patrick Molloy who was arrested first. All four men were subsequently convicted; Pat Molloy was convicted of manslaughter and given twelve years, and the others were convicted of murder and given life sentences. They protested their innocence from the start but Pat Molloy – who died in prison – had made a 'confession'. Pat always claimed that he was conned into making his confession by being shown a confession by Vincent. But the police said no such statement existed.

This confession was the focus for the conviction, but wasn't quite what it seemed. It was later subjected to a special forensic examination called Electrostatic Document Analysis (Esda) in 1990.

In 1978 the forensic staff said the confession documents were sound, with none of the tampering that had been suggested. However, when the Esda test was made it showed that one particular pad had Vincent Hickey's signature on it and the same pad provided the paper used on Pat Molloy's confession. Vincent Hickey's document was quite separate, so when an impression of his details and a signature was found on the Pat Molloy pad it led to some very uncomfortable questions. Molloy and Mr Vincent Hickey were held and questioned in different police stations.

It was unlucky in that the imprint had been covered by a label when produced as an exhibit in court, but lucky in that this label seemed to protect the imprint and it hadn't worn away with the years of handling.

When Vincent's solicitor, Jim Nichol, had his 'statement' examined, his suspicions were raised and confirmed: Vincent Hickey's statement had been forged. The officers who'd been at the core of the interviews, Detective Constable Graham Leeke and Detective Constable John Perkins, were heavily criticised. In fact, the Court of Appeal quashed the convictions; the trial hadn't been fair, as Pat Molloy's confession also was improperly obtained.

This was a second criticism of DC Perkins who also falsified evidence in a 1989 trial. He has subsequently died.

Vincent Hickey and his cousin Michael and Jim Robinson were all granted compensation but, in a cruel move, the Home Office deducted for their board and lodgings while they had been inside – this set a precedent. One has wonder how much money was saved by not prosecuting the police officers.

The Brighton Trunk Murders

On 10 May 1927, staff at Charing Cross station in London reported a stench in the left luggage office. They found the dismembered body of a woman.

Sir Bernard Spilsbury conducted a post-mortem. Her limbs had been cut off and the parts were wrapped in brown paper and tied up with string. Her shoes and handbag were also in the trunk. She'd died about three weeks before.

Seven years later, in June 1934, the overall temperature in England ranged from 29° to just under 8°, so flesh wouldn't decompose any quicker, but a peculiar stench was noticed at the left luggage office at Brighton station on 17 June. As it was in a locked trunk the Railway Police were called. When they opened the trunk they found a number of layers of paper and cotton wool, all of which seemed to have blood stains on, and they found a parcel that looked as though it had been tied with rope similar to sash cord. Inside was a human torso with rope holding the arms in place.

The chief constable put a call through to Scotland Yard straight away. Detective Chief Inspector Robert Donaldson was sent down and traced Mr Henry Rout, who'd taken the trunk in, but he couldn't remember anything about who left it.

The following day another trunk was discovered, this time at Kings Cross Station in London – it contained two limbs. So the question was: were these two later cases connected to the first? It was never made clear.

On 19 June, Sir Bernard Spilsbury performed a post-mortem on the 'Brighton body' and put the victim's age at about twenty-five; she was pregnant and had been struck on the head with a blunt instrument. There was very little to go on, apart from a piece of paper with writing on it.

The police looked at the cases of 700 missing women and they checked hospitals and known abortionists. This was the first case where the police appealed directly to the public through the press.

A journalist contacted the police and told them that a prostitute had disappeared in Brighton, a Ms Violet Kaye. However, she was forty-two years old. She lived with a man considerably younger than her, twenty-six-year-old Tony Mancini, who had convictions for theft.

In September 1933, Violet Kaye had moved from London to Brighton and had been in a relationship with Mr Mancini. Her real name was Violet Saunders, and she had been a dancer touring the country in revue shows. She had since turned to prostitution and was a heavy drinker and prone to irrational outbursts. She'd accused Mr Mancini of groping one of the waitresses in the café where he worked, a huge row erupted, and a few days later he told a work colleague that Violet had gone to Paris.

DCI Donaldson decided to interview Mr Mancini and it transpired his real name was Cecil Lois England, but he had to let him go. On the off-chance, DCI Donaldson thought the police might have a look at the flat Mr Mancini and Ms Kaye had shared in Kemp Street.

And there was another trunk. Neighbours had complained of a foul smell – inside the trunk was the body of Violet Kaye. Mr Mancini was now nowhere to be seen. Eventually, however, he was found in south-east London and arrested by two police officers from the Metropolitan Police, ostensibly for vagrancy.

Tony Mancini was charged with murder and appeared at Lewes Assizes, where Norman Birkett KC led for his defence. He pleaded not guilty, claiming a client must have done the killing. Dr Bernard

Spilsbury was called by the prosecution but Mr Birkett managed to convince the jury that his client had found her dead, and as he had a criminal record feared he wouldn't be believed. He panicked and put her in the trunk. It couldn't be proved otherwise and he was acquitted.

Years later a Sunday newspaper carried a story where he admitted killing Ms Kaye.

As for the body in the trunks at Kings Cross and Brighton railway stations (known as Brighton Trunk Crime – Number 1), the case was never solved, and there was no evidence linking Mr Mancini to either crime.

Brown, Martin and Howe, Brian
Killed by Mary Flora Bell – convicted of manslaughter

There were some areas in England where post-war austerity never really did get a good parole hearing, and some people in areas within cities suffered more than their fair share of social problems. Newcastle-on-Tyne stands high among the North-Eastern industrial conurbations, and fortunes were made – but not by many, and certainly none on the Scotswood council estate.

In 1999 the place was bulldozed; extravagant plans for a replacement were put up, but it was partly crushed by the credit crunch, so had no residents for a while. A joint enterprise is now putting things to rights.

What will never be put to rights is the fate of two little boys and, for that matter, two little girls from the estate. Martin Brown and Brian Howe were both three-year-old-boys who met tragic ends – both were strangled. The two girls weren't related but were both Miss Bell, Norma and Mary. Mary Flora Bell was convicted of the manslaughter of the two boys in 1968, and once had the gall to ask of Martin and Brian's parents, 'Where were they when their children were getting murdered?' which, not surprisingly, caused outrage. What also caused outrage at the very top was the payment of a huge sum of money to collaborate in the telling of her life story.

There is no question that Mary had a poor start to life; she experienced not just the poverty and hopelessness but she was also a victim of sexual abuse and her mother would bring men to the house for masochistic sex, as she was a sex worker. Nevertheless, other children have been brought up in the same social jungle who didn't kill, so one has to ask if there is any clue as to why she did what she did. Mary, of course, blames Norma Bell, not directly perhaps. The boys were taken away from where they'd been playing and strangled.

One of her teachers from school said Mary was pure evil. But is there such a force of evil like there is good? Is there a devil that will drive people? It seems that from people like me, writers, commentators, historians if you will, there is still almost universal condemnation of Mary. But she is an excellent example of the rehabilitation of offenders. She served twelve years and left prison in 1980. A vibrant young lady, she soon had a steady relationship and a daughter in 1984; she is now a grandmother. As far as I can tell, she hasn't broken the law since.

But it's the loss to the mothers of the children one can still relate to so easily – the mums and the dads and the grandparents. One can't say the hurt came back to haunt them the day the press went to town on the story that Mary was to get the huge sum from the book industry; it never came back to haunt them at all, because the hurt never went away. Apparently, Mary wanted the story told to try and help prevent any similar cases in the future.

By the late 1990s, she'd been working as a nursing assistant at an old people's home, and she said of her youth on the Scotswood estate, 'Everyone who lived up there at that time was partially responsible.'

It was said by a boyfriend that she was haunted by her crimes, that they play on her mind; she writes poems and essays about what she did. There is no doubt that, since her release in 1980, she's lived an itinerant life and has successfully hidden her true identity by using an assumed name.

Her boyfriend went on to explain that he didn't think she was responsible for her actions because she was so young; only a child. He said it was her childhood that turned her into a killer – one has to hope, then, that she's unique and others in her wake won't suffer the same.

It was said in court that she wanted to 'hurt' somebody, and, if her mother's clients were beating her mother, then to 'hurt' someone smaller than her and really quite helpless may have been a way to direct her anger. But there is a lot of assumption in this. When the child sex abuse scandals started to come out in the 1980s, most people held their breath, but with each passing year there is almost an escalation in what comes out from the abuse victims – that is to say, the severity of the abuse they suffered – to the point where a prominent UK politician had a prominent UK entertainer bring him teenaged boys he could rape and dispose of. So have we any idea of what Mary went through? Before anyone shouts, which they will, about other abuse victims (survivors), then one has to say that there are degrees. A twenty-year-old touching the breast of a fifteen-year-old girl is no more acceptable than a fifty-year-old throttling a thirteen-year-old so her death corresponds with his orgasm, but one can plot the degree of seriousness.

Her mother, it's claimed, used her as a sex toy for the gratification of her clients, and her legs are still twisted from the implements her mother used on her. Let's take this as truth for a minute. What did Mary do? Did she try and get away? Apparently she did, but social services and the police returned her to her mother's house. They might have been aware of what was happening, but it might have sounded too bad to be true. Her boyfriend argued that ten-year-olds don't normally murder people. So she may have had every right to be angry, but what she did with the anger we can only theorise.

What actually happened to Mary is something we might be better off not knowing. We know what she did – that's enough.

June Richardson was Martin Brown's mum and she kept the secret from her grandchildren for a long time before telling them about their uncle Martin's death. But Mrs Richardson did say about the tragedy, referring to Mary Bell, 'It's all about her and how she has to be protected. As victims we are not given the same rights as killers.'

There are no right and wrong answers, just a dreadful side to the swinging sixties.

Black, Edgar
The murder of Richard Cook and the last death sentence in Wales

The two friends fell out when Mr Black heard that his wife was having an affair with Mr Cook. Both were married and lived in Stockton-on-Tees. Richard Cook moved himself and his family to Cardiff, and Edgar Black took his family on holiday to Scotland. But whatever he did, he just couldn't move on with his life. Mr Black told police, 'I decided I must see him, and if necessary retaliate for the harm he had done to my family.'

The two men 'exchanged a few words' before Mr Black pulled the trigger of a shotgun he had. Mr Cook was killed instantly.

Mr Black later told the police how he felt. 'You know all about it. It is the eternal triangle, I aimed at his chest. I did not mean to kill him.'

But whether he meant to or not, he was charged with murder; because he had used a gun, the charge was capital murder.

Mr William Mars-Jones, QC, told the full story when it came to court in late 1963, saying that his client 'was obviously oppressed and tortured by the discoveries he made, the bottom dropped out of his world – and it was due to the action of one man.'

Mr Roderic Bowen, QC prosecuting, said that Mr Cook was shot on the doorstep of his home in Cardiff. Edgar Black was found guilty and sentenced to death.

The MP Sydney Silverman was quick to point out that the only reason Mr Black had been sentenced to death was because he'd used a gun; it wasn't as though he'd manipulated himself back into Mr Cook's friendship and then poisoned his beer, or waited in darkness and stabbed him in the back. It demonstrated what a farce the Homicide Act of 1957 was in practice.

Mr Cook's widow was quoted to have said, 'I am trying to put the unhappy past behind me. Hanging this man is only going to rake up all the misery again.' The press interpreted this as Mrs Cook campaigning for Edgar's reprieve – she later voiced her disgust at this.

The sentence was commuted to life imprisonment, which delighted his wife and their three children. They visited him when his reprieve had been announced, and his wife later said of the three daughters, 'They asked him when he would be coming home, and asked him why he was there. The children told him what they had bought him for Christmas. My husband kept saying that they looked well and kept telling them to look after their mummy for him. "I shall be here for a very long time," he said.'

Reprieve petitions had been arranged in both Cardiff and their home town of Stockton-on-Tees.

Mrs Black also said, 'Edgar has forgiven me and I will wait for him over the years – no matter how long. He is a wonderful man and I realise that now. As we said goodbye he said he had something worth living for now. And he has.'

In the fullness of time the daughters appear to have got married, but in three different towns and not Stockton. I couldn't find trace of Mrs Black but she never remarried; it was recorded that an Edgar Black died in Maidstone and that our Edgar Black died in prison. Only one Edgar Black was born in 1926 and his death record also includes his birth, so it looks as though Mr Black did indeed die in 1989.

Edgar Black was the last man sentenced to death in Wales and would have been the first execution since the miscarriage of justice had wrongly hanged Mahmood Mattan in September 1952.

Black, Robert
The murder of Susan Maxwell, Caroline Hogg, Sarah Harper and Jennifer Cardy

Robert Black was born in Sterlingshire in 1947. He was fostered early on, and from the age of eleven was in a children's home. He would become a killer of children in later life. By December 2014 he'd been convicted of four child killings, but is suspected of more. He was arrested in 1990 with a young girl in the van he used for nationwide and continental deliveries; police in France and Germany have open files.

At the age of twelve, with other boys, he attempted to rape a girl, but failed – he was then moved to a different children's home. By fifteen he had a job as a delivery boy in Glasgow and molested a number of girls, but he was convicted at seventeen when he took a seven-year-old into a derelict building and tried to strangle her – when she lost consciousness, he masturbated. He wasn't given a custodial sentence, though.

He got a job with a builders' merchants in Grangemouth and actually seemed to settle – he even had a girlfriend for a while, but she ended the relationship. He again escaped the law when he was nineteen, after he molested his landlord's nine-year-old granddaughter; he was simply told to leave his lodgings.

Mr Black moved to Linlochleven and sexually abused the

seven-year-old daughter of his new landlords. He went to borstal for a year and then moved to London. He'd always been a keen swimmer and secured a job as a pool attendant, but was accused of touching a girl, so was dismissed.

By the mid-1970s he was in his late twenties, working as a van driver, which took him the length and breadth of the country – he was even in Northern Ireland in 1981 delivering posters. Jennifer Cardy was abducted, sexually assaulted and murdered in August 1981 – Mr Black was to be convicted, but not for another thirty years.

In July of 1982 Susan Maxwell, aged eleven, lived on the England–Scotland border. She crossed the River Tweed to play tennis in Coldstream, but vanished on the way. Mr Black abducted, raped and strangled her. Her body was found in Staffordshire, well over 200 miles away.

The following July he struck again, this time in Edinburgh; Caroline Hogg lived in the Portobello area and went out to a playground near her home. This time he dumped the body in Leicestershire, about 300 miles away, and she wasn't found for ten days. The cause of death was elusive, but her clothing had been removed. Caroline was only five years old.

Sarah Harper, aged ten, went missing in Leeds in March 1986. She was only going to her local shop, and the shopkeeper later said she did come into the shop. But she never got home. Her body was found in Nottingham, in the River Trent – she'd been raped and murdered.

Police soon thought the three murders were linked and that the perpetrator travelled as part of his work. Fortunately the police could use computers to cross-reference details, which meant a copper's memory was a secondary tool.

In July 1990 Mr Black tried to abduct a girl, and was seen putting her into his van. The police were soon on the case and caught him. The girl was tied up and gagged and had been sexually assaulted; she'd been put into a sleeping bag.

Police raided his home and found a number of images of children in pornographic material. He came to trial and was convicted of abduction and given a life sentence. But the police weren't finished. They trawled through receipts from petrol stations to try and find out where he'd been and when. Subsequently they could charge him with the murders of Susan, Caroline and Sarah, and another abduction in 1988.

He stood trial in 1994, and the judge agreed to let the jury know he was serving a life sentence. He was convicted on all charges and given a number of further life sentences, with a minimum tariff of thirty-five years.

There are other cases where he is suspected but, as yet, evidence is poor. Genette Tate was thirteen when she disappeared in Devon in 1978; her body was never found. April Fabb disappeared in April 1969, and again no trace was ever found; April was also thirteen. Mary Boyle vanished from Cashelard in Donegal in 1977. An Garda Síochána know Mr Black was in the area. Mary was aged six. Suzanne Lawrence, a fourteen-year-old from Essex, has been missing since 1979, and Christine Markham, aged nine, disappeared on her way to school in Scunthorpe in 1973.

Blake, George

Treason

George Blake wasn't an Englishman, though he lived and worked here – he was born in the Netherlands, and during his service in Korea in their war he was easily convinced his heart lay elsewhere. I say his heart and not his loyalties because he was a double-agent, and with those, one never knows how much loyalty to a country was betrayed but how much personal friendships may have made him stop short.

It is said that several hundred British agents were betrayed, but the true figure will never be known, as a lot of Mr Blake's past would be manipulated to serve political rather than historic purposes.

What we do know was that his mother was Dutch, his father was Egyptian and he was educated in various locations, though Cairo loomed large. There he had a cousin, Henri, whose ideology appealed to him. He was in Holland when the Nazis attacked but managed to flee, eventually arriving in Britain. In the Royal Navy, he was a sub-lieutenant before being recruited to the security services. It is interesting that he wanted to marry an English girl but her parents prevented it due to his Jewish ancestry. In Korea he witnessed the Allies bombing small villages where civilians were killed.

Eventually, though, he settled in England and his work for the security services continued, but he was at some stage recruited into the KGB and became a double agent. He married and had three sons. In the early 1960s, his counter-espionage was stumbled on following the interrogation of another agent.

When he went on trial, the minimum he could receive in the way of sentence for the crime of treason was fourteen years, so when convicted on three counts he was given consecutive sentences rather than concurrent – a total of forty-two years. This was unusual. When he went from Wormwood Scrubs in 1966 it doesn't sound as though he was working alone, as others may have had an agenda, though not necessarily pro-communist. It was said George was a likeable fellow, and a forty-two-year sentence in pre-parole days was 'inhuman'. It hasn't often been topped.

George went to Russia via Eastern Germany, where he still lives. He divorced and remarried and published an autobiography. He has publically voiced his remorse for any individual who lost their life due to his actions.

His health isn't too bad for a man over ninety, though his eyesight has failed. As he was the son of a Dutch mother and Egyptian father and left the Netherlands for England to flee the Nazis, he felt he never belonged – and therefore feels he wasn't a traitor. You can only betray something you belong to.

Brinkley, Richard

The murder of Richard Beck and his wife, Elizabeth

Mr Reginald Parker was quite sure he hadn't seen Joanna Blume sign her will. The other 'witness' to the will was a Mr Harry Heard. Poor Mrs Blume had soon died and her granddaughter wasn't happy with her will; it left her house in Fulham to a Mr Richard Brinkley. The will had been signed two days before her death. So naturally validation was desired, but if Mr Parker hadn't witnessed a will then what had he witnessed?

The story would eventually come out that Mr Brinkley had told Mrs Blume she was signing up for a day at the seaside and she'd need to sign a form for it – she did so between two pencil marks, though the rest of the document was concealed. Mr Brinkley wanted a home and hers seemed suitable – this was his plot to get it.

He'd spent a good while working on Mrs Blume and gaining her confidence, but her granddaughter announced she'd contest the will. His answer was to offer her marriage, and her answer was a flat 'no'.

But if the witnesses were no longer available for any awkward questions about the will, then he would still inherit the house. So he travelled to Croydon to see Mr Parker – he had a bulldog which Mr Brinkley might be interested in owning. He took a bottle of stout with him to toast the deal.

When the two were out looking at the dog, Mr Parker's landlord,

Richard Beck, with his wife and daughter, found the opened stout bottle and thought it would be a nice treat. Mr Beck and his wife died soon after and their daughter was hospitalised – Mr Brinkley had put prussic acid in it to deal with Mr Parker's 'witnessing' of the 'will'.

The police investigated and found that a vet had supplied Mr Brinkley with the prussic acid and in an off-licence a man remembered serving him with a bottle of stout. He was arrested. In the summer of 1907 he stood in the dock at Guildford Assizes on two counts of murder and one count of attempted murder. He was hanged at Wandsworth Prison on 13 August 1907.

Mrs Blume died two days after making her 'will'. The great Bernard Spilsbury was called in to perform a post-mortem after they'd exhumed her body. However, no cause of death could be ascertained – what a coincidence and convenience her death might have been, but had Mr Brinkley actually got away with a murder?

Brinks-Mat Robbery, The

It might have been described as the 'crime of the century' at the time, but could equally be described as the 'curse of the century'. People have died, marriages have ended and friendships have been destroyed. It was early in the morning of 26 November 1983 that six robbers entered the Brinks-Mat warehouse at Heathrow Airport. It was an inside man, Anthony Black, who let them in, and as a 'straight goer' he was to be the gang's weakest link.

In one sense it was unfortunate for Mr Black, as his brother-in-law was Brian Robinson, one of the gang members, and it didn't take the police too long to make the link. As they interrogated the employees at the warehouse – they were the first suspects – the stories all confirmed each others', except Mr Black's. They had poured petrol over two of the men – one had keys and another the numbered combinations; these were frequently changed and, in the event, the staff member couldn't remember it.

The gang made off with £26 million worth of gold bullion, but this wasn't the original target; they had expected something like £3 million in cash. But the problem with having a few tons of gold was how to liquefy the asset. Kenneth Noye, who wasn't on the raid, was able to set up a smelting turn-round through a Bristol-based company before the gold was sold back to some of its original owners. One weak link here was the bank where the smelting firm conducted their business; it was noticed that the cash flow had increased considerably.

In court Anthony Black, Brian Robinson and Mickey McEvoy were all convicted – Mr Black sealed Mr McEvoy's fate, too; he got a twenty-five-year sentence. Mr Black seems to have gone off somewhere after his two years (originally six).

When Mr McEvoy was away he tried to negotiate the return of his share for a reduced sentence – only to find a lot of his 'whack' had disappeared. A high court ruling made him solely responsible for paying back £27 million.

It's a mystery, really, as to what happened to the bulk of the gold, and with some of the robbers never convicted it's anyone's guess who or where they are.

The banking group Johnson Matthey Bankers Ltd collapsed a year or so after the robbery, and Lloyds of London had a fairly hefty claim to settle. It has been suggested that any gold bought in the UK after the robbery may well have come from it.

Browne, Derek
Forger

If it was simply the case that 'I was pampering my ego to prove it could be done', then one has to ask why £5 notes were turned out 'in their hundreds'. Derek Browne was the owner of a printing company, so took a professional interest in forged currency notes and postal orders.

He pleaded not guilty at Worcester Crown Court in December 1975, saying he'd made the notes as his 'party piece' and he'd produced them so guests at parties could examine them – altogether, thirty-eight-year-old Mr Browne faced nineteen charges. He hadn't found the work easy. 'It took hours of work and I suppose it cost me £6 for each fiver in labour ... After I had produced a £5 note as good as I could my professional interest went and the whole thing was shelved.'

Apparently, the production of a Spanish bank note was comparatively easy. Mr Peter Crawford, prosecuting, explained that Mr Browne claimed that he'd tried to burn the forged notes while his wife was out of their home and some blew away in the wind, and travelled the length and breadth of a housing estate – he managed to recover some but a passer-by found some of the forgeries and handed them into the police.

Over 800 sheets of uncut £5 notes and in excess of 100 500 peseta notes were found in the workshop at his printing works, which represents, if this was his 'party piece', that he must have attended a lot of parties! But the notes were also found in his pockets.

The jury also heard that he'd presented the forged currency as payment for goods; when the police questioned him he was said to reply, 'I did a round trip between Bristol and Croydon. I suppose I must have made about £60.'

But the police also found the printing plates when they raided his firm in Upton-on-Severn. Further evidence came from the post office whose computer had picked up on the fact that some fivers had identical numbers.

After a three-day trial at Worcester Crown Court he was found guilty on ten charges of forgery and the use of the forging equipment. Mr Justice Kenneth Jones told him, 'Even if you started on this course out of technical interest, it was wrongful—and you knew it.'

He was jailed for five years.

Bryant, Frederick
Murdered by his wife, Charlotte

Charlotte McHugh was born in Londonderry, Ireland, in 1904, and her early years didn't see her achieve even the most basic academic standard. She couldn't read or write, but in her late teens, with her glorious mane of dark hair and eyes, she was popular with the men. Accordingly, she made the most of it, which has led to some labels that seem unnecessary. When she was twenty, she met Frederick Bryant, who was eight years older and was serving in Ulster with the Dorset Regiment. He was a country lad who found Ms McHugh attractive and she him, so when it was time to return to England she came with him.

Initially, they settled near Yeovil, in Somerset, where Frederick worked on a farm. Life in rural England had its attractions, but the local pub was the focus of activity and sometimes excitement was a little lacking. But after twelve-odd years of marriage, they had settled and had five children. Mrs Bryant was bored; she'd have a few drinks and sex whenever the opportunity presented itself. The villagers referred to her as a 'drunken slut', but Frederick seemed quite unfazed, even when he knew her income came from vice; he earned about 30s (£1.50) a week as a herdsman. 'I don't care what she does. Four pounds a week is better than 30 shillings.'

She'd entertain in their cottage and the arrangement seemed to suit all concerned. At the end of 1933, though, she realised there was perhaps more to life than just sex when she met a travelling peddler, Leonard Parsons. He'd been sleeping rough as he peddled his wares around the country, so was invited to the marital home, where Mrs Bryant was to peddle her wares. The problem was that Mrs Bryant developed feelings for Leonard. He didn't share the marital bed until Frederick and the kids were at work/school in the morning. Frederick wasn't too pleased, as this stretched the family budget rather than enhancing it, so Leonard had to go – but Mrs Bryant and two of the children went with him. She returned after a couple of days and life settled again, but Leonard would come round for his 'elevenses' and, eventually, they were back to square one. Early in 1934, Frederick was sacked from his job and they had to leave their cottage and moved to a small hamlet near Sherbourne in Dorset.

She didn't see Leonard, but their tenure was punctuated by Frederick suffering from bouts of what one of the attending doctors thought was gastroenteritis. He was creased up with severe abdominal pain. The symptoms lasted for about a week, but he recovered. This happened once more in the late summer of 1935.

One of her friends there, a widow called Lucy Ostler, became a little too friendly. Just before Christmas 1935, Frederick was taken ill again and this time the doctors wanted to get to the bottom of things so he was taken to hospital. There it was realised just how ill he was, and within a couple of hours he died.

As he'd died so rapidly, a post-mortem was performed and 'significant traces' of arsenic were found in his system. The police searched the cottage and pursued other enquiries regarding supply. A local chemist said he'd supplied a woman with arsenic, but neither Mrs Bryant nor her friend Lucy were picked out in an identity parade. Lucy was uneasy, though, and said she'd seen a 'tin' in the house and described it; the description matched that given by the chemist. Further questioning told the police that she'd thrown the tin out in the rear garden of the house and they recovered it – it contained arsenic.

Lucy was an important witness when Mrs Bryant was on trial for her husband's murder. On that last bout of sickness she said that Mrs Bryant had given him a beef drink, and that almost as soon as he'd swallowed it he became violently sick. Leonard Parsons was traced and gave evidence, to the effect that he'd seen Mrs Bryant with poison but she'd said it was weed killer.

Mrs Bryant gave evidence incriminating Lucy Ostler as it'd been Lucy who stayed with Frederick on that last night. However, Lucy hadn't been around for the first two bouts of Frederick's sickness.

It looked bleak for her, but the Crown had to establish she was guilty on the evidence, and not that she'd done it as she was the only likely candidate.

Dr Roche Lynch, from the Home Office, told the court that the ashes beneath the boiler contained an 'abnormally large' amount of arsenic – 149 parts per million, when he said the norm would be about 45 parts per million. So something with arsenic in it had been destroyed in the cottage.

After an hour's deliberation she was found guilty, convicted of murder and sentenced to death.

But it soon came to light that Dr Roach Lynch was inaccurate in his assessment of the usual residue of the ash of a boiler fire. It could range from 145 parts per million to 1000, so the fire ash at the cottage had contained below what might be considered as average.

This brought potential reasonable doubt and her legal team were soon busy. But the Court of Appeal was critical of the scientist and her death sentence stood. She was taken from Dorset and was hanged at Exeter Prison on 15 July 1936.

While in the condemned cell she actually learned to read and write; she wrote a letter to the king begging for mercy and suggesting another for the crime whose name was scratched out – if she said it was Lucy Ostler in court then it's unlikely to be any other, but she'd only 'joined' the household after two bouts of the illness. And if she said it was Leonard Parsons then he'd departed before the last, final and fatal bout of the illness.

Bulger, James Patrick
Murdered by Robert Thompson and Jon Venables

With a child's murder the imagination can get out of control, and take one's emotions with it. But when children are the killers then the whole thing ratchets up a notch or two. Many papers have been written as to why children murder, and the whys and wherefores are something psychologists will continue to look at. What most folk find unpalatable is the sheer brutality that can come from a child.

James Bulger from Kirkby on Merseyside was murdered in February 1993, and was found two days after his disappearance. In this world where it seems there's a camera everywhere, the two killers were seen behaving as if they were selecting out a target. They were also seen stealing from shops some things that were later found at the scene of James's murder. And there is one scene, which by now the majority of the world has seen, of James being led away by one of the killers.

They'd started their torture before they were out of public sight but people assumed as James was holding one of the boys' hands that they were together and nothing untoward was happening. Although two people challenged them, they were given answers that seemed to satisfy them; no criticism can be directed to these people.

James was taken up a railway embankment and led to an isolated spot. The boys' behaviour was then beneath contempt: they kicked him and stood or stamped on him. One of the boys had earlier been seen stealing some modelling paint which they threw into James's left eye. They also collected up bricks and stones and threw at him. There was also talk of batteries being placed in his mouth, and elsewhere on his anatomy, as well as a gross injury to his private parts. In all, there were forty-two isolated wounds, and pathologist Dr Alan Williams, giving evidence at the subsequent trial, was unable to distinguish which was the fatal blow; he added that James may well have lived for a few minutes after the reign of abuse had ended. One jury member was visibly moved when she felt the weight of an iron bar that had been dropped on him.

His socks, shoes, trousers and underpants had been removed and so one can't help but wonder if there was a sexual element to the crime. The boys at the trial wouldn't give any comment but they denied the insertion of batteries into James' rectum. This was something neither boy would discuss even later when they were paroled, but one of them was further convicted in his twenties for the possession of child pornography.

However, to return to the original crime scene, they partially disguised James so if a train ran over him, or rather when a train ran over him, then it might be assumed to have been an accident. His body was indeed later cut in two by a passing train. However, a skilled pathologist would soon tell that he was dead before the train hit him.

After the crime, it didn't take the police long to identify the boys on the CCTV images from the shopping centre. As the pictures appeared in the press, folk were critical of the people who'd seen them taking James, though this was very unfortunate. It does, however, give an indication of the anger felt with such a young child as a victim. In a way, it's understandable; anger is a bit easier if it has a target. One early suspect who was later cleared of any wrongdoing had been identified by the public, and his family left Liverpool afraid for their safety.

A lady who knew the two suspects were playing truant on the day of the crime and recognised one of them made contact with the police. The boys were arrested.

They were tried at Preston Crown Court and convicted. The case highlighted the difficulty of young offenders and how they should be punished and rehabilitated. It's a difficult area, because there is still a split among the population as to how adult offenders should be dealt with. At their release from detention they were given new identities.

Cameo Cinema Murder of Leonard Thomas and Bernard Catteril

George Kelly and Charles Connolly

It was the week after clothes rationing came to an end, money was short, but in March 1949 the Cameo Cinema in Liverpool wasn't doing too badly: *Bond Street*, starring Roland Young and Jean Kent, was showing that week. The manager, thirty-nine-year-old Leonard Thomas, had taken himself away to his office to count the night's takings – it was suggested the killer sat watching the film and waited for the cashier to take the money up to Mr Thomas's office. There he was joined by his under-manager Bernard Catterill, who was thirty. The killer and his accomplice then went to his office, and as one man stood as look-out, the other broke off the lock to the office and went in.

The takings that night were just over £50. As Mr Thomas struggled with the robber, shots were fired. Both Mr Thomas and Mr Catterill were hit. The money was found later, still in the office. The men were taken to Smithtown Road Infirmary, where they died. Mr Thomas left a widow and two children and Mr Catterill left a widow.

The police searched far and wide for the killer, but were having no luck at all until September, when a prostitute, her pimp and a conman said they'd overheard the planning for the robbery. Two names the police were given were George Kelly, an 'unemployed labourer' aged twenty-seven, and Charles Connolly, who was twenty-six; both men said they didn't know each other. Mr Kelly was living in Copperas Hill, which was just around the corner from Lime Street Station (he had the nickname of Ceaser of Lime Street), and Mr Connolly was way out in Huyton. They both denied any involvement in either the robbery or the murders.

But they were charged. They stood together in the dock at St George's Hall, but the judge ordered separate trials after the jury were unable to reach verdicts. Mr Kelly was the first to be tried, and the prosecution relied heavily on information given by the prostitute and her pimp – both had recently left prison. They said they'd been in a pub called The Beehive and that Mr Kelly and Mr Connolly were in the pub too. They overheard the plotting and saw Mr Kelly produce a gun.

However, Mr Kelly had an alibi because he was with a gentleman called James Skelly and they visited several pubs together that evening – but not The Beehive. He hadn't been far from the Cameo Cinema but wasn't involved, and witnesses could support his alibi.

There was no forensic evidence and no eyewitnesses, and the police hadn't found the gun, but he was convicted and sentenced to hang.

Mr Connolly thought he too would be convicted and sentenced to hang. He was able to 'plea bargain' through his lawyers and pleaded guilty to robbery. He was given a ten-year sentence but after his release he said that he wouldn't have pleaded guilty if hanging had been abolished because, quite simply, he was innocent. He said he'd have shouted his innocence as much as Mr Kelly. He died in 1997, still shouting his innocence.

George Kelly was hanged at Walton Prison, Liverpool, on 8 February 1950 by Albert Pierrepoint and Syd Dernley. The same couple of executioners would soon be at Pentonville Prison in London to send Timothy Evans into the next world.

George's family and supporters started shouting his innocence for him. Mr Kelly's daughter, Kathleen, employed solicitors to go over and over the evidence. Rex Makin, and later his son Robin, championed their cause, but it was a former Liverpool businessman who'd got to know Charles Connolly who did the footwork. Lou Santongelli believed Mr Connolly was innocent and sifted through the evidence: he made a discovery which would make most folk throw their eyes up to heaven in sheer disbelief, but anyone who has looked at crime in the post-war era would probably think the discovery was typical. A confession to the murder was found which hadn't been disclosed to the defence (the defence was led for Mr Kelly by Rose Heilbron KC).

By the new millennium the case had only got as far as the Criminal Cases Review Commission, and sadly Charles Connolly had died in 1997.

Going back to 1949, the police officer in charge of the case was Detective Chief Inspector Herbert Balmer and the Liverpool City Police call this his most 'notorious case'. What it comes down to is if the confession was made available to Miss Heilbron and the defence team, then there was a good chance of acquittal. George Skelly, who worked with Lou Santongelli in researching the case, has published a couple of books – one on the Cameo Conspiracy and another about Alfie Burns and Teddy Devlin, hanged for another murder which DCI Balmer was involved in; the *Liverpool Echo* refer to Mr Balmer as 'now-discredited'.

So who withheld the confession? No one will ever know for sure, but at the Court of Appeal in 2003 both George Kelly and Charles Connolly had their convictions quashed. Officially, they were cleared, and the Cameo Cinema case is an unsolved murder.

Camps, Professor Francis
Pathologist

Francis Camps was the son of a GP and, with Bernard Spilsbury and Keith Simpson, made a big difference to the detection of foul play. A couple of murderers in connection with Professor Camps are worth a mention – I'll come to these – but they're overshadowed by the more notorious cases of John Christie and Dr John Bodkin Adams. With Mr Christie, Professor Camps managed to 'rebuild' a skull from many, many pieces; with Dr Bodkin Adams he suggested over 150 souls had died in mysterious circumstances.

Professor Camps qualified in Guys in London in 1928, where he also took his 'House' jobs for registration. As a GP in Essex he had an interest in pathology and formed good relations with police and coroners, which took his interest further. He secured a part-time, and later full-time, position as a pathologist and later he was attached to the Home Office.

He knew that no murder investigation, unless it was a domestic affair, was straightforward and, as I will discuss, one particular domestic situation almost saw a murderer get away with it.

Stanley Setty was actually born in Iraq as Sulman Seti and became involved in some shady dealings after the war; when the black market was rife he made many a dubious buck. His partner in crime was one (Brian) Donald Hume. In October 1949 Mr Setty's torso was identified by fingerprints, and in Donald Hume's flat evidence of blood was found. Professor Camps could tell the police, when their investigation was flagging, that the corpse had been dropped from a 'great height', so the investigation team began visiting flying clubs. They discovered that Donald Hume had hired a light aircraft and further probing found that when he boarded the aircraft he had two large parcels – it was discovered that the parcels were no more.

Mr Hume claimed the parcels were printing equipment to forge food coupons, as food was still on ration. But he later admitted it had been Mr Setty's corpse. The story was that three gangsters hired him to dispose of the body, so a murder conviction looked unlikely, but he got twelve years for being an accessory.

Another triumph for justice from Professor Camps came in 1953, when Reginald Watters was found hanged in his quarters where he was stationed with the British Army in Germany. His post-mortem showed death had been consistent with hanging. But one of the Provost Police Officers wasn't convinced – when he heard Sgt Watters' widow had married his former best friend, he alerted Scotland Yard. Eventually, Professor Camps performed a second post-mortem and his view was death had been caused by a blow to the neck – martial arts style. Sergeant Frederick Emmett-Dunne was tried and convicted for murder; found guilty, he was given a life sentence – hanging had been abolished in Germany.

Professor Camps went on to research the effects of coal gas and carbon monoxide in suicide, and was later to publish on the detection of gas in the body after death.

He married his third wife just a few months before his death in July 1972.

Cannan, John
Abduction and murder of Shirley Banks

John David Guise Cannan was born in Sutton Coldfield, Warwickshire, on 20 February 1954. He was convicted in 1988 of murder and sexual offences, and given three life sentences with a recommendation not to be released. He was guilty of the murder of Shirley Banks in Bristol in October 1987, the attempted kidnapping of Julia Holman the previous day, and the rape of a woman in Reading in 1986. He's the only suspect in the murder of Suzy Lamplugh,

Mr Cannan was only aged fourteen when he indecently assaulted a woman in a phone box; he was placed on probation. He assaulted his girlfriend, Daphne Sargent, in December 1980, because she'd broken off the relationship. He then turned to robbery, and held up a petrol station at knifepoint in February 1981, and in March robbed a knitwear shop. This was especially evil; he tied up the assistant's mother and raped the shop assistant, who was in late pregnancy. He was apprehended soon after and was to serve five years of an eight-year sentence from the summer of 1981.

There were a series of rapes in the West Midlands, referred to as the 'House for Sale' rapes, which occurred from 1979 to 1981 – coincidentally, they stopped when he was jailed.

In the summer of 1986 he was on day release from a hostel at Wormwood Scrubs when Suzy Lamplugh disappeared.

His main ploy was that he was a businessman and would 'court' women with chocolates, flowers and sometimes champagne, but if rejected ...

In August 1986 when living in Bristol he had a relationship with a solicitor, which ended with him behaving threateningly. He raped a woman at knife-point in Reading in October 1986, calmly hailing a taxi afterwards; he was linked to this attack by DNA from semen, but evidence wasn't strong enough for conviction. An earlier DNA profile was inconclusive, but the Home Office ran the test again in 1988 and came up with a match, confirmed by ICI Laboratories. He later tried to abduct a thirty-year-old woman from a car park at gunpoint, but she fought him off and later identified him.

On the evening of 8 October 1987 he abducted Shirley Banks in Bristol city centre. Her husband, Richard, searched round a few places he thought she might be as they'd arranged to meet for a drink. There was no sign of Shirley and the following morning he rang her work place only to be told she'd phoned in sick with an upset stomach about a quarter of an hour earlier. He called the police. It was later thought she'd been held overnight in Mr Cannan's flat, and he'd persuaded her to phone work complaining of sickness, after promising to release her.

Over 100 officers from different police forces spent nearly 150,000 man hours looking for Shirley. They helped broadcast television appeals, and Bristol Docks was searched – her car was missing.

As in most of these cases they looked in every conceivable place for clues and then reviewed the clues they had – the phone call to work could mean she'd left of her own volition. Her husband was a suspect, but was eliminated. The police linked the case to the failed abduction the night before, also of course in Bristol. A *Crimewatch* reconstruction was scheduled.

Mr Cannan was arrested in Leamington Spa for a sexual assault at knife-point on an assistant in a clothes shop. Two passers-by chased him and the police were called. The police found a knife in a bag that was blood-stained and when they saw his hand was bleeding, they arrested him. They found his black BMW nearby with a length of rope and an imitation handgun.

The police thoroughly searched his car. This was a couple of weeks after Shirley had disappeared – they found the tax disc for her car in the glove compartment of his. Her Mini Clubman was found in the lock-up garage at his block of flats – it had been orange but was painted blue. Avon and Somerset police travelled to Warwickshire and arrested him for Shirley's disappearance.

The media linked Shirley's disappearance to Suzy Lamplugh's.

He said he'd bought the mini from a man at an auction, but he didn't have an alibi for the night Shirley disappeared. Later, a taxi driver told the police that a woman called a taxi to his flat at about 2 p.m. on the day after Shirley's disappearance, but Mr Cannan denied anyone had called from his flat. He'd alsoborrowed a vacuum cleaner from a neighbour and cleaned his car.

The police brought in Julia Holman, whom he'd attempted to abduct, and she identified him in the line-up. They'd found their man, but not the woman: Shirley was still missing. But they were hopeful she was still alive, and they released Mr Cannan's picture to the press.

A cleaning ticket was found for a dry-cleaner in Sutton Coldfield, where he'd dropped off a raincoat with red marks on it in late October. The red marks he said were from having sex in a park, but the police had the coat tested for blood.

Without a body the police were stuck, so they needed to discover if they could link Shirley to his flat. They matched fingerprints from home, her parents' home and her work, eliminating other folk also present, and had what they thought were Shirley's fingerprints. They compared them with all the fingerprints they'd collected from Mr Cannan's flat. In interview he was asked if Shirley Banks had ever been to his flat and he said she hadn't; they asked him if he could identify a document they found in his flat, which he did, but then they asked him to account for how Shirley Banks' thumbprint had got on to the document. Two days before Christmas 1987 he was charged with her abduction and murder.

Shirley's body was found the following April in the Quantock Hills. Her thumbprint could be taken and it was a match to the one lifted from the document in his flat. She'd been killed by repeated blows from a heavy rock.

After considering the evidence for over ten hours a jury at Exeter Crown Court found him guilty of the abduction and murder of Shirley Banks and two other attacks. Mr Justice Drake jailed him for life and suggested he would be a danger to women if ever released.

Carruthers, Glenis
Murdered by person unknown

It was in January 1974 that Glenis Carruthers left a twenty-first birthday party. She was found about an hour later – she'd been strangled. Her body was left just in front of Bristol Zoo and it was reported that her shoes were missing – there didn't seem to be any sexual motive, unless the killer had been disturbed.

Glenis was a student at Bedford College – she lived in the village of Little Chalfont, not far from Amersham in Bucks – and the birthday girl was her fellow student, Sandra Hardyman. Glenis herself was twenty and they were training to be physical education teachers together.

Detective Chief Superintendent Dennis Lewis, who was then head of Bristol CID, said, 'The girl was manually strangled but not sexually assaulted and it is difficult to guess at the motive.'

It was discovered that no-one saw her leave the house and it was thought she decided to walk to a telephone box. Under DCS Lewis, 175 officers worked on the case and over 16,000 people were interviewed, but the police were unable to shed any light on her killer or their motive.

There were no witnesses who came forward to say they'd seen Glenis after she'd left the party, but one of the keepers from Bristol Zoo saw a man lurking around the zoo at the right time. He described him as in his twenties and about 5' 10" tall. He had shoulder-length brown hair.

With so little to go on, it's no surprise the police were stumped. There are many tales of similar cases where the police just stumble over the killer later, or perhaps find a collection of girls all buried in the same back garden. They have also found the remains of victims of a killer blocking up a drain. With this seemingly isolated case it's difficult to draw any solid conclusions.

Her elder brother has spoken of the years of distress the family were left with, distress it is impossible to address. One has to ask just who suffers the most, the victim or their family. Finding the killer would at least help them, if not Glenis also, find some peace.

Chapman, David

The Last Death Sentence passed in England

Twenty-three-year-old Scunthorpe-born David Chapman was the last man to be sentenced to death in England. The sentence was, of course, commuted to life imprisonment, because just after the sentence the Abolition of the Death Penalty Act received its royal seal.

He'd worked at Scarborough's North Bay Swimming Pool for a few weeks when he broke into the place after a night's drinking. He'd been out with his friend and it was claimed he'd drunk nine pints of beer. It was late on the night of 22 June 1965 when the two passed the pool on their way home; they decided to go for a swim.

When they couldn't attract the attention of Alfred Harland, the night-watchman, they broke in, and Mr Chapman's thoughts had already gone from swimming to theft; accordingly he made for the office, where he knew the safe was. But on the way Mr Harland appeared, and he claimed that he lunged at him but couldn't keep his balance and fell in. Unfortunately, he hit his head on the way into the pool, and Mr Chapman said, '... he seemed to go limp in the water.'

His story wasn't believed. He had realised Mr Harland could and would identify him, so he simply left him in the pool. He had second thoughts, though, and his friend helped him pull Mr Harland out of the water. Mr Chapman later said that after this he went to find the safe and his friend let Mr Harland fall back into the pool again.

But the friend's story didn't match this. He said Mr Chapman pushed Mr Harland back into the water as he tried to get out – seemingly Mr Harland was still alive and active at this point. When he challenged him, Mr Chapman said, 'I had to do it because he recognised me.'

As the murder was in the furtherance of theft, the charge was one of capital murder, and they both pleaded not guilty when arraigned before Mr Justice Havers at Leeds Assizes in October 1965.

David Chapman was found guilty of murder and was the last man sentenced to death in England. The friend was found guilty of being an accessory after the fact of grievous bodily harm – but, as the counsel for the defence was to point out, Mr Chapman hadn't been convicted of grievous bodily harm, so how could the friend be convicted of being an accessory?

Mr Chapman served his time and was eventually released on parole. In 1982 he died in a road accident in the west country.

Chester, Peter
The murder of his niece, Donna Marie Gillbanks

If a man rapes a seven-year-old-girl and then murders her, he may have made the decision that he should silence the only witness to his act. If he then puts her in her bed with her favourite cuddly toy, then he has created a scene of horror that would shock a nation. It wasn't for several hours that her mother discovered she wasn't asleep, but dead. And that experience would ruin the rest of the mother's life.

June and James were a serious item, and Donna Marie was their only child. They lived in Mickleden Road in the Mereside area of Blackpool, with Lytham St Annes to the south-east; Blackpool to the north-east forms the third part of the triangle. Donna Marie's parents doted on her, though their marriage ended.

June's brother, Peter, lived about two miles away in Lytham Road. He'd recently married Carol.

It shook Blackpool to the core when he was arrested for the rape and murder of Donna Marie – his little niece. That was in October 1977, and in March 1978 the jury was unanimous. To add to

June's distress, he pleaded not guilty. He is one of only a few dozen prisoners who have served over thirty years. He's had numerous parole applications rejected, and is still in a high-security prison.

After one hearing it was reported that 'the Parole Board did not direct his release or recommend a move to open conditions as they concluded his risk factors had remained unaddressed and his risk remained very high to children, the public and known adults. Mr Chester therefore remains in a closed prison.'

June has asked, 'Who can say he won't rape and murder another child?'

The Parole Board has said within the last few years that they feel he still poses a threat. Penal reformers would argue that with him serving so many years over the twenty he was ordered to serve, before parole is a consideration, is harsh. But the twenty years is a minimum; it's not the case that the prisoner has an automatic right to freedom after his minimum. If the parole board think his 'risk factors are unaddressed', one might think he still poses a threat.

In more recent years Mr Chester has argued that prisoners should have the right to vote, and a lot of legal aid funds have been put at his disposal to fight the case. Perhaps a compromise would be that when he is deemed safe to rejoin society he should have the rights of other citizens. But until then …

Childs, John

The slaughter of Terry Eve, George and Terry Brett, Robert Brown, Frederick Sherwood and Ronald Andrews

Hire-purchase was loosely described as the 'never-never', so it was a surprise to read about a contract killer referred to as killing on the 'hire-purchase system'. One assumes he would kill first and be paid later.

A contract for an illegal act has no basis in law.

There were a couple of alternative names for the series of killings in this piece: the Poplar Butcher, and the Teddy-Bear Murders. In late December of 1979, forty-year-old John Childs was given six life sentences for murder. He fell into the category of underworld hit-man, but as one of his victims was a ten-year-old boy then all of this phraseology is washed away and the term 'evil' or 'vile' can find its way into Mr Childs' description.

At the trial in 1979, two of Mr Childs' associates were also convicted but were later cleared – they were convicted largely on his testimony. The murders, for which he pleaded guilty, took place between 1974 and 1978. He'd been arrested for something seemingly unlinked to the killings, a robbery in Hertfordshire.

Mr Childs was married with two children, so his family were sent away while their flat was used for the clandestine work. With a couple of associates it was decided, though each account has variations, that Terry Eve, who made children's teddy bears, should disappear; perhaps he should have an accident.

One major problem for a killer is disposing of the body, which is why the butchers' industrial mincer was bought and installed in a polythene-covered room in Mr Childs' flat. The process was completed with cremation in an open-hearth fire. But the mincing machine wouldn't work properly. Efforts to flush some of the remains down the toilet also failed, so a fire was started and for several hours after, the body was re-cut and burned. Finally, the ashes could be scattered on the Barking bypass.

Mr George Brett and his son Terry were next, and the killer(s) started to think they might make some money out of the murders.

They asked their associates if they had any 'contracts' they wanted 'completing', with a price-range of £2,000 to £10,000. An individual with a grudge against Mr Brett came forward. Mr Brett was a haulage contractor and Mr Childs fixed a meeting at a Dagenham factory – there was to be a chair to sit on and the victim should be shot from behind a counter with a Sten gun.

Again, though, things didn't run quite to plan and Mr Childs' car broke down, but with Mr Brett's help he managed to get it running again. However, his ten-year-old son, Terry, came out of the house to help and got into his father's car, which then went off to the factory. At the factory, Terry was given a teddy bear to play with while his father was shot. Then Terry was shot.

Mr Brett's car was dumped at King's Cross and the bodies of father and son were dismembered, put in polythene bags, and taken to Mr Childs' flat.Here the same incineration process took place for the next 24 hours.

Mr Robert Brown was the next to go because they thought he'd seen the killing of Terry Eve, although he hadn't. It was later established that he may have told the police about a false insurance claim they'd made, and it appeared they thought that he was too dangerous to live. Mr Childs was to carry out the task and the victim was actually on the run from prison at the time, so Mr Childs rang his landlady pretending to be from the prison service. Mr Childs offered to help him and was taken to his flat. Here he was shot twice in the back with a revolver, but didn't die – so a divers knife, sword and an axe were all used before Mr Brown and life parted company. As usual, the body was incinerated and this time the ashes were deposited in Wanstead Flats.

Next on the list was forty-eight-year-old nursing home proprietor Frederick Sherwood, a straightforward business job for £3,000: £1,500 as a down payment and three instalments of £500 – just like hire purchase. Mr Sherwood had a Rover for sale and Mr Childs rang him up to show his interest. After a drive to Dagenham the deal was completed. As they had a drink Mr Sherwood was shot at but the bullet caught Mr Childs in the hand, so he picked up a hammer and hit Mr Sherwood over the head with it. Another shot at point-blank range finished the job. They cleaned up and dumped the car in Earls Court before they dismembered Mr Sherwood's body. Phone calls were made and the three £500 instalments were made.

By now, the alcohol consumption of Mr Childs was getting out of hand and he couldn't sleep unless he was drunk. It was now 1978 as the final job was agreed but this was a problematic case, because the wife of Ronald Andrews was attractive and one of Mr Childs' associates simply wanted him out of the way. Mr Childs was to be paid £500.

The plan this time was that Mr Andrews' car would be found in a river at Wisbech in Cambridgeshire, but if Mr Andrews wasn't in the car it would be assumed he got out but had then been washed away. Mr Childs, posing as a private detective, would dupe Mr Andrews with manufactured evidence of his wife's infidelity. While talking about his wife he'd be shot. All went fairly smoothly and the body was taken back to the Poplar flat for incineration. After two and a half bottles of whisky, Mr Childs was through with the job and the criminal speciality.

His total income for the jobs was £3,180.00. The teddy-bear murder brought him £80; £600 for Mr and Master Brett. Mr Brown didn't attract a fee, and Mr Sherwood was a paltry £200. The final job came to £500; the remainder of the £3,180 came from 'other' profits.

Finally he was arrested or at any rate questioned about a robbery in Hertfordshire when he suddenly stopped talking about that and described, in a flat emotionless voice, the full horrifying story of the Hire-Purchase murders.

It is doubtful that he'll be released from prison.

Cochrane, Kelso
Murdered by persons unknown

A lot of people have been credited with lubricating race relations in the past fifty years or so, and leading politicians have all claimed some credit. But it's the ordinary chaps on the street just getting on with it that have done the most. It's true that in London there is still some tension and the so-called keepers of peace, the police, haven't always helped matters.

Incredibly, some political groups wishing to repatriate folk in the early 1960s actually believed some ethnic groups supported them.

Calming racial tensions hasn't always been easy or practical, but displays of cultural celebrations have sometimes helped; probably the most famous is the Notting Hill Carnival.

A short while before its inception, people like the British Union of Facists had established offices in Notting Hill and there was a single incident that made many in the country stand up and take note. A lad in his early thirties had hurt himself at work – he was a carpenter – and after treatment in hospital was making his way home. He was attacked and stabbed to death. His name was Kelso Cochrane, and if anything he strengthened the resolve of the Caribbean community.

A killer, though deceased, has now been identified and word has it that his guilt was an 'open secret'. If the police knew who was responsible, then it begs the question of why he wasn't prosecuted. One obvious reason is that any witnesses were terrified of reprisals and contemporary news reports support this; one woman said she saw five white youths attack a lone black man; and a headline in a newspaper at the end of May 1959 said the police thought that perhaps up to ten witnesses were too intimidated to come forward.

The name offered up a couple of years ago was certainly in the frame at the time and he was reported to have 'helped the police with their enquiries' for about thirty-six hours. No charges were ever brought and a cold case review was hampered by the fact that all forensic evidence was destroyed a few years after the murder.

Perhaps the way the Caribbean community have held their heads high ever since has been the outcome. At the time of the murder the police were quick to emphasise that the motive seemed to be robbery – murder in the furtherance of theft was capital and the killer would have been hanged. With race riots in Notting Hill only the previous August, 1958, the hanging of a white youth for the murder of a black youth would only have added fuel to the fire.

Confait, Maxwell
Murdered by persons unknown

At shortly after 1 a.m. on the morning of 22 April 1972, the fire brigade attended a fire in a house at Doggett Road in Catford, south-east London, which didn't present them with too many problems in controlling and extinguishing. But the police did have a problem with the fire, because the body of a man who'd been strangled was in an upstairs bedroom.

Within a couple of days, three youths were 'helping the police with their enquires', but the police weren't helping the case as they practically bulldozed the three into statements, into court and into prison or special hospitals; they had alibis, however. The three were either suffering learning difficulties or were minors, and the case led to severe criticism of police practice. Their alibis were scuppered by the wrong time of death being recorded, and they were convicted. However, their parents were not taking it sitting down and petitioned. When the highly reliable Roy Jenkins returned to the Home Office in 1974, and Sam Silken as Attorney General, then it would only be a matter of time before questions were asked.

The three youths were eventually exonerated as their alibis were deemed to cover the time of Maxwell's death, even though there had been doubt as to the time of death – his temperature hadn't been taken, which is usually the best indicator.

One of the original suspects, a man called Winston Goode, who'd split with his wife though they remained under the same roof, had raised the alarm. He later became very disturbed about

Maxwell's death and finally he committed suicide. It appeared the two men had a common passion which revolved around women's clothes: Maxwell was known to be a transvestite.

It was noted that Maxwell had been strangled but there was no sign of a fight or a struggle in the flat. This suggested he knew his killer, or at any rate that there had been some consent. It was suggested that partial asphyxiation may have been part of a sexual act and control was lost. Maxwell was a male prostitute, so the possibility couldn't be ruled out.

The crime remains unsolved.

Cook, Peter
The Cambridge Rapist

Just one week after the second general election of 1974, in a quiet bedroom in Cambridge, a twenty-year-old girl was raped at knifepoint.

Two weeks later another girl was subjected to the ordeal in a bedsit in the town, and the police, looking carefully at his methods, concluded that it was the same man. All they could do was to warn women, particularly those living alone or in bedsits, to securely lock their doors and windows. But as Cambridge is a university town there were many girls in this category.

On 11 November, a bizarre sight met a young lady as she opened her door in Huntingdon Road to find a man wearing a wig and just a blanket around his body. She didn't take any nonsense and eventually her would-be attacker departed.

Whether or not this angered the rapist, though the anger levels of these individuals are never easy to judge, two nights later he beat and raped a girl on a college campus. She was eighteen and was in a sound-proofed music room when he grabbed her – he dragged her out into the college grounds and into a shed.

Three weeks before Christmas he was in a block of flats, which he entered through a back door. It was 2 a.m. when he woke a girl, held a knife to her throat and raped her in the garden. Blindfolding her, he warned of his return if she told the police.

However, Detective Superintendent Bernard Hotson and his team of twenty detectives were getting to work in order to catch him.

Then, a return to the scene of his first attack, where a twenty-year-old girl was raped and stabbed. One thing the police had now established was the bizarre ways he escaped, wearing unusual clothing – this time it was a beard and a wig.

The crime of rape is said to be one of diminishing returns, and it looked as though the violence was increasing in severity and nature. But everything went quiet as 1975 began.

Four girls shared a flat in Marshall Road, but with three of them away the rapist was back with a vengeance – he broke into the flat through the back door and was dressed entirely in black leather. 'Do you know who I am – I'm the Cambridge Rapist.'

He raped the girl and left her so severely bound it took her six hours to get free.

But he was getting complacent and, in May 1975, he attacked in daylight for the first time. Mr Cook cut the girl's clothes off with a razor-sharp knife and raped her; he then stabbed her in the stomach. She was left bound and gagged. Unless he was caught he was going to kill.

Early on 8 June 1975, a twenty-eight-year-old Canadian student was asleep in her room in her hostel when she heard footsteps in the corridor. She got out of bed and opened the door. There was a man in a black leather outfit. In desperation, she tried to shut the door but a knife flailed around. She screamed with as much force as she could and was heard by two men nearby. They rang the police and the instructions were quite simple: 'Stop everything that moves.'

Detective Constable Terry Edwards was close at hand and saw an old lady's bicycle coming towards him. No lights, and the rider pedalled ferociously – DC Edwards stopped it, or tried to, because the only thing he could hold onto was 'her' hair, which came away in his hand. But it was enough to knock the cyclist off balance and, with the help of people awakened by the commotion, DC Edwards could overpower 'her'.

In the basket on the front of the bike was a carrier bag, and inside was a mask made of leather with 'rapist' painted on it. There was ether and a cloth pad and a small device for short-circuiting lights in homes to plunge them into darkness. The Cambridge rapist had been caught. The idea had been that an old lady on a push-bike would dupe the police into thinking she was an innocent pensioner and not a highly dangerous monster.

Peter Cook was convicted of raping six women, wounding two more and committing an act of gross indecency on another victim. Mr Justice Melford Stevenson gave him two life sentences, and recommended he spent the rest of his life in jail.

He died in Winchester prison in 2004, aged seventy-five.

Cooper, John William
Murder of Richard and Helen Thomas (1985) and Peter and Gwenda Dixon (1989)

Eleanor and George got married in 1938 and had eight kids, which boosted the population of Milford Haven in south-west Wales a little – the fishing industry was in decline by then, but the total population has only recently peaked at 13,000 or so. One of Eleanor and George's eight is now in prison, serving a life sentence for four murders and two rapes. John Cooper is also known as the Quiz Show Killer, as he appeared on a television quiz show. He was married and had two children – later in court his son, appearing as a prosecution witness, would explain how he'd carry a shotgun concealed beneath his coat.

In September 2011 he appealed against his convictions, but his appeal wasn't successful – now past seventy, it's highly unlikely he'll ever be released. Mr Cooper had a long history of crime and the offences he received his life sentences for were all committed in the 1980s. In 1998 he was convicted of robbery and served ten years of a fourteen-year sentence. He left prison early in 2009, but was arrested in May 2009. The two cases of double murder were regularly reviewed and advances in DNA, and forensics generally, identified a gun he owned as a murder weapon – blood was found on the gun and it was a one in a billion chance the DNA could have belonged to another person.

His first foray into murder was on 22 December 1985, when a grand three-storey farmhouse was burned to the ground. When the brother and sister who lived there – fifty-eight-year-old Richard Thomas and fifty-four-year-old Helen – were found, it was discovered they'd died of gunshot wounds. Helen Thomas was very active with local charities and was a supporter of Riding for the Disabled.

For over fifteen years fifty-one-year-old former RAF Flight Lieutenant Peter Dixon and his fifty-two-year-old wife Gwenda, who worked as a secretary, had taken holidays in the peaceful beauty of Pembrokeshire, but they were murdered as they took their last walk of the holiday along the clifftop coastal path. It was 29 June 1989 when they encountered Mr Cooper.

Before killing them, he forced them to the edge of the cliff and tied them up. He stole their bank cards, demanding their PIN numbers – Mrs Dixon was also sexually assaulted and he stole Mr Dixon's wedding ring. He shot them in the face at point-blank range and hid their bodies in bushes. He later took money out of their bank accounts through cash machines.

Mr and Mrs Dixon lived in Witney, in Oxfordshire; when they

failed to return home, anxieties were raised and their twenty-two-year-old son Tim reported them as missing four days later, so the case was one of missing persons to begin with, but just under a week later their bodies were found on the cliff path where they'd been concealed in the undergrowth.

With such a brutal attack, no less than 150 officers were assigned to the task of catching the killer and bringing him to justice. The local community were numb with shock and things weren't that different in Witney either when the story broke.

Mr Cooper also committed a horrific rape on a sixteen-year-old girl and then sexually assaulted her younger friend. He held them at gun-point. That was in March 1996, in a patch of woodland in Milford Haven.

The Dyfed-Powys police started reinvestigating the case in 2009, under the supervision of Detective Chief Superintendent Steve Wilkins, who described him as 'a very dangerous and evil man'.

But he was finally tracked down and faced the families in court. Arriving at the magistrates court he said, 'You must judge me after the trial and not before.' With a string of thirty violent robberies already under his belt, the police felt confident.

For the prosecution, Gerard Elias QC said, 'All the victims were subjected to the most terrifying of ordeals. They were murdered for pitiful financial gain and sexual gratification.'

He was convicted and sentenced to life imprisonment.

Crimewatch
'Don't have nightmares'

This is a programme transmitted by the BBC, usually every other month, and has had a host of presenters, including the late Jill Dando. It's also had a number of serving police officers assisting with the presentation of the programme.

The first case featured was the murder of Collette Aram, which has now been solved, and there have been some notable cases where evil people have been taken off the street. There are folk who may be frightened by the subject matter but it has been running for just on thirty years, so one hopes it's more than well-established.

There are, moreover, numerous reasons why the show should continue and with the power of television it could be seen as an extension of neighbourhood watch. It's been a springboard for campaigns to become law, such as the so-called Sarah's Law, which can notify as to the whereabouts of those convicted of crimes against children. So far as I know, as a result of Sarah's Law little has happened in the way of vigilante action.

It doesn't argue any sociological ideal, but presents the facts and merely requests more information if any is available. Naturally some will feel inhibited and even frightened at the prospect of getting their facts wrong, but the police do have a way of carrying out an investigation. The old days of PC Plod saying quite the wrong thing at quite the wrong time have long passed, and the police are now committed to serving a community rather than just 'banging up a few villains'.

Police work has doubtless become far more hazardous in the past few decades, and as soon as a warrant card is picked up or a uniform is donned it does increase the risk of violence to the officers. This is a fact – not an acceptable one, but still a fact. So again, it can be seen as a public relations exercise.

In a documentary a few years before the start of the programme, an assistant chief constable did say that 'most people are reasonably law-abiding', so the police officer and a *Crimewatch*-type programme can paradoxically be a source of comfort, and has doubtless reduced the feeling of 'them and us'. Some will feel cheated if, say, after a burglary the villain isn't apprehended. This is because police are there to investigate the crime and may need more evidence to have sufficient for the Crown Prosecution Service to progress, so it has to be remembered that some little tit-bit of seemingly useless information may be the link that's needed to complete a very large chain.

Crippen, Hawley Harvey
Murdered Cora Crippen, though there are doubts

John Trestrail is an American toxicologist and is 'the world's foremost authority on criminal poisoning and murder by poison'. One of his arguments seemed to me to be one of the most common-sense arguments in a poisoning case I've yet heard; it went along the lines of 'poisoners don't dismember and bury' – of course, they'd want the body cremated and the evidence destroyed.

So the case of Dr Crippen isn't over yet, but on Wednesday 23 November 1910 the authorities thought it was. Just after breakfast at London's Pentonville Prison, John Ellis pulled the lever that dispensed justice to Hawley Harvey Crippen as he fell through the trap-door with the hangman's noose around his neck. At the end of the drop, he stopped abruptly and his neck was broken – he was cut down a prescribed amount of time later and buried in the prison grounds. He'd been convicted of killing his wife.

Mr Crippen qualified as a homeopath with a doctorate in 1888, but his wife died and so he moved to New York to practice – they'd had a son, whom he left with his own parents. He met and married the daughter of a German mother and Polish/Russian father, and she used the name Corrine 'Cora' Turner – she was a dancer with the stage name of 'Belle Elmore', but her actual birth name was Kunigunde Mackamotski. In the theatrical world she occupied, fidelity wasn't noted. The couple married and decided to try their fortunes in London.

However, the qualifications he had didn't entitle him to practice as a medical doctor in England, so he worked as a distributor of patent medicines. Cora still aspired to a career in music and theatre and her social life revolved around this, but Dr Crippen seemed to spend an inordinate amount of time promoting her career. Therefore, his link with his American pharmaceutical company came to an abrupt end.

He managed to get work as a manager at the Drouet Institute in Regents Park Road, though this has been labelled as a 'quack institute'. He took up his position in around 1903, and also on the payroll of the 'institute' was a young typist called Ethel Le Neve.

This is a mystery, too, because I can find no record of her in birth records, nor in the census for the late nineteenth century, as Le Neve, Neeve or Neave. Nor can I find her father or mother (Walter and Charlotte) in Norfolk. One story says Dr Crippen hired her in 1900 and another claimed she was already at the Drouet Institute when he went there in 1903.

In 1905 Dr and Mrs Crippen moved into 39 Hilldrop Crescent, where they took lodgers, one of whom Cora had a relationship with. Dr Crippen took Ethel as his mistress. His financial status was far from good, and after a party at their home on 31 January 1910, Cora disappeared. He said she'd returned to America and later died. Ethel moved into the house and wore Cora's clothes and jewellery.

One of Cora's theatrical friends, Kate Williams, went to the police to discuss her disappearance, but when another of Cora's friends, Lil Hawthorne, spoke to her friend Detective Superintendent Frank Froest, the enquiry started. The house in Hilldrop Crescent was searched but little was found and Dr Crippen seemed to satisfy Detective Inspector Walter Dew, but did admit he'd fabricated the story as he didn't want the personal embarrassment that she'd left him for another man. But Dr Crippen and Ethel got the wind up and vanished, which didn't satisfy DI Dew.

So the police went back to the house and searched. And searched some more, and eventually they found human remains buried under the brick floor in the basement. Cora had had an operation, and the scar was enough to satisfy Dr Bernard Spilsbury that the location of the scar, together with her medical history, suggested it couldn't be anyone else. This sounds a bit of a thin criteria. The head and limbs and some of the skeleton were never found.

Meanwhile Dr Crippen and Ethel had made for Belgium where they set sail for Canada on board the SS *Montrose*. Ethel disguised herself as a boy and they sailed as father and son. But the captain was very astute and, as their pictures were in many continental newspapers, he thought it might be them. This vessel had a modern radio, and telegraphist Lawrence Ernest Hughes sent a telegram by wireless to the British authorities: 'Have strong suspicions that Crippen London cellar murderer and accomplice are among saloon passengers. Moustache taken off growing beard. Accomplice dressed as boy. Manner and build undoubtedly a girl.'

DI Dew backed the captain's hunch and travelled to Liverpool, where he boarded the White Star Line's most up-to-date ship, the SS *Laurentic*. He could arrive in Canada, which was still in the British Empire, ahead of Dr Crippen and Ethel, where he made contact with the authorities.

As the SS *Montrose* steamed into the St Lawrence River, there was DI Dew on the pilot's vessel, ready to come aboard, where the arrest was made.

Dr Crippen was quoted to have said, 'Thank God it's over. The suspense has been too great. I couldn't stand it any longer.' He maintained his innocence, but that doesn't seem consistent with his comments.

They stood trial, and Ethel was found not guilty. Dr Crippen was convicted, sentenced to death and executed on 23 November 1910.

It may be that at some time in the future we will see new developments. As I said, there was a tiny sliver of skin bearing the scar, which was examined by Dr Spilsbury for the Crown at that time, but a more recent examination strongly suggests the tissue was from a male. Scar tissue also does not bear sweat glands, while the sample did.

Cora Crippen has relatives alive and well in America.

The Criminal Cases Review Commission has said there is no possibility of referring the case to the Court of Appeal, but they would have to if there was 'compelling new evidence', and this is not now beyond the impossible.

Cummins, Gordon Frederick: The Blackout Ripper

The murder of Evelyn Oatley, Margaret Lowe and Doris Jouannet (Evelyn Hamilton)

Gordon Frederick Cummins was born in Yorkshire in the early spring of 1914. His mother, Amelia, had married John Cummins in 1912. They had another son in 1917 and a daughter in 1920. Gordon Cummins killed under the cover of the blackout in London in 1942; although only convicted of one murder, that of Evelyn Oatley, he actually murdered four women and attempted to murder another two. The police officer who brought him to book, Ted Greeno, had a son, who said that when he'd gone through his father's papers after he'd died, he found some photographs Mr Greeno had kept of the case and that Mr Cummins 'had made a real mess of them'.

He left Yorkshire and in late 1936 married Marjorie in London – there's no record of any children. Mr Cummins volunteered to join the RAF when war broke out and by the start of 1942 he was a member of ground crew – Leading Aircraftsman – but applied for aircrew training. He was described at the time of his trial as a 'cadet', which suggests he may have been working towards officer status, and the selection process was in February 1942 at Regents Park in London.

Evelyn Hamilton's body was found in an air raid shelter in Marylebone on 9 February. She'd been strangled and her handbag had been stolen – but there was the large sum of £80 in it. There didn't seem to be any sexual motive.

Evelyn Oatley was thirty-five and on Monday 10 February her naked body was found at her flat, which was in Wardour Street in the West End. She too had been strangled, but her throat had been cut and she'd been mutilated in her genital area with, it was thought, a can opener. But a big clue was left in fingerprints and, moreover, it seemed the killer was left handed.

Margaret Lowe was a forty-three-year-old lady, who'd worked as a prostitute and was murdered in her flat in Gosfield Street, Marylebone. She was strangled and her body was mutilated with what seemed to be a number of household items: a razor blade, a knife and a candlestick. Sir Bernard Spilsbury performed the post-mortem and described Ms Lowe's injuries as 'quite dreadful'. Doris Jouannet was murdered on Wednesday 12 February; she was thirty-two and had married Henri in 1935 – he was over thirty years older than her, and there were no children in the marriage. Henri worked as a hotel manager. It was said that Doris would 'pick up service men' but that she didn't 'work the streets' too often. Doris and Henri lived in a ground-floor flat in Sussex Gardens, just around the corner from Paddington Station. Again, she'd been mutilated, and the press started running comparisons with Jack the Ripper.

Greta Hayward was attacked on Friday 14 February in a doorway in Piccadilly Circus, but she managed to escape, thanks to a delivery boy on his rounds. The police gleaned more information; her attacker had been trying to make advances but she'd rejected him. Notably, he was in an RAF uniform and he left behind his gas mask, which was marked with a serial number, '525987'.

The police were now able to start putting the parts of the jigsaw together, but Mr Cummings wasn't finished yet. Kathleen

King was attacked in her flat which was, again, in the Paddington Station area.But the lights went out as the business was about to be concluded – he attacked her, but she kicked him hard and managed to fight him off; he fled, leaving his belt and £5 behind.

The newspapers weren't helping the police by piling the pressure on, but it was true that many women were scared to go out. Kathleen King reported the incident immediately.

The police were led by the clues to Mr Cummings, who was interviewed and arrested. His fingerprints matched those in two of the properties he'd attacked in and matched the fingerprints on the can opener used to mutilate Evelyn Oatley. Upon his arrest a statement was taken, but the most important thing Ted Greeno was looking for was which hand he signed it with – it was his left hand.

It was the case of Evelyn Oatley that the police presented to the Director of Public Prosecutions, and his trial proper started on 27 April. Christmas Humphries prosecuted and John Flowers, with Victor Durrand, defended. Mr Justice Cyril Asquith presided. It was all over in one day, with the jury taking all of thirty-five minutes to convict.

Gordon Cummings was hanged by Albert Pierrepoint at Wandsworth prison on 25 June 1942.

Dando, Jill

Jill was born in Weston-super-Mare in Somerset in November 1961; she had a brother, Nigel, who was a good few years older than her. She studied journalism in Cardiff, landing a job with her hometown weekly newspaper, the *Weston Mercury*, and stayed for a few years. She moved to BBC Radio Devon in 1985, but three years later she moved up to London to work in television. Jill was to present the news and also worked on *Holiday*. With the departure of Sue Cook from *Crimewatch*, she joined the programme in 1995.

Fulham was her base and she met Mr Alan Farthing, an Obstetrician and Gynaecologist, whom she was set to marry in September 1999. But on 26 April 1999 she was shot once on her doorstep at point-blank range. She died instantly. Jill was then aged thirty-seven and had received death threats which the BBC took seriously. It would seem her killer was waiting for her as she'd only just parked – she didn't visit her home very frequently, however, as she often stayed with Mr Farthing. A neighbour heard a shout but said it sounded more like a greeting.

The Metropolitan Police mounted an investigation. All and sundry, even her colleagues, were interviewed so the police could rule them out.

But a local lad who led a strange life, Barry George, was arrested. Jill had told her brother that someone was making a nuisance of themselves. Barry George probably wouldn't have the approach of what sounds like an experienced killer, but he was arrested, charged and stood trial. He was found guilty and sentenced to life in prison in 2001, but his conviction was quashed in 2008.

The killing, in which she was held just above the ground and shot in such a way that the bullet actually exited, sounds unlike normal domestic shootings. One theory was that it was ordered by a Serbian, as Jill had made appeals for the refugees from Kosova, though this seems a bit dramatic as she wasn't against the Serbian peoples. However, the Home Office were involved at some stage and circulated a description.

Then there was talk of a British underworld connection because of her *Crimewatch* broadcasting. There might be some credence to this, and again I'd mention the Home Office. The description they gave out was of a man something like 6' tall; he was dark haired, had what was described as a Mediterranean appearance and was well dressed. He appeared to be left handed – the bullet was said to be 'rare and unusual', which seems an odd claim to hear; the bullet was 9mm, which is very common. The gun was connected to a possible gangland killing, some while after Jill had been killed.

The police were asked to thoroughly investigate 'gun dealers, reactivated weapons and especially ... custom-made ammunition.'

Jill had been working on another project when a fatal helicopter crash killed her friend Matthew Harding – he was concerned about corruption in sport, including alleged money-laundering. Another friend of his, Veronica Guerin, who was a journalist in Dublin, was shot dead in a car in the Dublin rush-hour. It was said also that Mr Harding had been, like Jill, asking questions and 'rattling cages'. Jill was also pursuing the blood results of the pilot of the helicopter.

Going back to the murder weapon, the bullets were, as I described above, 'unusual'. But the gun was thought to be either old or have had some modifications – a weapon that a professional hit-man would be unlikely to use.

There was some rumour about a contract for Jill's killing which originated in Scotland's underworld, but as this was said to come from a Merseyside underworld source it might not be wholly accurate.

In the wake of the sexual abuse scandals of some television personalities, it's been suggested there was a link. Jill apparently received some complaints and passed them up the BBC hierarchy. The BBC have said they had seen nothing which would substantiate the claims, but some documents have a habit of wandering around – one can only hope they resurface at some stage.

For now, though, Jill Dando's murder is an unsolved crime.

Delaney, Robert Augustus
The cat-burglar

He might have been Robert Augustus Delaney, born in South Africa, or he might have been Robert Aloysius Delaney, born in

Dublin. The problem for any historian is what's true and what's not – this fellow broke the law in just about every way possible, ranging from burglary to pick-pocketing to bigamy.

He was the original cat-burglar and his sense of balance was quite incredible; he could shin up a drainpipe in a way the average man would climb a ladder. He'd pause and balance on the window sill just like a cat – that led to the title cat-burglar. In those days windows were almost all locked with a catch that he could slide a small pointed knife-like implement into and open up. One report said he used a silk rope-like length of material he could climb up. He was always dressed immaculately and almost everyone who came into his life lived to regret it.

But his main problem was confidence. He was so confident his crimes would always go undetected that he didn't take too much care in covering his tracks. Modern-day criminals would say he was careless.

He deserted in the Great War and settled down with a lady called Kitty Sharpe, who hailed from Swineshead in Lincolnshire; not surprisingly, she's described as a wealthy widow – she was twelve years older than him, and they married in 1915.

He was an accomplished conman, using the name 'Craddock', with the title of 'Captain'. He stayed in London hotels and stole money to support himself. He'd mix in fashionable circles and later burgle their houses – and it was claimed that he was so supremely smug, he'd sometimes leave through the front door. He moved on to forging cheques and he was bound over in September 1924. But he was arrested again just after Christmas, when attempting another burglary – there were a string of crimes, and he went to prison for three and a half years.

When he left prison he was out for just a matter of weeks. Teaming up with another man, he broke into a few places and stole more than a few things, including firearms. When he waved a revolver at a police officer the sentence when he appeared in court was double the last one – seven years. He was released in October 1933.

But he did stay out until November 1934, when again he was charged with the theft of jewellery, but more importantly he'd incited a teenaged boy into burglary. Also charged was his new – it seems bigamous – wife, with receiving. To this, add another break in at Bexhill-on-Sea, and he was now called a 'menace to society'. He went down for nine years. He appealed, and because he'd committed the latest crimes when out on 'license', he had just under two years added to his sentence.

He was out by 1940, and next he was charged for receiving! There were other crimes and he got three consecutive sentences of three years. He left prison in June 1945 but in December he was in Lewes Assizes for stealing jewellery; he got four years.

In her lovely book on the subject, Pamela Southworth explains all in great detail and asks, 'Will he never learn?'

Mr Delaney died in Parkhurst Prison on 14 December 1948.

Denning, Baron Alfred Thompson
Lawyer

Tom Denning was born Alfred Thompson in January 1899 and died 100 years and about six weeks later. He went up to Oxford and then went off to fight in the Great War. When he came back, he took up law as a barrister and took silk in 1938.

He was most distinguished in civil law and was one of the leading lawyers in his field; some have called him the greatest lawyer of the century. He became a judge in 1944, in Probate, Divorce and Admiralty, became a Lord Justice of Appeal in 1948, and Master of the Rolls in 1962. On his retirement he wrote a considerable amount and was very influential in the House of Lords.

His public profile was raised immensely when he reported on the

Profumo Affair in 1962 – available in paperback, it's an essential read. It was part of the cover-up for the witch-hunt against Steven Ward from the Home Office, but nevertheless, it was published. His learned colleague Reginald Manningham-Buller wrote up a far clearer and factual report, but it was subjected to the Official Secrets Act.

Tom Denning was referred to as the 'people's judge' but seemed to have a unique balance, because even though some of his judgements flew in the face of the law, government would sometimes incorporate his words in statute.

There were, however, a couple of areas where he is open to criticism. He lost his cool when discussing the role of the media after the work undertaken by the *Rough Justice* series of programmes. He maintained that cases from a court that had been dealt with by due course of the law and judged in front of a jury shouldn't then be taken up by the media. When pushed on the issue and asked if he meant that that it was acceptable that innocent people might be convicted, he said, 'Yes.' He later retracted the comment – one can only say that if he thought the retraction of the comment would change anything then he needs to have a look at the amount of 'confessions' taken from suspects by the police and later retracted.

He dropped a loud clanger when discussing the Birmingham Six. He felt that if they were allowed to proceed to trial, i.e. appeal, then time and resources would be wasted 'by many people for no good purpose. If the six men win, it will mean the police were guilty of perjury, that they were guilty of violence and threats, that the confessions were involuntary and were improperly admitted in evidence and that the convictions were erroneous'.

That was his reasons for wanting to block their appeal. This, taken with the above, demonstrates that some of the best lawyers on the planet were living on another one.

Dickman, John

The murder of John Innes Nisbet

John Alexander Dickman was hanged at Newcastle Prison in August 1910, and the case has divided crime historians ever since. His case was one of circumstantial evidence but it should be remembered that there are times when circumstantial evidence does give as good a picture, if not a better picture, as eye-witness evidence. When Mr Dickman was a citizen of Newcastle there were no such luxuries as forensics.

His mother died in childbirth so he was brought up by relatives. He initially worked with his father but would find other employment, which was mainly clerical. He married Annie in 1892 and things were settled until 1901, when he lost his job. Mr Dickman found another position, which was with a mining company that eventually he prepared for sale and in the event lost his job; he did receive £500 – something like £50,000 by today's values. He also picked up a couple of hundred pounds as a legacy. He lost most of it gambling, and eventually he was in debt to moneylenders.

On Fridays, some of the miners of the area were paid, which necessitated a member of staff travelling into Newcastle to collect cash. John Nisbet for his colliery was one, and he settled in his compartment for the return journey. The main question for the police, the court and for us now is whether John Dickman travelled in that compartment with him and shot him. Mr Dickman himself said that although he knew Mr Nisbet he hadn't travelled with him; he was going to yet another colliery and alighted before the train reached its destination – but the station he alighted at was not far from where the empty case Mr Nisbet carried the money in was found. Mr Dickman didn't get out at his intended station, so had an excess fare to pay. Along the way Mr Nisbet's wife was at a station for a quick chat, and although she saw another person in the compartment didn't positively identify him until court.

In the small community, other passengers also knew both men. Mr Charles Raven saw them together on the platform at Newcastle and knew them; Mr Dickman said he didn't know Mr Raven. Mr Wilson Hepple had known him, though, for over twenty years, and he said he saw Mr Dickman get on the train with Mr Nisbet – but how well did he know Mr Nisbet? Mr Percival Hall saw Mr Nisbet with Mr Dickman but didn't identify him until later.

But none of this circumstantial evidence proves anything; it was proved Mr Dickman got off the train but it wasn't proved at which part of the journey Mr Nisbet met his end.

Bank officials gave evidence of Mr Dickman's financial situation, assuming all of the facts were known. Professor Robert Boland recognised blood on his clothing and his coat had been rubbed with paraffin – a good cleaning agent. This also left proof wanting. And the identity parade saw some odd behaviour by police officers, letting a witness see Mr Dickman waiting in a room.

His own evidence suggested he was reading a newspaper and took no notice of his surroundings – that's how he missed his station. And he was unaware Mr Nisbet went to the bank on Fridays. But when he was found guilty he cried, 'I am entirely innocent.'

Neither the £370 stolen or the murder weapon was ever found. The governor of Newcastle prison received a letter signed C. A. Mildoning, confessing the crime; C. A. Mildoning doesn't appear on birth or death records or on the 1911 census.

John Dickman was hanged in Newcastle Prison on 10 August, 1910.

Dix, Glyn
The murder of Pia Overbury in 1979, and the murder of his wife, Hazel Dix, in 2005 showed two distinct methods

Between leaving the bakery shop where she worked on 2 October and being found partly covered in a wood three weeks later, thirty-two-year-old Pia Overbury had been abducted, raped and murdered. Pia had married James in 1968 and they lived in Gloucester with their two daughters, Maxine and Sarah.

Living not too far away was Glyn Dix, and matters took a turn for the evil in the latter part of 1979. Her daughter later explained that she knew Mr Dix through her mum's business, but he gave her (the daughter) a very uncomfortable feeling. After he'd murdered her, he partly covered Pia and she was found about three weeks later in a wood in Hartpury, which is about five miles to the north of Gloucester.

At first Mr Dix came up with some bizarre story that she was unhappy in her marriage and had begged him to shoot her; his solicitor told him to stick to facts. Eventually he did, pleaded guilty and was given a life sentence.

But part of why he said he'd killed Pia was that he'd been forced by the 'changing season', which suggested his mental health was far from satisfactory. Eventually, he was placed in Ashworth Hospital, which is a secure hospital up on Merseyside. His illness must have responded to treatment because in the 1990s he was back in the prison system.

He became friendly with a cell-mate and eventually he met his mate's mother. They would write to each other, and things started happening. Hazel had six grown-up children and was a fun-loving and popular resident of Redditch in Worcester. Lo and behold, they fell for each other and, when Mr Dix left prison on a life licence in 1999, they married.

Until 2004 everything was alright; the family were aware of his past, but only selected parts. He took up art and after a lot of hard work he finished a huge mural in the sitting room. It was along a satanic theme, though, and a later picture of Mr Dix was him folding two of his fingers down – the sign of the devil. Something evil was happening again.

The lad he'd met in prison was the only one of her children who still lived with them. He thought nothing of it when he went into the house, but a few minutes later, his sister, who lived directly opposite, was confronted by the lad shouting and screaming that Mr Dix had murdered their mother. Nothing could have prepared her for the sight in the kitchen when she went across the road to her mother's house.

Mr Dix had murdered her, but had quite quickly dismembered her body into sixteen pieces. When her daughter and son entered, he said, 'We had a little argument.' There was a suggestion that it was over a television programme, but there was something more sinister – he'd only just finished the mural in the lounge, with its satanic overtones, and he'd cut off two of Hazel's fingers, which could have meant he was trying to mould her hand into the sign of the devil.

Some of Hazel's children couldn't even go to the court late in 2005 to see his conviction; it's quite clear the tragedy is something they'll never forget.

Dobkin, Rachel
Murdered by her husband, Harry

At the time, in July 1942, it wouldn't have shocked as much as today, a builder removing a slab of concrete and finding a body underneath. It was a time when assumptions were often made that unknown folk would be killed in air raids – it was in a church, too, and it had been bombed just over eighteen months previously, when a hundred or so souls had died.

Nevertheless, the police were called in. The remains – which were fairly well preserved – were removed to Southwark Hospital Mortuary, where Dr Keith Simpson would do the formalities and perhaps the remains would find a more suitable resting place.

But straightaway he saw a problem, as there was unexplained

severing of body parts: all four limbs and the lower jaw were missing. Dr Simpson also found evidence of charring, so thought someone had tried to burn the body: quite a lot of effort had been invested to disguise the remains. However, the wrong lime solution was used to try and aid this, and it had the effect of preserving some flesh parts.

The remains could tell Dr Simpson quite a lot. It was a lady who'd been round about forty to fifty, had delivered after full-term pregnancy and had uterine fibroids removed. She'd had dark-greying hair, was 5' 1" in height and her teeth showed extensive dental work. Dr Simpson concluded she'd died about a year to fifteen months previously.

The police set about checking to see who'd been reported missing around about that time. Among many was a lady whose husband had worked next door. They were estranged and he'd been to prison for not paying maintenance. It was her sister who'd reported her missing. She was within the age range, was about the right height and had had dark-greying hair. Her sister could also tell the police she'd had treatment for a fibroid tumour. There were also full details of her dentist, who, when visited, said he'd kept records and described the lady's teeth and the treatment he'd given.

So they were now hot on the heels of a Mrs Rachel Dobkin, and once they secured a photograph of her and Guy's Hospital Medical Illustration had photographed the lady's skull then it was provisionally identified as Mrs Dobkin.

Mr and Mrs Dobkin's marriage only lasted a matter of days, but long enough to conceive a child that Mr Dobkin was obliged to maintain – he often defaulted and was imprisoned. The relationship between them had gone from bad to worse over the years, often publically. Their child was an adult by the time Mrs Dobkin was reported as missing.

Mr Dobkin, the husband, was interviewed by the police, who

initially had no real evidence, but as witnesses had seen them together in a café just before Mrs Dobkin disappeared and gave statements, together with her mother's statement that she'd not arrived to see her later that night, suspicions were aroused. Mr Dobkin said he'd seen her off on a bus to her mum's, but no one else had. He was arrested.

He stood trial in November 1942, with Mr Frederick Lawton defending and trying desperately to challenge the identification evidence; the jury took under half an hour. He was hanged at Wandsworth Prison on 7 January 1943.

Dryden, Albert
Murder of Harry Collinson, as recorded live

Albert Dryden built a bungalow without planning consent and over a number of years there was a dispute, which was finally settled by a court; the bungalow was to be demolished.

The bungalow was in the village of Butsfield, not far from Consett in County Durham, and on 20 June 1991 diggers were in attendance to demolish the building. Harry Collinson, the chief planning officer, was there in person, and over a fence Mr Dryden told him not to come onto his land. Though he was fully aware of what was to happen – the law is the law – Mr Dryden, who'd been obsessed with guns for most of his life, produced a gun and shot Harry Collinson twice in the chest, following up with a single shot to the head when Harry was slumped in a ditch. This was in full view of the cameras.

Stephen Campbell was a police officer on duty and he received a gunshot wound, as did Tony Belmont, who was present with BBC cameras. Mr Dryden was arrested later that day when armed police officers stormed the bungalow. Inside they found quite an arsenal.

Mr Dryden was given a life sentence for murder with a minimum tariff of eight years. That seems quite lenient, and when he took aim and shot he looked as calm and callous as one can imagine. When Harry Collinson was in the firing line he requested the gun be captured on camera, as the camera panned around Mr Dryden simply pointed the gun and shot.

One might be forgiven for thinking he wasn't responsible for his actions, but the court heard he was, and the jury convicted. It seems a few years into his sentence he described himself as a model prisoner, so if he was a model prisoner, who was clearly guilty, and was remorseful, then one would expect the parole board to look favourably.

But that is Mr Dryden's description, and it seems difficult to reconcile this with the turn his attitude was alleged to have taken later. He was quoted to have said, 'At the original trial, we ran a defence of diminished responsibility, but we have not yet tried provocation. I've been told I've got an 82 per cent chance of success.' One wonders how long the list is of possible pleas he can put forward.

The dispute had gone on for a number of years and the murder was televised. However, one recent claim was that Harry Collinson provoked him and he has a fairly lengthy dossier to support his claims.

Diminished responsibility and now provocation. There must be a word somewhere for the poor soul he murdered. But no. He wants to win his appeal, with the murder conviction overturned and one of manslaughter on the grounds of diminished responsibility substituted. 'If I won my appeal and the conviction was overturned, I'm in line for a £4 million payout. Manslaughter on the grounds of provocation carries a maximum of five years, so I will get £100 a day for all the extra time I have done.'

Mr Dryden has argued that the judge at his original trial set a 'minimum sentence of eight years'. My understanding is that in a life sentence the minimum tariff is merely the earliest at which a parole hearing can be applied for, not a minimum sentence.

He has applied a number of times for parole, saying, 'They don't want me out.' He seems to grasp some essentials, then. 'I'm so fed up now. I've spent all these years believing I would be released because I've been a model prisoner.'

A model prisoner might think of others rather than themselves, the one's they have wronged. He opened fire and then discharged a single shot through the brain.

The Dunblane Massacre

Thomas Hamilton

The entire incident was over in just five minutes, but the shock would fill most people with utter horror. A forty-three-year-old man with four hand-guns and several hundred rounds of ammunition had gone into a primary school in Dunblane in Scotland and opened fire.

Sixteen of the children, who were aged five or six years, were just killed at random; their forty-five-year-old teacher was also killed. There were twenty-eight children in the gym at Dunblane Primary School, as a PE lesson was under preparation.

Eileen Harrild was the teacher in charge of the class, and was no doubt surprised to see a strange man just walk into the gym. As she approached him to confront him about his presence he started shooting. Throwing up her arms to instinctively protect herself, she sustained injuries to her arms and chest. She managed to stumble to cover with some of the injured children. Mary Blake, the third adult present, was shot in the legs and head but managed to take other children to safety. What was going through the children's minds could have been incomprehension (until later), but for the two surviving adults it must have been beyond comprehension.

The attack seemed to be in three waves. The first of twenty-nine shots killed one child and injured several others; the gunman then walked up the gym where he fired six shots and then eight shots towards the far end of the gym. At the centre of the gym he fired sixteen shots at a group of children.

He saw a child look in the window so shot at him, but he was only injured by flying glass. The gunman then fired over twenty more shots before firing at random across the playground; in the cloakroom Grace Tweedle was wounded.

He left the gym and fired nine shots into a mobile classroom whose teacher had told her pupils to take cover. He re-entered the gym, discarded one weapon and took up another – he then put the barrel to the roof of his mouth and pulled the trigger. Death would have been instantaneous.

Of the school pupils and staff, sixteen were killed and sixteen injured.

Thomas Hamilton had been born in Glasgow in May 1952, and it wasn't until the early 1970s that his behaviour as a scout leader was questioned. It was enough for the Scouting Movement to request he leave. Complaints were made from members of youth groups he ran, but no criminal charges were brought.

Some documents have been subjected to a 100-year ban from public access. This is a long time and the main reason for this is that it might distress families. What could distress a family more than a gunman in a school?

This leads to the question – what don't we know? Thomas Hamilton's associates, for one thing. He was blackballed by the scouts, so how did he open boys' clubs?

East Anglia
Murders by person(s) unknown

No one knows the secrets of serial killers, and what murders they have got away with, but the police will follow up and a case of murder is rarely closed. When Norfolk made the headlines as five young girls' bodies were discovered within two weeks in December 2006, there were big questions about other unsolved murders in the area.

Natalie Pearman was only sixteen when her strangled body was found to the north-west of Norwich in 1992. She had a history of abusing drugs, and to fund her habit she sold her body – a risky business, and she paid with her life. However, her body was found about five miles from where she was usually to be found. The case is still open and the police have periodically reviewed it. They have DNA from Natalie – she'd had sex just before she died and the hope is eventually the police will find a link.

Amanda Duncan went missing the following July from the Portman Road area of Ipswich. She'd visited a house in London Road before she went to her usual haunts to sell herself. Mandy, as she was known, was to return to the house later but never did. In fact, she hasn't been seen since that night. As with Natalie (above), the police will keep the file open, but they were particularly interested in the driver of a Ford Sierra and a Ford Orion – Mandy was talking to the driver and this was one of the last times she was seen. The Orion was driven by a white male, thought to be in his late twenties. The car had a defective exhaust.

In both cases police are aware that some people may not come forward because of the association with the girls' street-work, but it's hoped that now twenty years have passed, they might be less uncomfortable about it.

But people were not uncomfortable to tell police they heard a sports car roar off into the night in September 1999 from the village of Trimley St Mary near Felixstowe. Others told of a local businessman who was seen in the vicinity of where seventeen-year-old student Vicky Hall lived – for the simple reason that he lived in the village too. So someone was seen in the early hours who owned a sports car. The arrest happened about fifteen months after Vicky's death, although police forensic experts could find no trace of Vicky or proof she'd ever been in the car. A tiny portion of earth said to come from the ditch Vicky was found in was in the car, but the defence's botany expert refuted this. It cost £2 million to get this man into court for a two week trial, at the end of which the jury took just over an hour to acquit him.

Vicky was neither a user of drugs, nor was she linked in any way to the vice industry. Her clothes were never found and even though she was found naked there was no evidence either of a struggle or of sexual assault or rape. It is a strange case, and one that baffled police: after the trial, through his grief, her father was quoted to have said, 'Unless someone owns up to their actions on that night and tells us exactly what happened, that is the only little bit of help we could have.'

His wife added, 'We have lost Victoria and nothing will ever change that, whatever happens. I don't think anyone can put into words how I feel today.'

Kelly Pratt came down from Newcastle to ply her trade on the streets of Norwich. After her disappearance her body was never found, so it's possible she is still alive, as Mandy Duncan might be, but it's extremely doubtful. These girls were just taken and murdered and, lest the moralists on their mountains preach, they seem to have done little harm in their lives. It is true (not of Vicky Hall) that they used drugs, but there is nothing to say they peddled or sold them. Public opinion, though, is against any major policy change for prostitution, though it isn't an offence for a woman to sell herself – it's the seedier side of brothels, kerb-crawling and pimping (to name but a few) that attract punishment.

The Association of Chief Police Officers feel that the decriminalisation of prostitution would be a step towards a safer environment for sex workers, though a House of Commons group, following a visit to a European city, concluded it wouldn't make much difference.

The murder of such girls has attracted ambivalent publicity, and there has even been criticism of the police for using so much manpower and money (the investigation into Vicky Halls murder cost over £2 million). But the point is that if a killer decides to kill – and it's largely down to a decision rather than a mental illness – he might kill anyone, not just target prostitutes; going back to the Yorkshire Ripper, Jane McDonald stands out as an 'ordinary' girl caught in the cross-fire.

Naturally, serial killers are charged for the crimes the police can get enough evidence on; with most serial killers, if not all, the head count of the victims is rarely fewer than reported or for what they are convicted on. The girls I have been discussing here were all from the Norfolk/Suffolk area, where a serial killer was later identified. With modern technology, the police and scientists can better tell if a person has or hasn't had proximity to a murder victim.

Edmund-Davies, Baron Herbert
Judge

The man who gave the Great Train Robbers such big sentences had one of the keenest brains in the judiciary in the sixties and seventies. He had been more of an academic, receiving a Doctorate of Law at Kings College. For a while he lectured at the London School of Economics.

Born in July of 1906, he came from a fairly ordinary background in Mid-Glamorgan and a lot of his education was through scholarships. He was called to the bar in 1929. His career was temporarily halted by the war and he served with the Royal Welsh Fusiliers.

His father was Mr Davies, who'd married a Miss Edmund, and he was always referred to as Mr Edmund Davies, so when he was elevated he hyphenated his last two names to become Lord Edmund-Davies, Lord of Appeal in Ordinary, in the seventies.

He'd built up a successful chambers in Swansea, where he was a formidable defence counsel in the 1950s – I'll mention a couple of interesting criminal cases shortly.

In 1952, he was appointed Recorder of Cardiff, and in 1958 Lord Kilmuir appointed him to the High Court bench. He presided over the trial of Gunther Padola, who'd shot and killed a police officer and was later hanged. In 1964 he added more to the legend of the Great Train Robbery with the sentences he meted out, which may have been an own-goal because it brought sympathy to the robbers, though it might have made a few of their followers think twice – but it may have prompted more violence to avoid being caught. Paradoxically, he was an advocate of penal reform and became a member of the Royal Commission on Penal Reform. Serious criminals, he suggested, could be reformed, but serious crime should attract serious punishment.

Lord Edmund-Davies chaired the enquiry into the Aberfan disaster. He was highly critical of the National Coal Board for building such large slag piles so close to the town.

He seemed to be a criminal lawyer by intuition, but it did him no favours: he'd often just take a quick sandwich for lunch, and later he'd pore over cases or consider judgements for the following day late into the night.

Shortly after going to the Lords, he chaired the Police Inquiry, which looked at pay and conditions of the service. His recommendations on a better pay structure weren't greeted with enthusiasm by government.

He was of the old brigade of judges who weren't forced to retire, but he threw in the towel in 1981 – he was seventy-five, and did have a family and other interests, not least of which was his passion for his roots.

At the bar he had two outstanding cases in South Wales in which he led for the defence, the first of which was in 1952, when Alicia Millicent Roberts was accused of murdering her husband John with arsenic and it looked as if the verdict of guilty was a formality. It was said Mr Edmund Davies and Elwyn Jones, his junior and Mrs Roberts' solicitor, worked fifteen hours a day. In evidence, it came out that her husband had been a 'brute' and made excessive sexual demands. His son (her step-son) also told the court his father had mentioned suicide. After the not guilty verdict they left the court to great cheers from the crowd at Swansea Assizes – Mrs Roberts was also given a conditional discharge for her attempted suicide while on remand. The children of both Mrs Roberts and her husband's first marriage were thrilled. The outcome of that case, although buried in years of obscurity, was hailed as a 'great demonstration of British Justice.' There was demonstrable doubt.

In 1953 George Roberts was accused of battering a retired school teacher to death. Mr Edmund Davies suggested to Mr Justice Devlin, after the Clerk of the Court had asked the defendant his name, 'The accused is a deaf mute – I do not think he can comprehend the question that has been put to him.'

George's uncle said, 'To my knowledge he has never been able to speak and cannot hear.'

After much arguing by the prosecution, Mr Edmund Davies' defence was simple: if a man can't hear the charge then he can't answer it. The jury agreed, when finding him mute 'By visitation of God', and delighted the village, who never thought he could ever harm anyone.

Baron Hubert Edmund Edmund-Davies died on Boxing Day 1992 aged eighty-six.

Ellis, Peter

Attempted murder of his wife, Lisa

Peter Ellis was adept at making money and was a successful businessman; he had a clutch of bed-sits in Cardiff, from which he lived very well. By 1993 he was married with two daughters, but had another lady-friend and didn't want to face a large divorce settlement. The answer was to wire up the bath to the electricity mains to kill his wife. But at flashpoint, she merely leapt out of the bath; had she grabbed the taps, bath rail or anything metallic, then she would have earthed the charge and been killed. A consultant forensic pathologist explained that if she'd been killed then the likelihood was that the death would have been attributed to a heart attack.

Mr Ellis was in his mid-thirties and had met his wife, Lisa, through his church, and every soul he met thought he was special. But the police said this was the usual front for a conman. Some years before, he had faced deception charges, so simply photocopied headed notepaper from South Wales Police, then forged the superintendent's signature on a letter to the court and lawyers saying there was no evidence to proceed; an eagle-eyed detective noticed the forgery, but he nearly got away with impersonating a police officer and perverting the course of justice – which was then added to the original charge.

He'd lied to and deceived both women for a good while; the lover and the wife discovered each other when the lover discovered his address and confronted him: with a slap and some well-chosen words.

The answer for Mr Ellis was that as he didn't want to share his money (he'd recently pulled off a scam netting himself £25,000 by fraud), he planned to kill his wife. Very few, and more by luck than anything else, can outsmart the police and forensic scientists. It was discovered there was an electrical charge through the bath – it actually melted the bath chain.

He'd also, just prior to the event, insured her life for over half a million!

In court he put up his defence that this was the scorned wife who made it all up, and that he was a good man and deeply religious: the prosecution told the court that 'his real religion was hypocrisy, selfishness and deceit'.

The jury at Cardiff Crown Court didn't believe Mr Ellis was anything but guilty. Mr Justice McKinnon praised Lisa for her strength and fortitude. He was jailed for fifteen years for attempted murder, with three years for a number of deception charges.

One hopes Lisa and his lover found future happiness. The sad thing is that his mother collected the rents on his bed-sits, and if he did serve his full term he'd leave prison with a six-figure bank balance.

Ellis, Ruth
Murder of David Blakely

I've never had any doubt that Ruth Ellis was guilty of murder – the conviction was sound, but the punishment was an obscenity.

Ruth was born in Rhyl in North Wales and had five siblings, though one is said to be the result of parental sexual abuse, and Ruth, it was said, was abused by her father. They moved south to Basingstoke in Hampshire before finishing up in London. Much of Ruth's schooling was in Basingstoke and she left school at fourteen.

She was employed initially as a waitress but within three years she'd given birth to her son, Andy. His father was a Canadian soldier.

After this time, she took up work in nightclubs, where she was popular with men for her retorts to their crude innuendoes. She also did a bit of nude modelling. When she was twenty-three she married an alcoholic dentist called George Ellis, and that marriage was doomed almost before it got off the ground. Her daughter Georgina was born in October 1951, but George refused to accept paternity and accused her of numerous infidelities.

He was soon off the scene, though he wouldn't stay away. Ruth was earning good money, some earned by the odd bit of duty above and beyond. However, one can't really identify much in her life that would help her self-esteem. The Little Club in Knightsbridge had an owner who, although seemingly generous, also had a large sexual appetite.

Then she seemed to meet the man of her dreams: David Blakely, a bit of a ladies' man who was moving up the success ladder – though not very quickly – at motor racing. The relationship was fiery, to say the least, and Ruth miscarried after he'd punched her in the stomach. They were both unfaithful, but it's clear to see that her self-esteem was getting lower still.

But then she met another man through mutual friends, Desmond Cussen, who was a good deal older than Ruth and David; he became besotted with Ruth. His dislike of David became open hatred. With Ruth's history of abuse – she also, it is claimed, had an illegal abortion – and David's violence, together with Desmond's 'input', there was a disaster waiting to happen.

But this is where I think the situation could have been saved, though on the other hand one has to recognise that it was a gradual 'wearing down' dynamic in which Ruth may not have seen how far she was moving into an impossible situation, in an impossible state of mind. It came to a head, but by the time it did she'd been drinking Pernod like it was going out of fashion. It's also recognised that Ruth admitted that Desmond did play a large role in the crescendo, but this wasn't made public, though the police and Home Office were aware at the time. Desmond wasn't prosecuted, as Ruth was the only witness and it was at the very end of her life that this came out.

It was late in the evening of Easter Sunday – 10 April, 1955 – that David and his friend, Clive Gunnell, left the Magdala pub in Hampstead. Ruth was outside, but he didn't see her. As he walked to his car Ruth called out to him and took aim with a Smith and Wesson revolver she'd taken from her bag. It was the second and third shot that felled him; Ruth walked up to him and pumped three more bullets into him.

One wonders if she saved the sixth and last bullet for herself but other reports say the shot missed and hit a passer-by in the hand. Ruth then turned to Clive and suggested he might call the police.

She'd obtained the gun and put it in her bag, travelled up to the Magdala and then waited. That shows intent. She then fired until the gun was empty; that is murder, no matter what people might argue of her past and present abuse, or that she was at the end of a number of months of provocation. Nowadays, one might suggest diminished responsibility but it would be for a court to decide. And with such a deliberate act, manslaughter would be a big uphill struggle for any lawyer.

An off-duty policeman was in the bar and made the arrest, but from that moment on, Ruth didn't resist any exercising of the law. Her police statement describes the victim's actions of running but is interspersed with quite matter-of-fact description. 'I took the gun from my bag and I shot him … I thought I had missed him so I fired again. He was still running and I fired a third shot. I don't remember firing any more but I must have done.'

She was charged with murder and her case, before Mr Justice Havers, opened at the Old Bailey on 20 June 1955. Leading for the Prosecution Mr Christmas Humphries QC asked her what she intended to do when she had the gun in her hand. 'It's obvious when I shot him I intended to kill him.'

Mr Justice Havers advised the jury that there was not sufficient evidence to suggest provocation as a defence so manslaughter couldn't be supported. '... there does not seem to be anything in it [her evidence] which establishes any sort of defence to the charge of murder.'

The jury were the next stage where choice didn't appear – they convicted in just under a quarter of an hour.

And finally Mr Justice Havers had no choice; she was convicted and sentenced to death, though he recommended mercy. But the Home Secretary, Gwilym Lloyd George, had the final decision on behalf of the Queen. He was quoted to have said, in rejecting the appeal, 'If a reprieve were to be granted in this case, I think that we should have seriously to consider whether capital punishment should be retained as a penalty.'

The matter was discussed by the Cabinet, and one can identify Ruth Ellis as a major contributor to the abolition of the death sentence a decade later.

But her execution was set. There was an outcry and petitions were signed in the thousands. Ruth didn't appeal, she was resigned to her fate – but is the word 'resigned' appropriate?

The last visitors departed the day before the execution and she settled to write a few letters. An apology went to David Blakely's parents, and another exposing Desmond Cussen, who supplied the gun.

With hundreds of people outside the prison shouting and screaming, Ruth Ellis was hanged at Holloway Prison by Albert Pierrepoint on Wednesday 13 July 1955. Her body was buried within the prison, but she was later moved to St Mary's Church in Amersham, Buckinghamshire.

It's difficult to see what possible argument there is to quash the conviction, but as long as the argument continues, the death sentence will remain a reminder of the barbaric times so recently tolerated.

Fabb, April
Disappeared without trace, April 1969

It was her sister Pamela's husband, Bernard, who'd had his twenty-eighth birthday the day before, which necessitated the trip. It was a very short trip and on that spring afternoon of 8 April 1969 she left home to deliver his birthday present – it was a packet of ten cigarettes. Pamela had been married to him for four or five years and their son, Duncan, was April's first nephew.

April Fabb was thirteen as she pedalled away from home that afternoon at about twenty minutes to two. She saw some friends along the way, but by 2.00 p.m. she was well on the way to Roughton, the village next to Metton, in Norfolk, where she lived. One of the farm labourers at Harrison's farm saw her just after. But between 2.00 p.m. and 2.15 p.m., she vanished. No trace was ever found of her – at 2.15 p.m., her bicycle was found in a field.

There were no signs found of freshly dug earth in the vicinity, so the most likely event was that she was abducted, or that someone local had hidden her somewhere, but in the huge police operation that followed she would have been found. If she were abducted she could have been literally anywhere; even though Metton is in north Norfolk, that wouldn't really have mattered.

There are two killers on life sentences, who will probably never be released, who may know something. Robert Black drove a van all over the country and Europe, and although he didn't have a drivers licence until much later there is nothing to say he didn't steal a van or a car in the area and do the deed, though his victims were mainly dumped and eventually found. Another had links with the area; Peter Tobin's victim number has yet to be decided but he did conceal some of his victims very well. Neither man has any real motivation to help the enquiry, as they will not be released from prison.

One frightening theory is that it may be someone who develops a different *modus operandi* for each crime, who might have several under his belt and has always stayed one step ahead of detection.

April's father died in 1998, never knowing his daughter's fate; his wife, April's mum, died in 2013. The agony of not knowing can never truly be imagined, but the police will never give up.

Fairley, Malcolm
Multiple rapist: The Fox

In April 1984, a seventy-four-year-old woman, who lived alone, retired to bed at 9 o'clock in her Linslade, Leighton Buzzard, home. She read for a while and then settled. She drifted off only to be awakened by a man in her bedroom. He held his hand over her mouth and indecently assaulted her. This, though, was just the start.

On 10 May, he broke into a house in Cheddington, where a man lived alone. The Fox stole £300 and a shotgun and cartridges. He thought he'd stay a while and confronted the occupier wearing a mask and brandishing the gun. He then indecently assaulted him.

There followed three burglaries without violence, but the Fox obtained another shotgun – he'd buried the previous one and later couldn't find it.

Three days later, he was in a property near Leighton Buzzard. He rearranged furniture and made a sort of liar, then waited, but raided their fridge when hunger got the better of him. He also made a pot of tea and thought better of it – he stole £130 and left. The owners found the teapot was still warm. But in the town of Leighton Buzzard a married couple were asleep and awoke to find him holding the shotgun and wearing a mask. He shot the husband in the hand but the husband still chased him away; he later told the police the gun shot was an accident which shook him.

But in the first week of July, at night, he entered a house in Linslade. He was armed. When his victims woke he tied them up and indecently assaulted the wife, who screamed, and he fled. Four days later he broke into a bungalow, where a family of four were, forced the wife to tie up her husband and indecently assaulted her. Her husband was hit with the butt of the gun and the Fox then raped his wife. He tied her up and made his escape.

In mid-August, an eighteen-year-old girl and her boyfriend were at her home together with her younger brother. All three were tied up, the girl in the bedroom – he took a drink and calmly raped her. Later he raped her again before he left.

He committed a series of burglaries in Milton Keynes, and shortly after travelled up to Durham (his home county). On the way, just where the M1 and M18 divide (just east of Rotherham), he 'parked' on the hard shoulder and made his way over the fields to a small village, broke into a house and tied the occupants together by the leg. He raped the woman, cut a portion of soiled bedding, and left.

Before travelling further he hid the gun, but more tellingly, he reversed the car onto a bush branch and left a paint mark from his car. In Sunderland, he committed two more crimes before returning south.

By now, the police were expanding the team of officers to catch him and the public were forming their own vigilante groups. The offences continued, now around the Milton Keynes area.

It was a good old police hunch that thought when he was on his way north and an attack occurred, then he might have stopped on the M18. Tracks were found leading from the crime scene at the bungalow to a spot where a car had scraped against a bush leaving the paint; there were tyre marks, too. The police also found the gun and a mask. They now knew his car colour – it was the break they needed.

The paint was 'harvest yellow' and it was a British Leyland car. So, with the vague physical description, it was time for the police officers to whittle down the list. A couple of detectives found a car with a scrape in the right place, and a garment missing a trouser leg – the same colour as fabric of the mask found just off the M18. He was the right height and build, and his accent was from the north-east. When invited to help the police with their enquiries, he confessed.

He received six life sentences.

Flannelfoot
Henry Vickers

Walter Hambrook was a policeman with the Metropolitan Police, whose most satisfying moment was when he saw Henry Edward Vickers sent to prison. But that was after Mr Hambrook retired as detective superintendent of the Flying Squad – a squad he'd helped to form.

Some years before, while a detective sergeant, Mr Hambrook had arrested a jobbing burglar who had the strange habit of wearing flannel around his shoes so he didn't make a sound as he burgled. He was sent to prison for just under a year and Mr Hambrook got on with his career.

In 1932 a spate of burglaries that were to total several hundred started, and eventually the local police called in Scotland Yard, headed by Mr Hambrook. After some while it occurred to him that he'd met this *modus operandi* before, and he wracked his brains: one evening, on his way home, he was recognised by a city gent. They got talking and it turned out he was the prosecutor from twenty-odd years before. DSupt Hambrook checked through the records: it was him! Henry Vickers was back. If the police could find him then the case would be cracked. *If* the police could find him ...

The burglaries continued, and on most weekends a spate of them would occur somewhere or other in the London suburbs. He laughed at the special precautions the press would report from police conferences. A map in Scotland Yard was marked with pins: Greenford, Stanmore, Sudbury Heights, Stoneleigh Park, Cheam, Wealdstone, Blackheath, Surbiton, Morden, Enfield, Acton and twenty other suburbs were highlighted. They must have considered taking the pins out and put them on the map where he hadn't raided.

Flannelfoot would leave home at about nine o'clock in the evening and catch a bus or tube to his targeted area, which would be a row of houses where the occupants were preparing for bed. He worked silently and quickly, scouring the house for cash or small valuables that could be sold on quickly with little possibility of being traced. He'd also relieve gas and electricity meters – and with the majority of suburban workers on weekly cash wages, it meant cash would be in the house. When one house was 'done', he simply moved next door. Typically, four or five houses in a row were entered in this manner. Sums of about £20 were not uncommon for the final haul, which today would be a fraction under £1,200. He would obviously wear gloves, and sometimes take a snack from the larder, and he would be endeared to the house dog. The public were getting irritated by the police's lack of progress; the police were getting more than irritated by the lack of progress.

He'd leave the flannel rags behind him as a sort of 'insolent calling card'.Sometimes they'd be pinned up on a picture frame, or left neatly crossed on the back doorstep. And he'd write to the police praising an officer who'd, for instance, given him directions to the nearest tube station when his night's escapades were over. 'Nice of the police officer to tell me ....'

Another first was how he'd ring up Scotland Yard and tell them: 'Just off to Brighton for a while. Will let you know when I'm back'. This would have incensed the officers. And at Christmas he rang up to wish them a merry Christmas and a happy New Year.

Mr Hambrook continued to wrack his brain and remembered Mr Vickers had married and had a daughter, but when Mrs Vickers was traced the story was that her husband and daughter had vanished. The thought was that they were in London, which didn't narrow it down much.

In June 1935 a beat police officer saw a girl of fifteen wandering aimlessly through the streets of London. She looked dazed and helpless. He spoke to her and found she was confused about her life and could recall few details. She became Patient No. 27 in Highgate Hospital – the girl without a name.

The hospital asked the *Daily Mirror* to help, and when they printed the picture Mrs Vickers was on her way to reunite with her daughter, Elsie. There was now her name, address and other more pertinent information. The detectives questioned her gently about her father and she explained that he went out some nights and came home early in the morning. 'He used to come in and pour money all over my bed,' she said.

She was frightened and ran away from her father, but any employment was met with questions she couldn't answer. However, the police now had an address, which they watched around the clock. He was followed everywhere he went. One Friday night – his favourite night, because pay packets were plentiful – they arrested him, peacefully and quietly; he'd never used force or violence.

During questioning he was shown a huge collection of theft and burglary reports and asked for a pencil; he ticked thirty four of them. In January 1937 he was sentenced to five years.

Mr Vickers died in 1942.

WPC Fletcher, Yvonne

Police officers are more likely to be hurt doing their job than most others. This is a fact, not an acceptable one, but a fact. Indeed, they'll put themselves between the public and a possible threat almost by nature, and most folk are appalled to hear of one of them murdered when on duty. Sadly, history has recorded many of them, but one soul who was mortally wounded was twenty-five-year-old Yvonne Fletcher.

It was on 18 April 1984 that she'd been on duty outside the Libyan Embassy in London, where a group of Libyan dissidents were showing their opposition to the Libyan government led by Muammar Gaddafi. Trouble was expected, not to put too fine a point on it.

At just after quarter past ten when pro-Gaddafi demonstrators arrived to drown the protest, shots rang out. Eleven people were injured and one bullet hit WPC Fletcher in the stomach. She was taken to hospital but died about an hour later.

There followed an eleven-day siege of the Libyan Embassy and the staff were finally expelled from the UK; sanctions against Libya were put in place. It's been suggested that this incident led to Prime Minister Margaret Thatcher allowing the US to base their combat aircraft in the UK to later attack Libya.

The Libyan Government expected that the murderer should get diplomatic immunity; the British Government eventually let the diplomatic staff depart, but diplomatic relations were broken off between the two countries.

Things went quiet between UK and Libya until the Lockerbie bombing. Eventually Gaddafi accepted Libya was responsible. Compensation or reparation payments were made, which was to include victims of the Lockerbie bombing, but this didn't come until 1999. After Gaddafi was removed from power the new Prime Minister, Shukri Ghaney, said that Libya wasn't responsible for

WPC Fletcher's murder and that they'd accepted responsibility merely to resume international relations.

Has he got a point? Were the occupants of the Libyan Embassy not responsible?

The official line was that WPC Fletcher had been killed by a bullet from the second floor of the Libyan Embassy.

But take a ballistics expert and two of the country's leading forensic pathologists and ask them if the bullet could possibly have been shot from the second floor of the Libyan Embassy. They will dispute it – with the velocity of the bullet and its supposed origin, it would have travelled at a 15° angle. But it didn't. It would be more likely to come from an adjacent building and from a higher floor. I daresay that eventually an alternative 'official' line will be adopted.

Gadd, Paul Francis – AKA Gary Glitter
Paedophile

It was in May of 1944 that Ms Gadd had a son, Paul Francis. She was single and her mother helped her to bring him up with his brother. The young Mr Gadd had a good singing ability and was a natural showman. He performed poorly at school and ran away to London, where he was fortunate, although his singing and entertaining career didn't immediately take off. But as 'Paul Raven' he did impress, and in the early seventies, with the coming of glam-rock, his singing, song-writing and entertainment prowess shot him to fame – he was now known as Gary Glitter.

His career declined somewhat as the seventies wore on, but he had a bit of a peak again in the eighties. By 1987 the rot had started to set in, with three drinking and driving charges that led to a ten-year ban, and he missed prison by a hairsbreadth. Some of his other activities were to come back to haunt him later.

In 1997 he took his laptop to PC World for repair, and in the course of this repair it was found to hold a number of pornographic images of children – the rot was now well established and was media fodder. He was convicted and sentenced to four months' imprisonment – the number of images ran into thousands.

He also faced charges of having a sexual encounter with a fourteen-year-old girl in the late seventies, but was acquitted. Now a target of national hatred, he left Britain and travelled far and wide, to emerge in Cambodia just after the millennium; from there, he was deported to Vietnam to face charges of child sex abuse – he was found guilty of 'obscene acts with minors' and given a prison sentence. He might have faced a charge of child rape, which would have carried the death sentence. However, he was sentenced to three years, and on his release in 2008 was sent back to the UK, where he was placed on the Sex Offenders' Register for life.

He gave an interview for the BBC, and inevitably the subject was broached; he gave an answer that was later said to try and minimise his offending. Christine Beddoe, who is the UK representative of the international ECPAT network (End Child Prostitution, Child Pornography and Trafficking), responded by suggesting we should hear from the children and not from him – that seems reasonable!

Mr Gadd blamed the press for his downfall, though it's difficult to see how. They may well have contributed; if they ran true to form, they may have exaggerated it. But he has been convicted in more than one country – the press don't convict, the courts do.

The Home Secretary of the time, Jacqui Smith, said he should be given a Foreign Travel Order (FTO), which would stop him leaving the country, thereby 'controlling' him – but a number of countries throughout the world have refused him entry.

He was going to appeal against his lifetime's entry on the Sex Offenders Register, but decided not to.

More recently, 'Operation Yewtree' was set up to investigate past sex crimes by celebrities. His association with Jimmy Savile was probed and in June 2014 he was charged with eight counts of sexual offences against twelve- to fourteen-year-old girls, between 1977 and 1980; he was subsequently jailed for sixteen years.

Goddard, Baron Rayner of Aldbourne
Judge

Rayner Goddard has been praised and criticised for his work in the judiciary. As Lord Chief Justice he was famous for dismissing cases with the utmost rapidity and he was to make sure Derek Bentley went to the gallows in 1953. But he also believed in penal reform and wouldn't imprison a younger convict if it could be avoided. The fact is, though, that his tenure as Lord Chief Justice from 1946 to 1958 saw a number of social changes and it was a time when crime was rising. Much as his actions may be despised with hindsight, it was a different world – it may have been necessary to take a firm line.

He was born in Notting Hill in 1877 and attended Marlborough College, and later Trinity College in Oxford; he graduated in 1898 and was called to the bar in 1899. Just under a decade later he married Marie and they had three daughters, but sadly she died during surgery in her mid-forties.

Mr Goddard, as he then was, specialised in commercial law, but towards the end of the Great War he was appointed as Recorder for Poole in Dorset; he then took silk in 1923. Briefly, he was Recorder for Bath, before moving down to Devon three years later.

In spring of 1932 he became a full-time High Court Judge and was knighted a few months later. Only six years later he went to the Court of Appeal as a Lord Justice, where his power and eloquence were noted in legal argument.

He received a life peerage as a Law Lord in 1944 and became Baron Goddard. In 1946 he became Lord Chief Justice, and with

Clement Attlee taking the House of Commons by a landslide it was time for peace, with a low crime rate. The war on crime had begun; Lord Goddard was to be its general, and it was thus that historians have tended to judge him, but he did feel a stronger arm of the law was a necessity.

There were a few faces who would become underworld generals. Derek Bentley, though, wasn't one of them, and even though it's accepted that there were social changes taking place in the country – which still had rationing in the 1950s – a fair trial was still his right. It's been suggested that the police officer who died when Derek Bentley was 'in custody' may have been hit by a police marksman's bullet.

Two years later, Lord Goddard let slip that his feelings for police officers was that they should be able to obtain evidence in any way they can, and the test of the evidence was whether it was relevant or not. This is quite frightening now, but things have moved on. It was qualified by the test of unfairness to the accused, but it still seemed to give the police the power to operate outside the law, although things have been tightened up since. His main concern wasn't the police but the 'Gangster's Charter', though one has to ask, just who were the gangsters?

He stepped down as Lord Chief Justice in 1958, but continued to attend the House of Lords and in April of the following year he actually returned to the Court of Appeal because a huge pile of cases had built up and he helped to clear them.

From the end of the war until the beginning of the 1970s, the moral infrastructure of the country changed almost beyond recognition and some really quite horrible crimes were committed. So when in 1970 he was asked about the Derek Bentley case, its small wonder his view had become that he'd hoped for a reprieve. But criticising David Maxwell-Fyffe the Home Secretary didn't particularly help his case, especially as he was quoted to have said, 'The blame for Bentley's execution rests solely with Fyfe.'

One can see his point, but, in conducting the trial, the defence wasn't given the latitude it needed and so Derek's trial was not fair; the blame for this falls squarely with Lord Goddard. Indeed, one of the barristers involved with the defence openly criticised Lord Goddard. John Parris was in hot water as a consequence. Journalist Bernard Levin thought he was a bully and said so publically. Lord Goddard's former clerk suggested he ejaculated when he gave the death sentence. But Lord Bingham said he was 'one of the outstanding criminal judges of the century'.

Baron Goddard died in May 1971.

Goozee, Albert William
The murder of Mrs Lydia and Miss Norma Leakey

Albert Goozee was a lodger with Lydia Leakey in Parkstone, Dorset. She was twenty years older than him, but a relationship bloomed. Her daughter Norma was nearly twenty years younger than Mr Goozee but, again, a relationship bloomed.

On 17 June 1956 the three of them went into the New Forest for a picnic, but they didn't come back. Lydia and Norma were stabbed to death and he was rushed to hospital with stab wounds. The police suspected Mr Goozee, and by the end of July he was fit enough to stand trial for murder, and at Hampshire Assizes it was alleged that he killed both Lydia and Norma.

He explained that Lydia's husband didn't treat her well and she'd told him how lonely she felt. He went on to say that Lydia wanted to get into bed with him and as she was crying he agreed. The next stage in the plot was that her daughter Norma came in and her mother suggested she got into bed too. Mr Goozee's statement went on to say that Norma gave him an ultimatum – he either had sex with her too or she would tell her father about her mother and him. When he refused, a bit of a row developed.

Mr Leakey became involved and after a fight Mr Goozee left the lodging house.

However, contact was either maintained or re-established and the three – mum, daughter and Mr Goozee – went for their trip into the New Forest. He and Lydia reclined together on a blanket and when Norma saw them, according to his statement, she attacked her mother. Her mother took refuge in the car where she produced a knife and when Mr Goozee went to take it from her he was stabbed. He apparently still managed to get hold of the knife and stabbed Lydia. Norma approached the car and screamed 'What have you done to my mother?' His statement concluded that, 'After that my mind must have gone blank.'

In his summing up Mr Justice Havers suggested that he'd got so inextricably linked in this triangle that the only solution was to kill them and then kill himself. As the jury weren't entirely convinced that Mr Goozee's version of events was true they convicted him. He was sentenced to death.

He was reprieved shortly before the execution was to take place. He served fifteen years.

Gray, Gilbert QC
Barrister

Gilbert Gray was labelled a 'formidable' barrister, and he had a reputation for not always following his clients' instructions. But this was mainly where he was defending the indefensible.

Mr Gray was born in April 1928 at Scarborough in Yorkshire; his father was a butcher and local magistrate. He went to Leeds University, where he switched from theology to law; he was also president of the students' union.

He was called to the bar in 1953 and took silk in 1971. John Poulson was a client, as were senior executives of Matrix Churchill

– and Peter Wright, who wrote of his MI5 activities. He was active in the Brinks-Mat case as well as civil cases, including *The Herald of Free Enterprise* in the late 1980s. Mr Gray was also called on in the case of James Kelly who died in police custody – Mr Kelly was punched, sat on and had his testicles squeezed; he died of heart failure because he 'exerted' himself.

But when Mr Gray was retained for the almost impossible task of defending Donald Neilson, the Black Panther, his name made the national headlines. Mr Nielson pleaded guilty to kidnap and blackmail, but denied murder, leaving Mr Gray with an almost impossible task. Mr Gray tried to persuade the jury that even though Mr Neilson was bad, he wasn't quite so bad to earn the title of the Black Panther. He explained, 'You have heard much about Mr Neilson and the Black Panther; but you may, when you have heard of this man's pathetic attempts to 'make it big', think rather of the Pink Panther and Mr Peter Sellers.'

But Mr Neilson was determined not to be caught; three sub-postmasters were shot dead and much carnage surrounded those raids. Mr Neilson also shot a security guard, and when he kidnapped a teenage heiress his activities turned to the unspeakable.

Apparently Mr Neilson fixed Mr Gray with a 'stare of rage' at this 'enormously unwelcome' line of defence. It didn't cut any ice with the jury, but it's difficult to imagine what would – Mr Neilson was given several life sentences. The case had attracted huge media coverage throughout and it's difficult to imagine how a jury member could stay immune from such publicity.

Following on from this Mr Gray was called upon to defend John Lambe, who was called the M5 rapist as his crimes were often in the vicinity of that artery or its tributaries.

It was in 1981 that the case came to court and if rape is about the perversion of power then Mr Lambe satisfied his bizarre needs, but there might have been ways he could have achieved his objectives with fewer people caught in the crossfire. His rationale was that he'd been in a remand home early in his life and had developed a sense of injustice – it wasn't the ladies he attacked that were his primary targets; he wanted to challenge and humiliate the police. When one thinks that it took something like three and a half years and the attention of several hundred police officers to catch him, then he might have achieved what he set out to do. But, as I say, it was a shame so many were caught in the cross-fire.

With the guilty plea, however, Mr Lambe saved his victims (survivors) an ordeal in court. In his final speech Mr Gray said his client was 'utterly remorseful and totally apologetic ... [the crimes were] quite overwhelmed by so many other factors and features, and one feature of immense gratification far in excess of the sexual side. All the time he was rejoicing in the prospect of causing the police confusion . . .'

Mr Gray became a Crown Court Recorder in 1972 – an appointment made by the Queen on the Lord Chancellor's recommendation – and held the post until 1988. It's the basic grade of judge. But his strength was as a barrister and he didn't retire until his death in April 2011.

Twice he stood as a parliamentary candidate for the Liberal Party in the 1950s, but was unsuccessful. Mr Gray was married to Dilys in 1954 and they had four children. He worked for charities and his generosity was usually in favour of the Royal National Lifeboat Institute, which came from engagements as an after-dinner speaker – his wit was also noted in the barristers' robing rooms.

The Great Train Robbery
Cheddington, Buckinghamshire, 1963

This crime wrote headlines around the world. At first it was merely called the Cheddington Mail raid, but as soon as the press got hold of it they just asked their readers to sit back and watch the figure go up. And that's the direction it went.

The local police sent a couple of police constables along with the report of a theft at Cheddington Station. This was closed at night, with minimal cash kept on the premises – just enough for the float for the ticket office till. When it was realised that a train had been stolen then it suggested a bigger crime; when it was realised it was the 'up special' travelling post office, which could be carrying cash, it grew bigger still. And when it was known the train was carrying far more bags of money than at first thought it was declared a huge crime.

Senior police officers were called in. Scotland Yard was involved virtually from the start. The British Transport Police and the Post Office Investigation Branch were all called together for a meeting to see who was to do what. There were two jobs – to catch and prosecute those responsible and to recover the money.

By now it was called the Great Train Robbery, and media from around the world wanted to know all about it. A gang of fourteen men with two extras – one of whom was their own train driver, the other his 'minder' – were at the trackside. The signals were rigged and the train stopped, was divided and moved a few hundred yards to where it could be relieved of about 120 bags, containing over £2 million. Then they left the train and went to their hideout – the money bags were carried in a lorry and the men in two Land Rovers. The hideout was a 'farm' just under thirty miles away.

The public were carried away with it all; the audacious plan had actually worked like clockwork. But there was one issue that blighted the robbery from then on. They beat the driver of the train when they hi-jacked it, which is well publicised, but they also scared the living daylights out of the fireman and the five men in the carriage when they smashed their way in with crowbars, coshes and axes.

The Metropolitan Police's Flying Squad were the focus of the enquiry as it was fairly clear that it was an organised gang from London – and they had a very good idea of who the membership of the gang consisted of. The arrests started in Bournemouth and continued through London; three men were never charged.

The full might of the law was ready to flex its muscles when the trial opened in Aylesbury early in 1964, with Mr Justice Edmund Davies presiding. There were few surprises, except perhaps that one of the robbers had left his fingerprints on a monopoly board, which was said to be a portable object and so the judge ordered an acquittal. At the end of forty-odd days the jury filed back into the court; Aylesbury Court was too small for all the accused, their lawyers, the Crown's lawyers, the jury and all the rest of them, so the council chambers were modified for the job. The foreman of the jury answered each of the verdicts for each of the charges for each of the accused: it was described as a 'litany of guilty verdicts'.

The first to be sentenced, and on a guilty plea, was told, 'You will go to prison for twenty-five years.' So those who'd pleaded not guilty would get more – 'You will go to prison for thirty years.' Even the lawyers were shocked. The robbery had made the headlines, and now the punishments were doing the same.

Escapes were planned and expected, with one chief constable suggesting nuclear arms would be utilised to get them out. Two escaped, Ronnie Biggs became a household name and Charlie Wilson went to Canada. Three of the robbers were not caught in the main thrust. Jimmy White, when caught a couple of years after the robbery, got eighteen years and Buster Edwards, who gave himself up, was sent away for fifteen years. The so-called mastermind of the raid, Bruce Reynolds, was captured in Torquay in 1968 and got a twenty-five-year stretch.

Books were written, films were made. Most of the robbers were released after roughly twelve-year stretches. In the meantime, the driver and fireman had both died, Jack Mills of pneumonia

– which is a story in itself – and David Whitby of a heart attack. The innocent man caught up in it all, Bill Boal, died in a nursing home a week after being released from prison early, due to a brain tumour.

And as for the money, only a fraction was ever recovered. The main share of the first man to be arrested, Roger Cordrey, was just over £140,000; £101,000 was discovered in a wood in Surrey and over £30,000 was discovered in a caravan belonging to Jimmy White. There was £50,000 (or £70,000) left in a phone box as part of an immunity deal, and that same night, Roy James had about £12,000 with him when he was arrested. Most of the rest is a mystery, but life on the run is expensive.

The robbery was called the 'Crime of the Century' by some, but Mr Justice Edmund Davies called it a 'sordid crime inspired by vast greed'. To some it was the job to end all jobs, but very little happiness was enjoyed and it changed many lives.

Gutteridge, PC George
Murdered by Frederick Browne and William Kennedy

These days the M25 cuts through Essex, with Stapleford Tawney on the north-eastern side and Stapleford Abbotts on the south-eastern side. The area is about six miles north of Romford, and in 1927 the parish of Stapleford Tawney had a population of about 400, who were mainly agricultural workers. William (Alec) Ward was a postman, and he was driving a post van from Stapleford Abbots towards Stapleford Tawney. It was about 6.00 a.m. on 27 September.

The previous night, at about 11.00 p.m., PC George Gutteridge left his home and made his way south to meet his colleague Police Constable Sydney Taylor, who was stationed at Lambourne End. After the meeting, the two parted.

Alec Ward noticed something out of the ordinary and pulled to a halt. It was the body of a police officer, propped up against a bank with his legs protruding out into the road. He was in full uniform, though his helmet was off and was in the road quite near. He had his notebook out and in his right hand was his pencil. He had four bullet wounds – including one in each eye.

A doctor was to estimate that death had occurred about four or five hours before discovery. George Gutteridge was thirty-eight, married to Rose, and they had two young children, Muriel and Alfred (Jack). George had joined Essex Police in 1910.

The evening before the shooting, Dr Edward Lovell of London Road, Billericay, had his car stolen. It was a blue Morris Cowley and had some of his medical instruments and some drugs inside. The car was soon found, but miles away in Brixton in South London. There were blood splashes on the body work and later a spent cartridge was found inside the car.

Detective Inspector John Crockford headed up the enquiry, but Scotland Yard was called in and it seemed as though PC Gutteridge had stopped a car and was about to make notes when he was shot. Chief Inspector James Berrett attended from Scotland Yard.

The spent cartridge found in Dr Lovell's car had a curious mark, which suggested a fault in the breech-block of the gun that fired it. This was discovered by ballistics expert Robert Churchill when he examined it and he thought the weapon was probably a Webley: two had recently been found in the mud of the River Thames, but Mr Churchill ruled out both as the murder weapons.

Little happened to help the enquiry until the following January when the Metropolitan Police arrested a notorious criminal who had a garage in Clapham. Frederick Guy Browne had stolen a Vauxhall car, which he'd sold. When the police raided his garage they found a number of firearms including a revolver in the glove compartment of the car he used for running around in. They also found plenty of ammunition and a small revolver. When they searched his home they found another revolver.

The police considered Mr Browne's known associates and one had recently gone to ground. He was William Kennedy and he had a considerable history of crime. Liverpool Police soon tracked him down, but he returned to London in mid-January to get married.

Robert Churchill matched up the bullets from PC Gutteridge with a weapon found in Mr Browne's possession, so he was arrested. When Mr Kennedy arrived at his garage on 21 January he found the place locked up with two men he didn't recognise – he wondered if they were police officers. Not taking any chances, he and his wife returned to Liverpool. But he was well known to the Liverpool police. When they went to arrest him he tried to shoot one of the officers, Detective Sergeant William Mattinson, but he'd left the safety catch on. DS Mattinson then subdued Mr Kennedy and called for help – three other police officers were soon in attendance.

The following day he was interviewed at Scotland Yard by DI Berrett, who didn't waste time; he asked him if he knew anything about the murder of PC Gutteridge the previous September. After some hesitation he made a statement that was long but not rambling. In the statement, he said that although he hadn't murdered PC Gutteridge, he had been present, and that it'd been Frederick Browne who'd shot the officer.

By 23 April the prosecution was ready, and at the Old Bailey the trial began. Mr Browne denied having any connection with the crime, claiming that he was at home and in bed when it had happened. However, the main notable event of the trial was the evidence Mr Robert Churchill could give regarding the marks on the cartridge case found in Dr Lovell's car, which he said had been fired by one of the guns in Mr Browne's possession. This proved the case against them conclusively, though Mr Browne offered the defence that he'd only recently acquired that particular gun.

The jury didn't accept it and both were found guilty of murder. Frederick Browne then went to the condemned cell at Pentonville Prison and William Kennedy went to Wandsworth. They were executed on 31 May 1928.

Haigh, John George
The murder of William Donald, William and Amy McSwan, Archibald and Rosalie Henderson and Roberta Durand-Deacon

John George Haigh was forty when he was executed for the murder of six people from September 1944 to February 1949. He either battered them or shot them and then attempted to dissolve their bodies in acid. Sir Hartley Shawcross led for the prosecution and Sir David Maxwell-Fyfe for the defence. Mr Justice (Travers) Humphreys was the judge and Mr Haigh was sentenced to death, which was carried out by Albert Pierrepoint on Wednesday 10 August 1949.

One boast he had was that he'd killed nine people, but there's no evidence to support this; he felt he had a foolproof method to dispose of the bodies and without them he couldn't be prosecuted. He was to be proved wrong in two ways. Firstly, the acid didn't completely dispose of the bodies, and secondly, he appears to have mistaken the 'body' in *corpus delicti* for a literal body, rather than 'a body of evidence'.

He was a fraudster and forged consent documents, enabling him to sell off some of his victim's belongings – this brought him a large sum of money.

John Robert and Emily Haigh were pleased in 1909 when God had sent them the gift of a son, John George. They were members of the Plymouth Brethren, so his upbringing (he was their only child) excluded outsiders and he was lonely. He apparently had a recurring dream in which blood was either drunk or was in a drinking vessel. There wasn't even any sport, and the Bible was a major source of family socialising. He was educated at Wakefield College after he'd won a scholarship. The family lived in Oatwood in Yorkshire and when John George married, he brought his bride home. He was jailed soon after for fraud and his wife departed his life; his parents suggested he departed from theirs.

Accordingly, he headed for the bright lights of London and got a job as a chauffeur to a wealthy owner of amusement parks. Mr Haigh had served part of an apprenticeship in mechanics, so was well suited and could also help maintain the amusement machines. But he set up a business as a solicitor, which led to a four-year sentence for fraud, and was frequently returned to prison. Prison gave him time to think and it was here that he dreamed up his plan for murder and then to put the body into acid. There would be, he concluded, no trace left.

His old employer William McSwann was his first victim, and then later Mr McSwann's parents, William and Amy. The releases for property he'd forged netted him several thousand pounds on the sale of the property.

The acid bath was initially located in the basement of his home in Gloucester Road, but later he rented a workshop in Leopold Road, Crawley.

Dr Archibald Henderson was next, and then his wife, Rosalie, after him. They had been fairly wealthy and Mr Haigh sold off their possessions, too, and took the money.

He lived in the Onslow Court Hotel, where another resident, Mrs Olive Durrand-Deacon, was taken to his workshop in Crawley on a false pretext, murdered and dissolved. But she was soon missed; detectives started to ask questions at the Onslow Court Hotel and soon discovered Mr Haigh had a criminal record.

The police searched his accommodation thoroughly and found the forged papers regarding earlier victims' property. They also wondered what he was doing with a receipt for Mrs Durrand-Deacon's fur coat. Suspicions were raised and so they took a trip to his workshop in Crawley. Professor Keith Simpson went with them and he saw three stones, which he thought might be gall stones – as they eventually proved to be. Acid hadn't dissolved these, nor had it dissolved a part of Mrs Durrand-Deacon's dentures, which were traced back to her dentist.

The police arrested Haigh. The jury were only out for a few minutes before returning a guilty verdict.

Hall, Anthony

The murders of Miss Jacqueline Thomas (1961) and Miss Sylvia Whitehouse (1969)

In August 1961, James Ponting lived in the Bordesley Green area of Birmingham; he worked in an office, so it might have been some relief to get home, put the lead on his dog Mick and go out for some air. Quite close to his home were disused allotments and Mick could have a run off the lead; like most dogs, Mick would be more interested in what was off the path. He'd gone into some long grass and James called him a couple of times, but Mick had found something interesting. When James discovered just what, he turned around and ran to the nearest phone box to call the police. They attended just a few minutes later.

About a week before, fifteen-year-old Jacqueline Thomas had gone to a fun fair in the Ward End district with friends and had been seen at about 10.30 p.m. with a man. She wasn't seen alive again, and it was Mick who now led James to the body.

Jackie's parents called police at around midnight on the night she disappeared. The police then had to break the heartbreaking news that the body was their daughter, found only a few hundred yards from home.

Jackie had been raped and strangled. The crime had happened probably four or five days previously, and it was likely she was murdered where she was found. She had no 'defence wounds', but the realisation that horror is at hand can often trigger a fear that may result in a form of 'freezing up', which might inhibit movements of defence. But one strange point here is that she was strangled with her own underskirt, so there might have been a willingness to go into the old allotments, but it later became clear Jackie didn't want to go further than she felt comfortable with; she had also been seen kissing a man at the fair earlier. The other odd point is that her watch stopped at 12.15. The watch may have run down, but equally, it might have been damaged during her murder and therefore shown the time of death. However, as there were no defence wounds, the latter option is unlikely.

The police started to search. They soon discovered that Jackie had been with her friend Annie that evening so arranged a reconstruction with another girl wearing Annie's clothes to see if anyone who'd been to the fair could help.

A twenty-four-year-old man was brought to their attention who had been seen with Jackie that night; the police traced him and found he was married with a young baby. They didn't find any evidence against him.

But the hunt for the killer grew; police showed Jackie's photograph to workers at the fun fair and they knew she'd worn a fairly distinctive pair of white jeans and a black sweater. Her past and present employers and their staff were also questioned.

Over a thousand homes of friends, relatives, old school chums and anyone who the police thought could help were visited in the search for clues. They worked around the clock, posters were displayed, schools were visited and requests for information were put out by tannoy at St Andrew's football ground, where Birmingham City played.

Police liaised with the Director of Public Prosecutions but, despite months of investigations, they couldn't find the evidence to bring Jackie's killer to justice.

Fifty-three witnesses gave evidence at the inquest held later that year, including the twenty-four-year-old man whom the police had suspected. His name was Anthony Hall; he admitted he'd been with her and that they had shared a kiss and cuddle, but denied rape and murder. His mother gave him a false alibi because he didn't want his wife to know he'd been 'larking about' with girls. He was questioned at the inquest for forty minutes and concluded by saying, 'When I left the girl that night she was alive and well.'

The inquest also heard from forensic experts who said they found nothing to link him to the case. The jury had to conclude that Jackie was 'murdered by person or persons unknown'.

It was over forty years before the police were to charge Anthony Hall with Jacqueline Thomas's murder; when he attended court he was described as having 'no fixed address' because he'd been given a life sentence for the murder of another teenager, about eight years after Jackie.

In answer to the charge of Jackie's murder, he pleaded 'not guilty'. Mr Justice Chapman said Jackie's murder was 'just too long ago' and he was worried he wouldn't have a fair trial. Another problem was that evidence hadn't been kept, over twenty of the original witnesses were dead and others were either ill or too old to be able to give reliable evidence.

The police, though, were satisfied that they weren't looking for any other suspect, and hoped new evidence would one day present itself.

It was nearly eight years after Jackie's murder that sixteen-year-old Sylvia Whitehouse was found dead. However this was a quite different *modus operandi* to Jackie's murder.

A lorry driver found Sylvia's partially clothed body hidden behind a hedge in Bickenhill Lane, in Marton Green, in December

1968. She'd been the victim of a frenzied and sadistic attack, suffering well over forty stab wounds. The venue was quite secluded and was popular with courting couples.

Sylvia had been walking home after leaving a youth club in Small Heath. Police called in the army to use metal detectors to try to find the murder weapon. Scotland Yard were also called in to oversee the investigation.

However, it was only a few days before Mr Hall found himself in police custody on suspicion of the killing.

He was now aged thirty and had separated from his wife. The case came to court the following March, when it was established that he'd offered Sylvia a lift in a car he'd stolen from Manchester a few days prior to the murder. He'd later tried to set fire to her belongings in an empty bedroom at his house at 5.30 the following morning, but the fire got out of control and the fire brigade were called. They were struck by the fact that the fire seemed to have been started deliberately so informed the police. When a close examination was made of the car he claimed was his, there was forensic evidence to link the car to him, and also to Sylvia.

At the murder scene, tyre marks were also found to link the car to the crime.

The case wasn't difficult for the jury; although Mr Hall claimed the car had been used by a friend that night, they simply didn't believe him. They were shocked to hear of his previous record of burglary, house breaking and indecent assault. They also soon learned that he'd been the major suspect of Jackie Thomas's murder all those years before.

He was, of course, jailed for life. Mr Justice Stable said, 'The sentence imposed by law is life imprisonment. I think, in your case, that sentence means what it says and that no other sixteen-year-old girl will be subjected to the appalling experiences to which you subjected this child.'

Hall, Archibald

AKA Roy Fontaine: The Monster Butler
The murders of David Wright, Walter and Dorothy Scott-Elliot, Mary
Coggle and Donald Hall

Only a few hundred paces from Knightsbridge Underground Station, down Sloane Street, is a very ordinary-looking set of double doors, which is the entrance, or one entrance, to Richmond Court, where a flat will cost somewhere in the low millions. Most residents are fairly well-to-do, and would have staff. One resident, Walter Scott-Elliott, who was a former Labour politician, and his wife were pleased to appoint a new butler in late 1977. Mr Fontaine came with excellent references, was well-spoken and smooth and demonstrated his abilities almost immediately. But Mr Fontaine wasn't all he seemed. In fact, he wasn't Mr Fontaine at all – he was Archibald Thomson Hall, who had a criminal record for jewel theft and had shot and killed his partner, David Wright, at his previous place of employment.

Mr Hall was forty-three and his criminal career stretched back to his youth. In prison he could polish his accent and manner; on one occasion he was a 'Lord', but he went to prison for seven years in the early sixties and got an extra five years when he escaped. Until 1977 he'd never used violence, let alone killed.

However, he'd met David in prison and when they both worked for Lady Hudson at Kirtleton Hall in Dumbartonshire he'd murdered him for threatening to expose him as a conman. One day they went out to shoot rabbits, but Mr Hall shot David in the back of his head. Then he moved south to London.

At some stage he teamed up with Michael Kitto; one report was that he met him through Mary Coggle, whom I discuss shortly. In early December 1977 he began to plot and plan a fraud – he could sign blank cheques from Mr and Mrs Scott-Elliot – but a conversation was heard by Mrs Scott-Elliot, who wanted to know what they were doing and who the accomplice was. She died shortly after when the pillow Mr Hall held over her face suffocated her; he put her into bed and tried to make the body look as though she was merely asleep.

A further accomplice joined the plot to masquerade as Mrs Scott-Elliot, one Mary Coggle. They drugged Mr Scott-Elliot and, wearing her clothes, Ms Coggle seemed to carry off her part of Mrs Scott-Elliott fairly well. Mr Hall, Mr Kitto and Ms Coggle, with a heavily drugged Mr Scott-Elliot and a dead Mrs Scott-Elliot in the boot, headed for Cumbria and then to Perthshire where Mrs Scott-Elliott was buried.

They carried on as far as Glen Affric, way up in the remote Highlands of Invernesshire, where they murdered Mr Scott-Elliot and buried him. Back in Perth they sold some of Mr Scott-Elliott's antiques, and sold some more in Edinburgh.

They went back to Cumbria, where Ms Coggle was murdered with a poker. By now, Mr and Mrs Scott-Elliot had been reported missing. The two men drove over the border and dumped Ms Coggle's body in a stream. All then went quiet for a while, and Mr Hall travelled back to Richmond Court to steal more of his former employers' valuables to sell.

Mr Hall's brother Donald joined them, freshly released from prison – he had a chloroformed cloth held to his face and became the next victim.

They bought a Ford Granada and fitted false number plates; Donald was put in the boot. They went to the Blenheim House Hotel just outside Edinburgh where the manager had a hunch about these two guests. When the police attended it soon came to light that the tax disc on the car carried a different number to the registration plates, and they shortly found Donald's body in the boot.

They were arrested and Mr Hall made one of a number of suicide attempts, but they were convicted and given four life sentences (Mrs Scott-Elliot's case was left on file) in courts in Scotland and England. Mr Kitto was given a fifteen-year tariff but Mr Hall was given a full life sentence – he confessed to all and explained he had no remorse.

His autobiography, *A Perfect Gentleman*, was published in 1999. He died in 2002 in Kingston Prison in Portsmouth.

Hall, John

The law was refreshingly compassionate ... to his father, Charles

The year of 1953 will be remembered as the year Queen Elizabeth II took the throne, and post-war austerity claimed yet another year. Peace was eight years old and the optimism of the post-war era was slowly establishing itself. But that year two quite horrifying executions took place – those of Derek Bentley and John Christie. The two cases are linked by the fact that both included a miscarriage of justice which saw a vulnerable person hanged; Derek himself didn't have a fair trial, and three years before Timothy Evans had been executed for a murder in Notting Hill that had actually been committed by John Christie – that of his wife Beryl.

Something unusual happened in Swindon and Sheffield that year, too – guilty pleas in murder cases. One lad smashed his landlady to death and was full of remorse, pleaded guilty and was later hanged. But in Sheffield Mr Charles Hall lived with his son, John, who had learning disabilities. In those days, there were huge hospitals to look after folk such as John, but the choice was to send him to such a hospital or look after him at home. These days, a huge amount of support is on offer and is multi-agency – in those days there was nothing, just the parents and any family members.

His mother died, which left just the two of them and Mr Hall soldiered on. In mid-October 1953, tragedy struck when they were both found in a gas-filled room of their home. Coal gas in those days could be lethal – John died but Mr Hall survived.

Their neighbour, Mrs Olive Mayhew, had become concerned when she hadn't seen them; after knocking repeatedly she asked another neighbour to contact the police – they broke in as concerns were so high for the safety of John and his dad. Mr Hall was taken to hospital to recover.

The problem was that the police couldn't just walk away; law said this was murder. In late November Mr Hall was in front of Mr Justice Sable at Leeds Assizes where he pleaded guilty to John's murder. It wasn't a long trial and Mr Justice Sable asked the counsel for the defence, Mr James Drabble QC, 'Have you fully explained to him the implications of the course he has taken?'

Mr. Drabble explained his actions and he felt that Mr Hall fully understood the implications – his legal team had suggested other paths were possible.

The full story then began to come out – John couldn't talk or see to his most basic of needs and Mr Hall and his wife had dedicated their lives to looking after him. Mrs Hall had died of cancer some four years previously, but Mr Hall had continued to plod on. It was said the strain had led to a breakdown in his health.

He began to exhibit the symptoms of cancer, and became convinced he would die of the same illness as his wife. The doctors told him he hadn't, but this is very common in someone whose mood is low – he had suffered a bereavement and it doesn't sound as though he could grieve properly. It's common with depression to feel real pain of a non-physical origin. This is called psycho-somatic, and Mr Hall would be a clear candidate for this. In those days, though, there was little knowledge of this, let alone treatment. It would be a completely different picture now.

Mr Hall felt unable to go on as he and his wife had for all those years. How he must have felt is anyone's guess; he saw his and his son's deaths as the only answer.

In court Mr Drabble had said he couldn't see how Mr Hall could answer to the charge except by the truth, and that was 'guilty'.

The prosecution, led by Mr J. Basil Herbert QC, was asked by Mr Justice Sable if there was 'any reason why I should not accept the plea'. Mr Herbert said he couldn't see any reason, which gives the impression that neither man was content at the position in which the law put them.

Mr Justice Sable asked 'He is fully rational and fully aware of the course he has taken?' Mr Herbert replied 'It seems to be so.'

Charles Hall was then sentenced to death, which was the only course available to the court. But the folk of Sheffield were not going to take it lying down – within days, a petition had attracted 3,000 signatures and another had attracted 1,300 from just one of the steel works. He was reprieved.

It's refreshing that compassion was at hand and the mess the criminal law was in at the time, with this and other cases from that year, would help the final abolition of the death penalty. With a guilty plea, of course, the case never went to the jury.

Just a year later, Mr Hall was on his way home; his reprieve from the death penalty was dealt with by the Home Office quite quickly. Some might feel uncomfortable at the fact that civil servants had a major say in his fate – but the politicians had made the law and the lawyers were duty bound; if anything, the most compassion came from the civil servants. Not that I suppose for one minute that Mr Justice Sable, Mr Drabble and Mr Herbert – or, for that matter, their juniors – would have criticised the Home Office.

Mr Hall's neighbour, Mrs Mayhew, had taken over the tenancy of his house, seemingly with the full blessing of the Sheffield Council, to keep the house in order until he could come home. The police, who had no choice but to act according to their obligations, had worked to sort out Mr Halls affairs so he could come home with no pressures on him. Mr Hall's former employers paid the travelling expenses so Olive Mayhew could visit him in prison, and they offered him a job when he came home.

And finally, his canary, Peter, was said to be singing as he walked in the front door.

Hanratty, James
Michael Gregston and Valerie Storie
The A6 Murder

James Hanratty is a name everyone will have heard of and he was one of the last men to be executed in England; just over two years after his death, capital punishment was abolished.

It became known as the A6 murder. The two victims were Michael Gregsten and Valerie Storie, and they were parked just off the road on the edge of a field. They'd been having a relationship and had been to a pub, having met at work. Both were civil servants; Michael was married with a couple of kids and Valerie was single. She said some years later that the relationship was beginning to fizzle out.

The crime itself was horrible. No murder is otherwise, but this was a prolonged agony for both Michael and Valerie and it seemed motiveless.

It was the evening of 22 August 1961, and Mr Hanratty approached their car in the field, which was near to Maidenhead in Berkshire. He wore a handkerchief in an effort to disguise his appearance and tapped on the car window with what turned out to be a revolver. He got into the car and then for the next five hours ordered them to drive around parts of west and north-west London, until eventually they pulled into a layby on the aptly named Deadman's Hill, which is on the A6 in Bedfordshire.

It was here that he shot Michael at point-blank range in the back of his head, twice: he died instantly. Following this, he raped Valerie before forcing her out of the car. The revolver was, said Valerie, reloaded. He pointed the revolver at her and just opened fire. Several bullets entered her body. Mr Hanratty then left them for dead and drove off. The car, a Morris Minor, was later found abandoned in Essex.

Valerie survived. She was paralysed and faced the rest of her life in a wheelchair, but she could drive and so she had some freedom. Her health was such that she struggled on at work for another twenty years. One has to admire that courage. She also had a very clear memory of what her attacker looked like and she easily identified him in an identity parade. The car light had come on and she saw him full in the face and clearly – even if an early Turnball-like warning was given to the jury, it was still a sound identification.

However, from the date of execution, 4 April 1962, doubts began to creep into the verdict. Even the rich and famous, who could attract publicity, questioned the verdict. Books were written, films were made. The 'pro-Hanratty lobby' grew in number and strength, which was reinforced by the strange confessions and comments about another suspect: Peter Alphon.

The police investigated but didn't conclude he was the killer, even though some spent cartridges from the murder weapon were found at a hotel he'd stayed in on the night of the killings. Valerie didn't pick him out of the identity parade. Another guest at the hotel that night was a J. Ryan, an alias used by Mr Hanratty – he had a long criminal history.

Mr Hanratty had gone to ground after the shooting but was finally arrested in Blackpool. The police knew he used the name of Mr Ryan occasionally, and it was this that led them to him. One strong clue was how he pronounced some words, with an 'f' sound instead of 'th', particularly 'I'm finkin''. And, of course, there were his icy steel-blue eyes. He was also seen by a couple of witnesses driving the car.

Mr Hanratty told one of his criminal counterparts that he would often dump any incriminating evidence under a bus seat – especially the back seat – and it may not have been much of a coincidence that the murder weapon was found in exactly such a place.

But crucially his alibi changed from being in Liverpool – his presence wasn't noticed by the people he was supposed to have been with – to being in the town of Rhyl in North Wales, but his witnesses were vague and the landlady couldn't be relied on.

Also, three things he was supposed to have said to people came back to haunt him. He confessed to, or at any rate discussed it with, another prisoner, and if the integrity of that might be doubted, he also was quoted to have said to a fellow member of the identity parade, who was in the RAF Police, 'I know I did it but I don't think they can prove it.'

When the verdict was announced he made another slip; when he was invited to utter the last words in his defence before he was sentenced he said, 'I am not innocent ... I mean guilty.'

It's difficult to know why so many folk thought they had the wrong man; Peter Alphonse was 'politically undesirable', but that seems a weak argument. Even when the DNA from his exhumed body was examined and compared with some from Valerie's clothes, and was the only male specimen found. Any sample or piece of male DNA that matched Mr Hanratty was conclusive.

There was talk of contamination of the DNA, but the scientists could rule out any other male DNA from her underclothes.

Before giving Valerie Storie the final word, which she deserves after forty years of insinuations she was wrong or just lying, one has to look at what the late Michael Sherrard QC, counsel for the defence, was quoted to have said – 'The wrong man was not hanged.'

One can't but admire Valerie Storie as she stuck to her belief for nearly forty years. 'I just had this great belief that somewhere, somehow, I would be proved to be right ...'

Harsent, Rose
Murder by person unknown

William Gardiner was a carpenter and lived in the small village of Peasenhall, about twenty-five miles or so to the north-east of Ipswich. Mr Gardiner was married with six children, a well-respected man in the local community and a lay preacher in the Methodist Church. He was choir master, and in the choir was a twenty-two-year-old woman called Rose Anne Harsent.

Rose was a domestic servant employed by William Crisp, who was a clergyman and lived at Providence House, where Rose also lodged. On 31 May 1902, Rose received what was referred to as an anonymous letter – but it can be taken as almost certain that she was aware of who the writer was, and later the police were certain it was written by Mr Gardiner. The gist of the letter was that the writer wished to meet Rose in the kitchen of the house at midnight, so it was thought she'd made her way down to make the rendezvous.

However, it was rumoured in the village that Mr Gardiner and Rose had been having a relationship and some while before two local lads, seeing them enter a building together, heard the associated 'oohs, aahs and gasps' and promptly told all and sundry what they knew – or surmised. An experiment measuring noise for a television documentary about a hundred years later put their claims into doubt. But in 1902 in a small village it was something to talk about!

But back to the midnight meeting Rose attended. Her father was also a local man and he'd arranged to meet her at Providence

House the following day. To his horror, he found his daughter dead. She was at the foot of the stairs and her throat had been cut. She was in her nightdress, which showed evidence that someone had tried to set it on fire. Had she tripped and cut herself on the glass from the oil-lamp she'd carried and some of her clothing had caught fire? This seems preposterous now, and when the doctor was called the true picture began to emerge – quite simply, she'd been murdered. The killer had tried to set her alight and evidence of newspapers and an empty bottle containing paraffin was found close by.

In those days pathology was in its infancy and it's likely the same doctor who pronounced her dead performed the post-mortem. Rose was six months pregnant. With the letter they'd found, which was almost certainly written by Mr Gardiner, and with the 'scandal', it was assumed he'd murdered her.

The police started a half-hearted investigation, which mainly involved digging up what dirt on Mr Gardiner they could. It transpired the couple had continued their relationship even after it had been made 'public'. But even so, Mr Gardiner denied any involvement in Rose's murder and at midnight he was at home with his wife. She was unshakable in her support.

But now, to consider the evidence.

Neither Rose nor her employer, or anyone else at Providence House, read the particular newspaper that was used to set the fire.

The bottle the paraffin had been brought in was an old medicine bottle, and the medicine had been prescribed to one of Mr Gardiner's children.

Mr Gardiner had a knife which had blood stains on it and had a bonfire the morning after the murder.

However, reconsidering that, I couldn't find out if Mr Gardiner subscribed to the particular newspaper. Is it likely he would take a bottle with paraffin in it which could so easily be traced back to him?

The blood on the knife couldn't even be proved as human in those days. The bonfire might have destroyed any bloodstained clothing, but was this proved?

It was in November of 1902 that he was tried at Ipswich Assizes, where Mr Justice John Compton Lawrence presided. Ernest Wild KC led for the defence and Henry Dickens KC led for the prosecution. At that time a jury had to be unanimous, so at the end of the trial, with eleven 'guilty' and one 'not guilty', it had to go to a retrial.

So it was in January 1903 that Mr Gardiner was back in the dock at Ipswich Assizes. The interest locally was as keen as ever, with a large crowd for the small public gallery; the police had to turn people away.

The defence had a few new witnesses, but it was expected that the prosecution would present a similar case. Counsel was the same as in the first trial and again, Mr Justice Lawrence presided. One rumour had it that the last trial had an anti-capital-punishment sympathiser so the judge explained what their oath meant, and why their opinions could obstruct justice.

Mr Dickens presented the case for the Crown and emphasised the lewd goings-on that were said to have been overheard, and the ensuing scandal. The pregnancy of Rose was the motive for the murder.

But what had been overheard by the two lads was strongly refuted by Mr Gardiner and it was him who had told Rose of what was being said around the village, or so he said.

The trial at its conclusion showed a staggering difference in verdict to the first. The eleven guilty and one not guilty turned around to two guilty and ten not guilty. Accordingly, a retrial was again ordered but the Crown entered a plea of *nolle prosequi* (unwilling to pursue) and that was the end of that, apart from the fact that it's fascinated crime historians and local historians ever since.

The key question revolves around his guilt or innocence, and how Mrs Gardiner went to great lengths to prove his innocence. Perhaps one should ask who was giving whom an alibi – Mrs for Mr or Mr for Mrs.

Rose Harsent seemed to enjoy her short life, though, and was said to have had other boyfriends in the village. The police found some pretty racy poetry in her belongings and some quite suggestive notes written too.

Hart, Michael

The murder of Angela Wooliscroft

In November of 1977, Michael Hart was on bail and signing twice a day at Basingstoke Police Station. He'd been involved in a serious crime in France where a taxi driver had been stabbed and police came under gun-fire, so extradition procedures were underway. At home, the police were resisting bail due to his recent history of house-breaking.

One morning he attended the bail signing and left the police station – later that afternoon he returned and signed for the second time. In the interim he stole a car, robbed a bank and shot a bank clerk dead.

He shouldn't have been on bail at all. The bank clerk was twenty-year-old Angela Wooliscroft, and her father said, 'If this man had not been let out on bail our daughter would be alive today. There is obviously a need for the whole system to be tightened up.'

Bail had been refused on the previous four occasions when Mr Hart appeared before magistrates, but Detective Sergeant Derek Luke, who had 'spelled out' to the magistrates what his record was, didn't attend court on a fifth appearance.

The raid landed him £2,500; he burned his clothing and threw the gun, a sawn-off shotgun, into the Thames. Meanwhile,

Barclay's bank had offered a £50,000 reward – the largest ever in the country at the time.

Mr Hart told the police, 'I asked the girl for money and banged the gun against the glass ... I hoped to break the glass. The gun went off as the girl raised her head. I had no intention of shooting anyone. It just went off.'

He tried hanging himself in a cell but survived to appear at the Old Bailey accused of murder.

The jury heard how, a few days after his attempted suicide, he made his confession to his wife in front of police. He was alleged to have admitted, 'I did shoot the girl, but it was an accident. I am sorry about all the publicity. I done it, love.'

Mr Michael Corkery QC, prosecuting, said Michael had gone to Barclay's bank in Ham, near Richmond, and gunned down Angela with a sawn-off shotgun as she handed over £2,500 in cash. Mr Corkery told the jury, 'It would have taken 6½ lb of pressure to fire the gun.'

The forensic experts tried all manner of things to get the gun to 'go off' but none worked: even though 6½ lb may be a middle average it will still need considerable pressure. The cartridge had blasted through the glass, which was over half an inch thick.

Michael Hart was found guilty on a majority verdict and given a life sentence with a minimum of twenty-five years.

Twenty years later, Mr Hart was a reformed character and attended a conference where he told teenaged school children that a life of crime is not beneficial to anyone. He left prison and now lives peacefully with his wife in the south of England.

Heath, Neville
Murder of Margery Gardner and Doreen Marshall

There were three boys born as Rupert Brooke/Brook during his lifetime, but I doubt either ever claimed to be a Group Captain.

The Rupert Brooke/Brook I want to briefly discuss here was actually born in Ilford in Essex in June 1917 as Neville George Clevely Heath, and he is one of Britain's most notorious sex killers.

His father was a barber but he wanted his son to have the best start in life and he sent him to grammar school in Merton Park, South London. When he left, he joined the army and enjoyed military life. In 1936 he joined the RAF, but was court-martialled for being absent without leave and left the force in 1937. He was soon on the wrong side of the law.

He was sent to borstal in 1938 for three years for theft, but put that behind him when he joined the Royal Army Service Corps after war had broken out and was sent to the Middle East. He was commissioned and was soon in trouble again, but this time for fraud. He went AWOL again, and on his way back to England escaped to South Africa, where he joined the Air Force. Things settled, but at the end of the war he was dismissed for wearing decorations he hadn't won.

In June 1946 he was in a hotel in Notting Hill with Ms Yvonne Symonds, whom he claimed to be married to. They had a nice evening and she left the following morning.

A few days later he met Margery Gardner, an artist and actress who was a few years older than him. They had a considerable amount of alcohol before retiring. The following morning she was found naked, bound and gagged. Her nipples had been savagely bitten. She'd been whipped with what appeared to be a leather riding crop with a diamond pattern. A large object had been forced into her vagina. The cause of her death was suffocation, but Professor Keith Simpson had thought this was after she'd been whipped.

Mr Heath went to Worthing to see Yvonne and her parents were taken by this handsome young man. However, the police were on the lookout for him and the press ran a story. Yvonne saw the story and contacted him, whereupon he said he'd clear up the matter – he actually knew the lady and had 'lent' her his room so she could entertain 'Jack'. He wrote to the police explaining that he had returned to the room in the early hours and found the body; he'd left as he thought he'd be wrongly suspected.

He went along the coast to Bournemouth and booked into the Tollard Royal Hotel as Group Captain Rupert Brook(e).

On 3 July he met Doreen Marshall and they enjoyed tea and agreed to dine together that evening. At about 11.30 p.m. she left to walk back to her own hotel and Mr Heath accompanied her. That was the last time Doreen was seen alive. The manager of the hotel she'd been staying at contacted the police two days later, and also Mr Relf, who was the manager of the Tollard Royal, where Mr Heath was a guest. Mr Relf told him that the lady with whom he'd dined two nights previously had vanished, but Mr Heath said this must be a misunderstanding and he'd contact the police to clarify matters.

Doreen was found on Sunday 7 July, when a lady out walking her dog noticed an abnormally large swarm of flies round a rhododendron bush. There was Doreen's body, naked and mutilated; there were 'defence' wounds on her hands, which had been bound, as had her ankles. She'd been beaten around the head and one of her nipples had been bitten off; her throat had been slit. Again an instrument had been forced into her vagina, and she had a long wound from her inner thigh up to her breast.

Group Captain Brook(e) was invited to the police station to view a picture of the missing girl, and another officer thought he looked like the man in the photograph circulated by Scotland Yard in relation to the previous murder. Detective Inspector George Gates was informed, but Mr Heath insisted it wasn't him. He wanted his jacket, but when the police went to get it they found a cloakroom ticket and a railway ticket. Thinking the cloakroom may be on the station, they recovered a suitcase with Mr Heath's clothing and his name. They also found a blood-stained hat and scarf, and a leather riding crop with a distinctive diamond pattern.

He was arrested and taken to London where he was charged with the murder of Margery Gardner.

On 24 September 1946, his trial opened at the Old Bailey, where he entered a plea of insanity. Two psychiatrists didn't agree and the jury took about an hour to deliver a guilty verdict.

On the morning of 16 October 1946 he was offered a tot of whisky prior to the arranged proceedings and suggested to the governor, 'You might make that a double.' Neville Heath was led through to the execution chamber, where he was hanged by Albert Pierrepoint.

Hewart, Viscount Gordon
Judge

Gordon Hewart was born in Bury in Lancashire in 1870; he wanted to be a lawyer but started off as a reporter. Eventually he was called to the bar, aged thirty-two, in 1902. He joined the Northern Circuit and soon became well known and in demand – he rose in stature and in only ten years he took silk.

Mr Hewart was knighted in 1916 a few months after taking office as the Solicitor General, and later in 1919 he became Attorney General.

When he was called to the bar he also joined the Inner Temple, and from 1917 he was a Bencher of the Inner Temple, who are the Masters – the Treasurer, which he became in 1938, is the leader of the Benchers.

He was also a Member of Parliament for the Liberal Party and represented Leicester before the constituency became South Leicester.

From very early on he had the main ambition to become Lord Chief Justice and this he achieved in March 1922, although some have said his tenure was not particularly groundbreaking. He did take an interest in criminal law, especially with the jury system.

But cracks began to show through the veneer. It was said his decision making was too rapid compared with his ability to consider evidence – or he was prone to making decisions before he'd heard everything. It was alleged he lacked social niceties and would sometimes be downright rude, a habit he also practiced with fellow benchers.

When he published his book, *The New Despotism*, it appeared as though civil servants were to be in line for his vitriol, and he openly attacked the Lord Chancellor. It has been suggested the genesis to this lay in his realisation that the Lord Chief Justice wasn't as powerful as he'd like. At times it might have been open warfare – in words – between him and the other senior law makers. Although he'd been a politician, he didn't like what was described as 'delegated legislation', which was the brief of civil servants.

Again, these were examples where his bad judgement let him down. He thought the government, whether or not in cahoots with the civil servants, wanted to take over the judiciary and its functions. History has demonstrated this just wasn't so.

On the other hand, he has been described as a great believer in and supporter of the jury system, saying that the system was 'impeccable'. But in his Court of Appeal judgement in *R* v. *Wallace*, he found that the jury had convicted William Wallace of the murder of his wife against the weight of the evidence. The jury was wrong!

The adage 'not only must Justice be done; it must also be seen to be done' was attributed to Viscount Hewart, though some have said he'd paraphrased another judge or he'd been misquoted.

He had children through his first marriage and remarried after his first wife died. He died in May 1943.

Hill, William Charles (Billy)
Gang leader, smuggler and conman

Billy Hill is largely forgotten now, but only recently Wensley Clarkson has published a biography of him and Billy's son has also had his autobiography republished only a few years ago. He was the original 'villain' in London, who more or less invented organised crime.

William Charles Hill was born into a family where crime was rife and his first stabbing was dated to the mid-1920s; he was born in 1911, so he'd barely got into his teens! He was to stamp his mark on the London underworld using his gift of intelligence, not just brute force.

His first forays into crime came later in the 1920s as a burglar, when he'd team up with others to raid, among others, jewellers; he practiced this throughout the 1930s and became quite adept at the 'smash and grab' type of raid. The best opportunity for one with Billy's pedigree then presented itself – the Second World War. This is when he became better organised, and with many of the younger police away fighting he could run rings round most of the older ones. It was a good time for the black market, and Billy was a dab hand with food and petrol – that's what people on the street wanted and they were prepared to pay, as were servicemen who wanted to opt out of the more dangerous activities in the war and desert; Billy could supply them with the right type of documents. For a while, he and Jack Spot teamed up but in the late 1940s he had to leave England in a bit of a hurry; he was promptly returned and went into one of Her Majesty's prisons for a warehouse robbery. From the 1950s onwards he never went to prison again.

He met a young lady, Gypsy Riley, with whom he was to have a lifetime's relationship; she was subsequently called Gyp Hill. They had a son, Justin.

By the coming of the 1950s Billy had built up a criminal empire, one which included smuggling and protection rackets. He had a reputation for using violence; but for all that, he still managed to come up with a plot to fleece high-society gamblers on card tables.

Billy was thought to be the main brains behind the 1952 Eastcastle Street Post Van robbery, which netted over a £¼ million (in 1952 values), and two years later he was involved in a gold robbery – these two crimes have become quite notorious, but no one was ever convicted. However, the authorities were closing in and the Home Office approved a plan to tap his phone. He was by now at loggerheads with Jack Spot and his gang. Frankie Fraser was in the thick of it and was reputed to be Billy's bodyguard; when he attacked Jack and his wife he got a seven-year prison sentence.

The phone tapping caused a bit of a row in the House of Commons and things were generally hushed-up. Concurrent with this was an investigation into Billy's legal team – a barrister was subsequently disbarred.

His fleecing of the rich card players re-emerged in the 1960s, and it was said John Aspinal, who'd included Lord Lucan as one of his closest friends, was instrumental in the fraud. The cards were variously bent (and straightened out), but Billy's men could see enough detail in the card to see if they were 'high or low' and so his card sharks could gain a substantial advantage.

Billy had interests overseas as well as his smuggling operation, and Gyp had a night club in Tangiers that she ran well into the 1970s. Another sideline came when Mickey Spillane was acting in *The Country Girls*; they needed a particular pistol and Billy got them an original, along with a couple of spares. He was also a good leader for the Kray Twins and helped them set up their empire – they remained good friends.

He'd use a knife, but was always careful to avoid possible damage to an artery; his aim was to damage and not kill. 'Only mugs do murder.'

He retired from crime in the 1970s and died on New Year's Day, 1984.

Hogan, Terry
AKA Harry Booth

'Lucky Tel' was born in London in 1931 and became what is loosely described as a career criminal. From his early twenties he had a reputation for reliability, and his first few jobs were in Billy Hill's gang. He was involved with the Eastcastle Street Robbery, which netted the equivalent of about £8 million (by today's values). The raid itself became the turning point for British criminals as these lads were now far more able to plan a robbery, execute it and then get away with it.

Among his other associates were George 'Taters' Chatham, who took Terry in hand and taught him all he knew about burglary, along with Peter Scott – probably the most 'up-market' group of London's underworld at the time. Terry became a perfectionist at the timing of a robbery and its detail. He was a member of the famous 'Bowler Hat Gang', who dressed up as city gents to perform a wages snatch at London Airport, and many of his contemporaries were together a few months later for the Great Train Robbery. He was said to have given the Kray Twins a very wide berth.

The Airport job in 1962 was one of his last pieces of work; as with the Great Train Robbery, the gangs were getting bigger, and the bigger the gang the more likely a 'grass' would emerge. He was in France at the time of the robbery but did help in the distribution and custody of some of the prize. Bruce Reynolds, Buster Edwards and Charlie Wilson were life-long friends, and the latter two died in dreadful circumstances.

He went straight from the early 1960s and into the linen business, settling down with a degree of respectability, but as life went on his need for alcohol increased.

It doesn't sound as though Terry ever found true happiness, although he doted on his family; he wanted to give his three kids the education and start in life he never had. His own upbringing had been abusive; crime was one way of escaping the poverty. He was deaf in one ear due to a beating he received growing up.

He took his own life in 15 January 1995, jumping from a top-floor flat window. He'd recently asked his daughter to keep some of the personal letters he'd exchanged with his former associates who'd spent many years in prison.

He wished desperately in his final years that he'd 'taken a different road in life'. It was sad that he could never recover from the way he started, that is to say, with crime. He sounded like more of a gentleman than a thug and this is borne out by his later criminal associates.

His daughter became a well-respected journalist, who tried to find the truth about her dad's end but was told, 'There was nothing his family could have done to save him; it was all in his childhood.'

Hoskins, Percival Killick
Journalist

Percy Hoskins was born in Bridport in 1905 and was to become a foremost crime reporter. He joined the *Evening Standard* in 1924, which started a fifty-year career, finishing up as chief crime reporter for the *Daily Express*. He didn't have a desk there and was apparently loath to have his employer know the hours he kept. It sounds as though his approach to crime reporting was almost a vocation.

He had a number of 'scoops', but two of his most notable pieces of work were the belief that John Bodkin Adams was not guilty and that Michael Fagan popped in for a natter with the Queen.

His friendships included Alfred Hitchcock – they could easily have passed for brothers – Bing Crosby and J. Edgar Hoover. He didn't do too badly for a journalist either, as he lived in Park Lane.

In 1956, a doctor in Eastbourne had rather a lot of patients die, and the circumstances were enough to rouse the suspicions of

Scotland Yard. Most of the rest of the country were waiting for a guilty verdict, and most of his Fleet Street cronies were baying for the gallows – Percy was unmoved, and when Dr Adams was acquitted he had the exclusive. His employer, who also happened to be a friend, phoned him when Dr Adams was acquitted and told him, 'Two people were acquitted today', which became the title of the book Percy wrote on the case when Dr Adams died in 1984.

His contacts were mainly police officers, and one friend said, 'If you were in trouble with the police, you rang Percy before your lawyer'.

Author and broadcaster Michael Bywater asked the secret of his success. He replied, 'Whenever you are interviewing somebody, always have this question in the back of your mind – "Why is this bugger lying to me?"'

The 'visit' to the Queen by Michael Fagan saw steps taken to hush up the story, so Percy was keen for it to hit the headlines. Michael Fagan scaled a drainpipe at Buckingham Palace and had a potter round and a glass of wine. It has been said the Queen had a chat with him and that he managed to do it because the police guards were changing shifts. Whatever happened, the story has a number of variations. At the time it was a civil offence and the Queen didn't appear to pursue the matter, but it's now a criminal offence.

Percy Hoskins died in Hove, Sussex, in February 1989; he was eighty-four.

Hindley, Myra and Brady, Ian
Murder of Pauline Reade, John Kilbride, Keith Bennett, Lesley Anne Downey and Edward Evans
The Moors Murders

In Gorton Lane, Myra Hindley recognised Marie Ruck, who lived next door to her mother, so she ignored Ian Brady's signal to stop and pick her up. Round the corner was Froxmer Street, which was once residential; these days it's a trading estate. It was in July 1963 that Pauline Reade saw Ms Hindley's car pull up, and out of the window she asked her if she could help her look for a glove. Pauline was later murdered, and on that night in July a series of events started that nauseates most folk in Britain to this day.

Pauline was aged sixteen and was on her way to a dance when she got into Ms Hindley's car. She may not have noticed the motorcycle behind them as the car headed north-east toward Saddleworth Moor. When it stopped, Mr Brady took Pauline onto the Moor, where she was raped and stabbed – her throat was cut and she was buried in a shallow grave. Here she lay for the next twenty-four years until the couple finally admitted the murder. Pauline was found, but only after a search that went on for two or three months.

After Pauline's death the couple distanced themselves from one another, but Mr Brady later contacted Ms Hindley again.

Twelve-year-old John Kilbride had gone to a market in Ashton-Under-Lyne, where he was approached by Ms Hindley. It was late afternoon on 23 November 1963. He was offered a lift home but the journey took him to Saddleworth Moor, where Mr Brady sexually assaulted and then strangled him. Mr Brady had also tried to slit his throat.

Mr Brady took one of John's shoes as a 'trophy', and it was the shoe they'd left on him that helped identify him. The police finally managed to find John because the couple had taken photographs smiling at each other.

On 16 June 1964, twelve-year-old Keith Bennett was heading for his grandmother's house. He was taken up to Saddleworth Moor, but only Mr Brady knows any more as his body has never been found. It has been suggested he was buried close to a gully, near to a stream. He was asphyxiated. Despite a number of searches over the years his body has never been recovered.

Mr Brady was ready for another method, and the level of depravity was to get worse. Lesley Anne Downey was ten years old, and on Boxing Day 1964 she was at a fun fair in Ancoats, to the east of Manchester, not far from Oldham. She was abducted and taken to their house, where she was posed for a camera and a tape recording was made – I understand police officers wept when they saw and heard the deeds of Mr Brady and Ms Hindley. Lesley was raped and probably strangled before she, too, was taken out to Saddleworth Moor.

But thank God for David Smith – although initially he was suspected as an accomplice. Seventeen-year-old Edward Evans was battered to death with an axe on 16 October 1965. David Smith witnessed the murder and the aftermath, when he was throttled with some electrical flex.

But David was terrified – would he be the next victim? Shortly after, they had dinner, where Mr Brady openly boasted about killing. David's terror remained with him even when he left them and could get to a public telephone to contact the police.

The killing was over. 'Wicked beyond belief' was how the judge described them as he sentenced both to life in prison.

Ian Duncan Stewart Brady was born in Glasgow. His parents weren't married, and indeed the identity of his father isn't clear – his mother was in her late twenties. It sounds as though she arranged a 'private' adoption, and as he grew up she saw little of him. As a teenager he had a girlfriend who he threatened with a flick-knife, and part of his 'punishment' was to go and live with his mum, who'd moved to Manchester and married Patrick. It may have been thought that this would bring him some stability, but he was soon in trouble and had a couple of stints in borstal.

He did try to turn over a new leaf, teaching himself

book-keeping. This astonished his mother, but he was also taking an unhealthy interest in Hitler and the Third Reich: he taught himself German to study *Mein Kampf*. But for all of that, he got himself a job in Millwards Merchandising, a chemical distribution specialist in Gorton. A year later, Myra Hindley joined the firm.

Robert and Nellie Hindley lived in Gorton where Ms Hindley grew up, but she mainly lived with her grandmother after her younger sister was born. What effect this had is impossible to assess, but her father was a heavy drinker anyway. He also encouraged her to fight if anyone hurt her and she did.

Her grandmother didn't send her to school as often as she should, but she still got good grades in exams and enjoyed sports. She also seemed trustworthy, often baby-sitting.

Swimming was a huge attraction, but one day she didn't go swimming and her friend Michael drowned. This caused her much pain, and as she was such a strong swimmer she felt that if she'd been there she could have saved him.

When she was eighteen, she got a job as a typist at Millwards Merchandising. Here she met and fell in love with Mr Brady, though he was slow to respond. But after a Christmas party he walked her home and they started to go out together. He somehow managed to convince her that rape and murder weren't wrong.

Whatever the chemistry was between them, their world became evil and remained evil. It was on 19 April 1966 that Mr Justice Fenton Atkinson opened proceedings and on 6 May the jury found them both guilty of the murders of John Kilbride, Lesley Anne Downey and Edward Evans.

Initially, Mr Brady went to Durham Prison and Ms Hindley to Holloway.

In 2002 Myra Hindley died in prison; she was sixty. Mr Brady is in Ashworth Special Hospital, Merseyside.

Humphries, Travers Christmas QC

Christmas Humphries was the son of a noted barrister and judge, and was usually called Toby by friends and family. He reached his peak at the bar following the war and prosecuted in some noted cases: Ruth Ellis, for example, who was guilty but suffered a barbaric punishment. Derek Bentley was innocent but was denied a fair trial, and Timothy Evans was simply innocent; it was the system that provoked the controversy.

He was called to the bar in 1924 at about the same time as his other passion in life also led to the spotlight; he founded the London Buddhist League, the forerunner of the Buddhist Society. He would publish and edit over three dozen books on the theme.

In his legal climb he started off in criminal defence, but was appointed Junior Treasury Counsel in 1934, which put him in the prosecutor's role. This change led to him gaining a reputation for efficient prosecutions. After the war, he was a junior at the Tokyo War Crimes trials. By the early 1940s he had a part-time judge's post as Recorder in Kent. By the end of the decade he became Senior Treasury Counsel, then became a Queen's Counsel; he took silk in 1959.

His progression to judge was made in 1962, and he would regularly be found at the Old Bailey, where he served until his retirement in 1976.

Sadly, his later years as a judge were not his best, and the sentencing of a fraudster following a very lenient sentence on a knife-wielding rapist caused a public outcry. The Lord Chancellor defended him to a hostile House of Commons, which sounded like a 'closed rank' defence, though he was also supported by the Probation Officers. But the House wanted his resignation, which he tendered soon after.

The legacy of Christmas Humphreys isn't to be under-estimated, though, as the three cases introduced above all contributed strongly to the abolition of the death penalty. In the case of Ruth Ellis, part of his prosecution agenda was to ask a direct question of what she'd intended when pointing the gun at her lover – 'I intended to kill him'. It was said that Ruth had a difficult past and the last type of lover she should have had is the one she fell for.

In the case of Ruth Ellis, the conviction was sound, though one can argue mitigating factors by looking at her past. The punishment showed the barbarism the country still suffered, and a lot of its citizens were unhappy about her hanging. The law is the law, but attitudes were changing.

England's barbarism had given a particularly loud show a few years earlier, when Derek Bentley was denied a fair trial by the Lord Chief Justice, Lord Goddard. Derek, barely above the intellectual level of an eleven-year-old, became the victim of a vicious vengeance when Police Constable Sydney Miles was shot dead in Croydon. And Timothy Evans, who could barely function in the adult role his chronological age put him in, was thoroughly duped by one of the most evil men of his time, John Christie.

Christmas (Toby) Humphries died in April 1983.

The Hungerford Massacre
Michael Robert Ryan

Dorothy Coleman married Alfred Ryan in early 1958. They lived in Hungerford, just under seventy miles from London. They only had the one child, Michael, who was born in May 1960. He wasn't a great achiever and didn't mix with other kids, but he reached adulthood without major mishap, though his mum would often need to bail him out financially and as time went on she'd have to tell many folk that the various stories he told about himself were not complete fabrications.

He attended college, but that didn't work out and there is no mention of any relationship with girls. He was in a local gun club but only went there to shoot rather than for social interaction.

Tragedy hit in May 1985 when his father died. He'd been twenty years older than his wife and was fifty-five when his son was born. Both parents doted on their son, and a lot was made of Michael's relationship with his mother, which was mere conjecture.

Wednesday 19 August 1987 was a pleasant day, although he'd just lost his job. His recent irritability wasn't unusual. Mrs Ryan went out shopping and her son went out killing.

Not far from Hungerford is Savernack Forest, just south of Marlbrough, in Wiltshire. Thirty-five-year-old Susan Godfrey had taken her two young children for a picnic. Michael pulled up in his car and approached them. When Susan saw the handgun she knew it was trouble; he told her to put the children into the car, which she did. He told her to pick up the picnic groundsheet and walked behind her. It's not difficult to guess what fears were running through her mind, but he just shot – thirteen bullets. The children were unharmed.

He drove off and stopped at a petrol station. The lady at the till, Mrs Kakoub Dean, looked up to see him aim a rifle at her. She ducked, and a bullet came through the glass, he'd seen her dive, so he went into the shop with a handgun. Pointing it at her at close range, he pulled the trigger, but nothing happened. He left. Mrs Dean later described him as not looking at her, but rather looking through her. What was going through his mind will never be known. He returned home to South View in Hungerford.

At about a quarter to one, he was putting weapons into his car, but when he tried to leave, the car wouldn't start. Apparently, he shot at the car five times and neighbours said he seemed agitated. He went back into the house and shot his dog, poured petrol over the place and set it alight – the resulting fire destroyed their house and two others. He took his guns out of the boot of his car and murdered two neighbours who were in their garden – Ronald Mason was shot in the back and Sheila, his wife, in the head.

At the end of South View there is pedestrian access to Hungerford Common, where he shot two more people: Marjorie Jackson, who had watched him from her window, and teenager Lisa Mildenhall, who stood outside of her house. Mr Ryan smiled at her as he shot. Both survived, but Lisa was hit four times.

Kenneth Clements was walking his dog when Mr Ryan took aim. Mr Clements lifted his hands but was murdered where he stood; fortunately, his three kids managed to get away.

With all the gunfire it was inevitable that someone would call the police, and when Police Constable Roger Brereton entered South View he was greeted with a hail of twenty-three shots, four of which hit him; he lost control of his car, which crashed into a tree. He managed to radio for help before he died.

A Volvo 360 followed PC Brereton, quite by chance, and eleven bullets were dispatched. Alison Chapman, who was in her teens, took a bullet in her thigh and another bullet hit her mum, Linda, in the shoulder. He reloaded and Linda kept her cool enough to reverse out and away. She drove to the doctors' surgery.

George White next turned into South View with Ivor Jackson in the passenger seat. Mr Ryan opened fire and killed George, but Ivor, though severely injured, survived. He had as much courage as Linda Chapman, because he just stayed where he was and didn't move, playing dead.

On the corner of South View and Fairview, Mr Abdul Khan was in his garden; he was shot and killed. By now, the alert had gone out and armed police were on their way.

Alan Lepetit, who'd helped build the gun display unit Mr Ryan kept in his bedroom, was shot but only wounded.

An ambulance arrived, and he opened fire at this too, as well as the fire engine that arrived shortly after. In the ambulance, paramedic Hazel Haslett was injured but was able to speed out of range.

It was at about this time (though accounts vary) that Mrs Ryan arrived back in South View – she could see what had gone on and guessed what was happening. She pleaded, 'Michael, Michael', but he took aim and shot her dead. Betty Tolladay had heard the shooting and came out to ask him to stop, thinking he'd merely been shooting at targets. He opened fire and wounded her, then ran down the pedestrian path to Hungerford Common.

Francis Butler was out with his dog and was shot dead. Michael then shot at Andrew Cadle but missed; Andrew pedalled frantically to get away as the gun jammed.

Marcus Barnard, who was in his minicab and who had been redirected away from the town centre by the police, was shot in the head and died. Mr Ryan shot at Douglas Wainwright, who also died, and his wife, who was wounded. Kevin Lance was wounded in the arm. He shot at Eric Vardy, who died, and John Storms, who was badly wounded. He shot at twenty-two-year-old Sandra Hill, who was wounded and later died.

Numerous others received minor wounds – at another time and place these would be called major; such was the nature of it.

Mr Ryan broke into Jack and Myrtle Gibbs's house and shot them both dead. They were the last two fatalities on the day, but Ian Playle died two days later; Ian's wife and children survived. He shot and injured Michael Jennings and Myra Geater from Mr Gibbs' house, and outside he shot and injured George Noon in his garden.

Finally, Mr Ryan holed up in the John O'Gaunt Community Technology College. He shot at helicopters flying overhead. Negotiations were tried. He shot himself just before 7.00 p.m.

The folk of Hungerford have wanted to put it behind them. To some, the building of houses in South View and the demolition of Jack and Myrtle Gibbs' house is the turning point in the journey to forget.

Reverend Andrew Sawyer arrived in Hungerford three years after the slaughter. He should have the last word. 'The town has moved on. What Michael Ryan did that day is only a small part of Hungerford's history; it doesn't define it.'

Ireland, Colin
The murder of Peter Walker, Christopher Dunn, Perry Bradley, Andrew Collier and Emmanuel Spiteri

Colin Ireland was born in Dartford, Kent in March 1954. His mum was seventeen and his father quickly departed. In his thirties he was to murder five men.

But that was the climax of his criminal activities, which started when he was in his mid-teens, though he hadn't shown any outrageously violent tendencies. However, he decided to murder homosexual men. He was heterosexual and had been married twice, seeming to start relationships quite easily though not sustaining them.

He claimed he was homosexual only to meet men and kill them. He was well-organised, and carried rope, handcuffs and a clean set of clothes. After the murder, he'd clean the victim's home to try to remove any forensic evidence linking him to the scene. He'd also stay at the scene to avoid being spotted leaving late at night.

Mr Ireland was raised by his mother; money was in short supply and they moved a number of times. His mum remarried in the early 1960s, but when she fell pregnant she placed him in care, though he later went back to her. In the mid 1960s she married again, though little is known of this marriage.

As a teenager Mr Ireland was sent to borstal for theft, and while there, he set fire to another resident's belongings. He returned to borstal training aged seventeen when he was convicted for robbery.

When he left school his life didn't look as if he were to achieve greatness. He was in the army for a while and then had a number of labouring jobs. In late 1975 he was convicted of car theft, criminal damage and burglary; on his release in late 1976 he went to live in Swindon with a lady friend and her children for a while.

He left Swindon but was soon in trouble again. In 1977 he was convicted for extortion and was away for eighteen months, gaining a two-year sentence for robbery in 1980.

Mr Ireland married Virginia Zammit in 1982 and, together with her daughter, they lived in Holloway, London. He was sent down for conspiracy in 1985. They divorced in 1987 and he remarried two years later – allegedly he was violent to Virginia and stole from her. In the early 1990s he moved to Southend-on-Sea, where he lived in a hostel. He later moved to a flat, from where he would visit a London bar to find his victims.

Peter Walker, forty-five, was a choreographer and into sadomasochism. They met and returned to Mr Walker's flat, where he was bound and ultimately suffocated with a plastic bag over his head. Mr Ireland placed teddy bears in a 69 position on the body, and locked Mr Walker's dogs in another room. The day after, he didn't hear any news reports of the crime, so he called the Samaritans and a journalist.

Christopher Dunn was a thirty-seven-year-old librarian from Wealdstone: he was found naked in a harness, and his death was initially believed to be an accident during an erotic game. As he lived in a different area from Mr Walker, a different set of investigators worked on the case, and the two cases weren't immediately linked.

Perry Bradley was a thirty-five-year-old American businessman who lived in Kensington. They went to his flat and Mr Ireland suggested that he tie Mr Bradley up – but he wasn't keen. He told him he was unable to perform sexually without elements of bondage, so Mr Bradley was soon face down on his bed, with a noose around his neck. Mr Ireland then demanded money and his bank PIN under the threat of torture. He said he was a thief and would leave after getting his PIN. He thought of leaving him unharmed, but realised Mr Bradley could identify him, so he used the noose to strangle him. He placed a doll on top of the dead man's body and stole £100 from the flat, and £200 from his bank.

Andrew Collier was dead three days later – Mr Ireland hadn't received any publicity even after three murders, so killed again. At the pub, he met Andrew Collier, a thirty-three-year-old housing warden, and they went to his home in Dalston. There was a disturbance outside and both men went to the window to investigate. He'd gripped a metal bar which ran across the window, which he later forgot to wipe to remove fingerprints during his usual clean-up phase. The police were to find this fingerprint. Mr Ireland killed Mr Collier's cat and then strangled him. He'd tried to get bank details but failed. He placed a condom on Mr Collier's penis and placed his cat's mouth over it; he placed the cat's tail in Mr Collier's mouth.

Maltese chef Emanuel Spiteri, aged forty-one, was next. They met in the same pub as the others. Mr Spiteri was handcuffed and bound on his bed. Once more, Mr Ireland demanded his bank PIN but didn't get it. He again used a noose to kill. After cleaning and clearing the scene, he set fire to the flat and left. He rang the police later to tell them to look for a body at the scene of a fire.

There were suggestions that police homophobia delayed the linking of all the murders, but they eventually did make the connection. The crimes were widely publicised through the mainstream media and it was clear that a serial killer who specifically targeted homosexual men was at large.

Mr Spiteri had travelled home with Mr Ireland by train, and a security video captured them on the platform at Charing Cross. He recognised himself and told the police he was the man with Mr Spiteri but he wasn't the killer – he said he'd left Mr Spiteri in the flat with another man. However, police found Mr Ireland's fingerprints in Mr Collier's flat; the evidence was mounting.

He was charged with the murders of Mr Collier and Mr Spiteri, and confessed to the other three while awaiting trial. He told police that he didn't have a vendetta against gay men, but picked on them because they were the easiest targets. He robbed those he killed because he was unemployed, and he needed money to travel to London when hunting for victims.

After the first murder, Mr Ireland contacted the media to tell them what he'd done; he wanted to be famous as a serial killer. After killing three more men, and a cat, he phoned the police to ask why they hadn't linked the murders.

When his case came to the Old Bailey on 20 December 1993, he admitted all charges and was given a life sentence for each. Mr Justice Sachs said he was 'exceptionally frightening and dangerous', and added, 'To take one human life is an outrage; to take five is carnage.'

He got his notoriety, with the name 'The Gay Slayer' and 'Jack The Gripper'.

Colin Ireland died at Wakefield Prison in February 2012.

Jeffreys, Professor Sir Alec
Genetic Fingerprinting

It was a failed experiment that opened the door for Professor Sir Alec Jeffreys (as he is now), when he saw, on what looked like an X-ray card, a pattern from human DNA. He thought this was the first DNA fingerprint, which was unique to an individual. DNA is Deoxyribonucleic Acid, and is largely to do with biological information storage – and has been around since man and probably before. In 1927 it was called a giant hereditary molecule described as what gave an octopus eight legs, humans two ears and snakes venom. But breaking it down still further, it explained why some folk have particular family traits – 'Oh, he's got his dad's ears', and so on.

But Professor Jeffreys went even further, to identify that even between close relatives DNA might be similar but not identical (actually, identical twins do have identical DNA but different fingerprints!). Professor Jeffreys felt that he was developing the world's first genetic 'fingerprint', very similar to your sibling/parents but quite different from the chap across the street. With it, one could find out if you, your dad, or the chap across the street had fathered a child around the corner. It went yet deeper – but I'll leave paternity (and immigration) cases for now.

DNA is in every cell in the body and each cell joins another to form the body. At conception the egg and sperm form one cell, which then divides, and the divided cell divides and so on. There are a selection of different cells, which all go through this process as an embryo is developed. Cells form tissue, tissue forms systems and all the systems together form the body. Different cells with slightly different genetic (DNA) programming form differently to do different jobs. Ignoring the Latin names, bone tissue makes bones, muscular tissue makes muscles, connective tissue makes skin, cartilage and so on. Zooming in more, the cell has a centre, or nucleus, where the DNA is held: chromosomes hold it there.

Professor Jeffreys identified that DNA is exclusive to each person and will have significant differences from other people's, which can be measured. If you like, my DNA is quite dissimilar to my wife's but very similar to my children; my wife's DNA is quite dissimilar to mine but very similar to our children. This is because the children's chromosomes come from two different people. The chromosomes are twenty-three pairs, though one pair is sex. Chromosomes hold the DNA in the cell. Without going any further down this road we can thankfully go back to Professor Jeffreys.

He devised a measure, or, as part of an experiment, found a measure of what he called 'bars', which were in a sequence. He had taken specimens from a number of people, and their bars were all different, so – quite crucially to us now, but not particularly then to him – the 'fingerprint' could be identified with precision. It could be seen where the DNA came from mum or dad to form a composite. Then his team began brain storming – where could they get DNA from, apart from the living body? Would it be at a crime scene? Would it be in a hair pulled from the perpetrator of a crime? Could it be found in semen from a rape victim?

As they got deeper, they could ask themselves – if a person sheds about eight pounds of dead skin a year, where do they shed it? Does 'live' DNA live in dead skin?

One of the first applications was in a paternity case, so brought immeasurable joy to a mum whose child could be proved to be hers and could stay with her – it was an immigration issue. Now, more and more people could be proved to be British through DNA, now called DNA fingerprinting. A private company was set up to inform the Home Office of paternity issues with people whose nationality was questioned.

Then something quite ghastly happened. Two girls were raped and killed – a good while apart, but the *modus operandi* was similar. The question was, did the same man do both? The police had a suspect who had actually confessed to one of the killings. The police asked Professor Jeffreys if the technique would show he killed the other girl. Much to everyone's amazement, it didn't, but to even greater amazement it proved he hadn't committed the crime he'd confessed to!

Professor Jeffreys was supported by the Home Office and his work with them, and his 'innocent' finding with the DNA of the murder/rape suspect was vindicated with a 'not guilty' from the jury. But that misses the point; an innocent man was cleared, which meant the guilty man was still at large. And as Professor Jeffreys said, 'The real perpetrator could have gone on to kill again.'

Then another amazing event happened. The police actually wondered whether, if the DNA testing had proved one man innocent, it could prove who the guilty man was. Local men from seventeen to thirty-four around the village of Narborough in Leicestershire were asked for a blood specimen. 4,000 came along quickly and were eliminated. But one of them gave a blood sample for someone else – and when the police discovered this they arrested both men.

One was innocently duped, but the other one gave a DNA sample that matched semen from both the murdered girls. In January 1988 Colin Pitchfork was jailed for life for the rape and murder of Linda Mann and Dawn Ashworth.

Professor Jeffreys was knighted in 1994, though he is modest about his achievements. 'I was just lucky that I got to discover DNA fingerprinting. If I hadn't, someone else would have done it by now.'

Jenkins, Billie-Jo
Murdered by person unknown

Almost everywhere one looked in Hastings in early 1997 was a poster with the question, 'Who killed Billie-Jo Jenkins?' But many years on, the only question answered is, 'Who didn't kill Billie-Jo Jenkins?' And that's her foster father, Sion. But the police decided he had, so they spent all of their time building a case against him. The press helped out immeasurably. Then trial by the English legal system could almost be called a formality, or a farce.

But Mr Jenkins wasn't prepared to play ball.

It was pure coincidence that Billie-Jo went to live with foster parents of the same name, and this girl, who'd been called 'difficult', soon settled with Mr and Mrs Jenkins and their four daughters. Things seemed to go very smoothly for her over the five years or so before her untimely end.

It was on the 15 February 1997 that she was murdered at the family home – she was beaten over the head with a metal tent peg. Billie-Jo was working at home alone, painting, to earn some extra pocket money. Mr Jenkins told police that he'd found her in a pool of blood when he returned from a visit to a DIY centre to the north of Hastings – and the police later discovered he'd not taken the most direct route! Clearly a suspicious piece of behaviour. He explained why, as the farce gained momentum, and was accused of taking two of his daughters, Annie and Charlotte, along for an alibi.

In a two-hour interview with Mr Jenkins' wife Lois, the police told her it was him. Neither his wife nor their four daughters could at that time shed any light on his guilt, but even if he'd been dropped from the enquiry then his marriage and family life was ruined.

Mr Jenkins was charged and convicted, but always maintained his innocence. An appeal in 1999 failed, but after a second appeal in August 2004 his conviction was deemed unsafe by the Court of Appeal and a retrial was ordered. In the first retrial the jury couldn't agree; in the second retrial they couldn't agree either. A 'not guilty' verdict was recorded in 2006.

The bill for all of this so far was reaching many millions of pounds.

After his acquittal, he still maintained his innocence. At some stage, investigative journalist Bob Woofinden, believing from the outset that the spots of blood on Mr Jenkins' jacket that the case revolved around could have been exhaled by the girl as she died in his arms, said, 'The prosecution case was dead in the water'. Or it should have been.

Bob went on to argue that the issue was how a dying girl may have been breathing and there was no scientific consensus from the boffins, except 'we don't know'. Personally, I think whether she was alive or not is immaterial. When a body is moved, especially by picking her up in the way I understand Mr Jenkins did, then the trunk is slightly compressed and some air left in the lung could easily be expelled by the pressure, thus sending the blood droplets flying. It could be said that, on occasion, the forensic people get too bogged down in their own field and forget simple rules of physics. Ask any nurse who has 'laid out' a dead patient just what happens when you roll them over to wash their back and clear up any incontinence; they groan as air is pushed out with their turning or moving.

But there is something else and you can try this at home. Take a melon as a substitute for a head and a rolling pin as a substitute for a tent peg. A video camera with a decent slow-motion replay is an essential. Place the melon in a shallow dish and set the video camera at right angles to it, but far enough back to completely track what happens when you beat the melon with the rolling pin. With a nice white shirt, sleeves rolled down, then it might be possible to count more than 158 microscopic particles of melon and see on the video – and this is the point – that the splashes on impact are not the issue: its where the raising rolling pin distributes. The splashes will go outwards (some on the shirt), but the distribution of particles 'extracted' from the melon on the rolling pin being retracted and made ready for the next blow will follow the retraction direction, i.e. all over one's nice clean shirt. And there will be more like 1,580 great big blobs of melon, not 158 microscopic ones. If he'd beaten her with a tent peg, Sion would have been covered in blood.

Interestingly, it was following a two-year investigation by the Criminal Cases Review Commission (CCRC) that Mr Jenkins' case was referred to the Court of Appeal. The CCRC said, 'There is evidence, not before the jury, that suggests Mr Jenkins could not have committed the murder'. The cost of the jury not hearing this has been shown.

The police investigation, the trials and the appeals – not to mention the cost of a few years 'inside' – are estimated to have cost £10 million. 700 witness statements were taken by the police, and jurors spent thirty-six days deliberating in the three trials.

At the time of the murder, or at any rate just before, there was known to be prowlers in the area and Mr Jenkins and family had stepped up security on their house. More recently, the suggestion has been made that a convicted serial rapist was in the area, but DNA from Billie-Jo and him would have both been on police records.

Officially the crime is unsolved.

Jones, Harold
Probably only killed twice

It was in the second half of the nineteenth century with the coming of the first deep coal mine, sunk in 1843, that the town of Abertillary, then in Monmouthshire and now in Gwent, began to grow. Its population was still increasing in 1921 when two most heinous crimes were committed – and the murderer was a fifteen-year-old boy. The horror was exacerbated when the killer was actually acquitted of the first murder and committed the second within only a few days of his acquittal.

Fred Burnell was a little concerned that his daughter Freda had taken longer than usual to make the trip to Mortimer's Stores in Somerset Street. He'd sent her there to buy grit as he kept poultry. His concern grew into anxiety, so he thought he'd walk to the shop himself to see what had happened. Freda did visit the shop but had left, explained Harold Jones, who was the assistant in the shop – she'd left at about 9.15. By then, Freda was probably dead.

However, Fred didn't know and he wanted to search around

the town. By mid-afternoon, with no sign of her, he contacted the police. They went back to the last person who'd seen her, Harold Jones in Mortimer's Stores, but they couldn't pick up on any clues. The February afternoon matured into evening and dark descended.

With the strong community spirit the mining towns tended to garner, many other townsfolk helped with the search. With the coming of midnight and the cold night air, the search was abandoned until first light. Just after 7.30 the following morning, in a lane in the town centre, an off-duty miner found Freda's body. The police were shocked by the savagery with which she'd been attacked; the doctor timed the death as occurring sometime the previous morning.

The local police wasted no time and sent for Scotland Yard. In the week that followed there was a lot of activity, which culminated in the arrest of Harold Jones for Freda's murder on the Thursday. He was subsequently charged. Mortimer's Stores had a shed from which screams had been heard, and Harold had the only key. An axe was found, which was thought to be the murder weapon, and also Freda's handkerchief.

In court he denied murder, and the evidence wasn't conclusive so he was acquitted on 21 June. The town all appeared relieved that the killer didn't seem to be one of their children. Harold went back to Abertillary to a warm welcome.

July soon came, and on Friday 8 July he struck again, against eleven-year-old Florrie Little, who lived in the same street as Harold. He took her into his home, where he attacked her with the same ferocity he'd shown against Freda those few months before. He hid the body in the attic. It was almost inevitable he was going to be discovered, but he seemed to keep an eerie coolness. With Florrie missing, the police decided to do house-to-house searches, and Harold's father invited them to search their house. Harold adopted a low profile but it was his own father who caught him and handed him over to the police.

He made a statement admitting to Florrie's murder, and also told the police that he'd murdered Freda the previous January. Because he was only fifteen years old, he escaped the death penalty. He told the court he'd experienced a 'desire to kill'. He was given the mandatory life sentence, or, as it's politely termed, 'detained until His Majesty's pleasure be known'. Harold Jones did return to Abertillary, but not until years later, and then only to visit; it has been suggested that the visit was to the graves of his victims.

Twenty years later, he was released from prison aged only thirty-five, and by 1947 he was in London. He lived in Fulham with his wife and child.

So the question is, did he kill again as an adult? He'd attacked the two girls with some ferocity and there seemed very little evidence of sexual content to his attacks. But after twenty-odd years, few policemen would have connected the two murders in Abertillary with the possibility that he was involved in a series of murders with a similar *modus operandi* in the mid-1960s – dreadful violence but little sexual content. In the series of murders he's been lately connected with, the assailant left the girls undressed, hence the poor title – Jack the Stripper. If leaving his victims naked isn't sexual then it's confusing to think what is. Sexual content in a crime is often an expression of the assailant's desire for power, sexuality often being a vehicle to communicate that power. There is also the fact that he was keeping a low profile between leaving prison in 1941 and turning up in Fulham in 1947 – which was many years before the Jack the Stripper murders.

Harold Jones died in 1971.

Joyce, William Brooke

Lord Haw Haw. Hanged for treason

William Joyce, alias Lord Haw-Haw, is now considered by many to be a sad and almost comical figure, some would even say pathetic. But at a crucial time in the last war, he was listened to – and although that might not have made a great deal of difference, it did seem to affect morale. He was a great speaker, and when the familiar 'this is Germany calling, this is Germany calling' came over the radio the Nazi propaganda machine was away. He was considered a traitor, and the feeling of the time from almost every household in the land was that he should be severely punished. The Treason Act was passed at about the time of his capture.

He was actually born in New York – his father was Irish and his mother English – but they moved to Mayo in the Irish Republic when he was three, and they moved again when he was fifteen, to England.

When he was around eighteen he became involved with the Fascist movement, and it was at this time he received a terrible wound to his cheek. It could have been caused by anyone, but he believed it was the work of 'Jewish Communists', and it also seemed to have an emotional effect on him; it gave him a constant reminder of where he wanted his hate targeted.

In October 1932, he was in his mid-twenties. He joined Sir Oswald Mosley's British Union of Fascists and soon came to prominence, but alarmed some members with his extremism. Nevertheless, he became their deputy leader. Mr Joyce and Sir Oswold were very different; Mr Joyce was a bad-tempered individual whereas Sir Oswald was quite charming. He lost his job as the party lost support and he was made redundant.

He made little effort to disguise admiration for Adolf Hitler and made up his mind the Jews had caused the Second World War – but with the war would come internment in the UK, so he fled to Germany.

Mr Joyce soon found his niche as a speaker for German propaganda transmissions and his broadcasts to England were infamous – he was christened (if that's the appropriate word) 'Lord Haw-Haw' by the *Daily Express*. It was illegal to listen but millions did, and he was able to give some useless but highly accurate information, which suggested more traitors actually active in England than was first thought. As the tide of war turned after the Battle of Britain, however, less people were swayed by the propaganda.

He was decorated by his 'leaders', but his life was falling apart due to his heavy drinking; indeed, in his last broadcast, which may not have been broadcast – the tape was found later – he was said to be slurring. He did, however, say that Britain would never be the same and would be heavily in debt by the end of the war. Credibility seemed to have deserted him. His last words were 'Heil Hitler'.

Mr Joyce was caught just as the war ended, and his appointment with the hangman was now a mere formality. The government passed the Treason Act as he boarded an England-bound aeroplane.

He took German Nationality on 26 September 1939, but he was charged with treason from the day war started until 2 July 1940, when his British Passport ran out. He was born in America of English/Irish parents and took German Nationality, but it was considered that as the holder of a British passport he should have remained loyal to the Sovereignty. He was found guilty and executed on 3 January 1946 at Wandsworth prison in London.

It's been suggested he was a double agent working for MI5, but he was considered a laughing stock by the British public by the end of the war. Given his American birth and German nationality, was he a traitor? It's not for us to say now, but, with the hatred of anything pro-fascist at the end of the war, it was suggested he was. He had said some pretty vitriolic things and undermined the morale of the country in the early stages of the war, and it had an effect.

It's a sticky one, because it has been claimed he got his British passport illegally; he wasn't so much anti-Britain as pro-fascist, and only went to Germany to escape internment. But then there is the argument of the other fascists in England, who were interned in England and clung to their political beliefs. Ironically, the entire war was waged in part so that people could believe what they chose.

Kiszko, Stefan
The Murder of Lesley Molseed

It was on Christmas Eve 1975 that Stefan Kiszko was arrested for the October murder of eleven-year-old Lesley Molseed. She was abducted in Rochdale in Lancashire and found on moorland. She'd been stabbed eleven times and her killer had ejaculated over her clothes.

Stefan lived with his widowed mother and had a steady job as a taxation clerk, but he also had a growth problem, which I will discuss later. His father had died of a heart attack in 1970.

He was unknown to the police, but when three teenaged girls made complaints that Stefan had indecently exposed himself, the police interviewed him. This was done without a proper caution, and when the police did arrest him they took a confession from him. It was later demonstrated that no solicitor was present for this interview, and Stefan was a quiet, easy-going sort of chap, who gave into the brow-beating, bullying type of questioning. On the promise that he could go home if he made a written statement, he cooperated with them.

In 1976, before Sir Hugh Park at Leeds Crown Court, he was found guilty of the murder and jailed for life. As well as the lies of the three teenaged girls there was fabricated evidence from the police and also the forensic services. He was represented in court by Mr David Waddington QC, who could see he was in grave danger of conviction and tried to limit the damage.

Sixteen years later it came out that the three teenaged girls had lied – they should have faced charges. It emerged that Detective Superintendent Richard (Dick) Holland and Mr Ronald Outteridge of the forensic service had also lied. The DNA in the sperm that had been ejaculated over Lesley didn't lie – nor did Stefan or his body, because he had hypogonadism, which meant he couldn't produce sperm.

DSupt Holland and Mr Outteridge were charged but not convicted, and they blamed Mr Jack Dibb, who, as detective chief superintendent, had led the hunt, and had subsequently died. The magistrates didn't think the two men would receive a fair trial.

Stefan's mother, Charlotte, never believed her son could be capable of such a crime, but in court she was an ineffective witness. As a campaigner for his release, though, she was tireless. Eventually she met Campbell Malone, a solicitor who promised to have a look at Stefan's file. He was deeply disturbed by what he found.

A letter was written to the Home Secretary in a plea for a review of the case. By some irony, the Home Secretary was David Waddington, who had defended Stefan in his original trial. His successor, Kenneth Baker, finally referred the case back to the Court of Appeal.

Mr Holland had retired by now and he was quoted to have said, 'Words can't express the regret I feel for the family and for Kiszko. The inquiry was done diligently and honestly within the terms that were legally andscientifically available at the time.'

One also has to acknowledge the hurt Lesley's family had to go through again; her father said, 'The police have a lot to answer to and we can't let the matter rest.'

He was one of the few who actually apologised to Mrs Kiszko. Chief Superintendent Ken MacKay of Lancashire police investigated the role of the police and forensic scientists. West Yorkshire Police resumed their investigation.

Prison isn't tolerant of sex offenders, and Stefan was the target of a lot of insults and several beatings while he was inside; eventually he was diagnosed with a severe mental illness, which was still being treated at the time of his release.

Charlotte Kiszko wasn't in the slightest bit tolerant of the system that had jailed him for sixteen years – but it wasn't the system that was at fault, it was a few of the people in it. 'His ordeal has destroyed his life,' she said. 'Nothing can compensate for it. Nothing whatsoever will bring back his lost years.'

When his conviction was quashed and he went home his relief was short-lived. On Christmas Eve (again) 1993 Stefan was found at home; he'd died of a suspected heart attack aged only forty-one. At least he'd had his conviction quashed, but had less than two years to recover. The following May his mother Charlotte died, just one day before Mr Holland and Mr Outerridge were charged with perverting the course of justice.

The torment for Lesley Molseed's family continued until Ronald Castree was convicted of her murder in 2007. He has later said that he has the right to be forgotten and removed from internet sites. Campbell Malone, in the absence of Stefan or his mother, deserves the last word. 'Ronald Castree will never succeed in any attempt to have his actions forgotten ... His murder of Lesley Molseed, his silence at the arrest prosecution and conviction of Stefan Kiszko and his devastation of two innocent families has been comprehensively documented.'

Kray Twins

Reggie Kray was born ten minutes before Ronnie, on 24 October 1933 in Hoxton in East London. Almost from the start the twins were a force to be reckoned with, and elder brother Charlie has said he was their punchbag.

By the time the 1950s drew to a close they were involved in many illegal activities, and in 1960 Ronnie was imprisoned for protection racketeering; Reggie moved on to nightclub management and was an associate of Peter Rachman, a vicious landlord who exploited his residents, who were mainly immigrants. Another associate was Alan Cooper, who was a financier and helped with money laundering and also established a mafia connection, which later fizzled out.

But the legitimate side of their businesses were well patronised and they made several useful connections, though information is difficult to come by.

There were links to homosexual relationships, and these tended to prevent pressure from the major political parties being placed on the police to curtail their notorious violence, as none of the parties were keen for the press to cover the affairs. Ronnie was associated with the conservative peer, Lord Boothby, and later with Labour politician Tom Driburg. The Lord Boothby issue, where the politician stood accused of being supplied with young men by Ronnie and attending orgies, was settled with Kray twins' threats and an infusion of money to Lord Boothby.

Their rival gang, south of the river, were the Richardson Brothers, who had one George Cornell as an associate. The rivalry between the two gangs came to a head over Christmas 1965, with Mr Cornell allegedly insulting Ronnie's size and sexual orientation. George Cornell was a vicious mobster who was said to fear no one; on 9 March 1966 he was drinking in The Blind Beggar pub in Whitechapel Road – well into the Krays' territory – and Ronnie Kray went into the bar and shot him dead. Ronnie later said the murder was because Mr Cornell had threatened them.

In December 1966, they assisted Frank Mitchell to escape from Dartmoor Prison. Frank was a large man with a mental disorder, which made him a handful, but he was coerced into a van to be taken to a 'safe house' and shot; later he was put into the English Channel. Reggie later said he regretted having anything to do with Mr Mitchell.

In October 1967, an associate who did the odd bit of work for them was paid to murder a former business associate Leslie Payne; he was Jack 'the hat' McVitie. The murder didn't occur and Mr McVitie was said to have been heavily dependent on drugs – he was a known drug dealer. In the event it was Mr McVitie who was murdered and this is what led to the Kray twins' downfall. It was also suggested Ronnie had egged on Reggie to do the deed but Mr MvVitie's body has never been found, though I gather his liver was flushed down a toilet somewhere.

Leonard 'Nipper' Read was an astute copper and knew that the Krays had some friends in Scotland Yard, so when he was briefed to investigate them with a view to their arrest and conviction he hand-picked his team, based them away from Scotland Yard and told them they were always to go everywhere in pairs. But as well as Scotland Yard being a weak link, there was a virtual wall of silence from all others. By the spring of 1968 the police thought they had enough evidence and on 8 May there were seventeen arrests.

In the later court case there was one acquittal and sixteen convictions. Mr Justice Melford Stevenson said, 'In my view, society has earned a rest from your activities.'

Reggie and Ronnie were each given life sentences and should have served thirty years before eligibility for consideration for parole. In the event, neither were paroled. Ronnie was diagnosed with a severe mental illness and was transferred to Broadmoor, where he died in March 1995 aged sixty-one. Reggie Kray was released on compassionate grounds with terminal cancer in August 2000 and died in October 2000.

Lamplugh, Suzy
Murdered by persons unknown

The potential purchaser may have had second thoughts about a property in a busy street and decided to think about a house in a quieter, more residential area. He may have planned to convert the older property to flats when events intervened. Whatever his explanation to the estate agent, her car was found across the road from another house her company were agents for. Of her, there was no sign, and there hasn't been since that day in late summer of 1986.

Susannah was born in Cheltenham in Gloucestershire in 1961. She'd worked in a few jobs in the beauty industry, but by her mid-twenties she worked for Sturgis and Co., an estate agent in Fulham. She'd bought a flat in Putney and had a regular boyfriend, though someone was lurking in the background – either with her blessing or not.

A client had contacted the office and asked to view a property in Shorrolds Road and Suzy (as she was known) left her office to meet him at the property. His name, Mr Kipper, was false and the address he gave was also false.

Her white Fiesta was seen in Shorrolds Road at lunchtime but was a mile away at another property soon after, and the car was later found to be unlocked, with her purse in the door pocket. The seat had been pushed right back, which might suggest another driver. Forensic examination of the car yielded no clues.

The police interviewed far and wide. The lady in the house opposite to where the car was found was pretty sure of the time the car had arrived, although she didn't see Suzy or 'Mr Kipper'. The only way the car could have got there without someone leaving forensic clues is if Suzy left it there.

Her family were devastated, although they turned tragedy into help for women alone, either working or just going about life, with the Suzy Lamplugh Trust.

The police investigation was huge but nothing was found. What is known, or is as close to fact as one can dare to suggest, is that she was abducted and later murdered.

But how can someone be abducted in Fulham at lunchtime, when there are people milling around and actually men working on the road close by?

The police have named a suspect, which is unusual. But looking at his usual methods, one finds he used all sorts of 'restraining tools', for example, handcuffs.

Related, but on a different tack, if one is purchasing a house in London it might be a normal question to ask, 'Where's the nearest tube?' which, even if answered, can still mean the asker goes to the passenger side of their own car – not Suzy's. In the glove box is a conveniently placed A–Z directory, which the buyer opens up at the pre-arranged page. The driver's door is open – parked on the wrong side of the road – and one would ask, through the open door, 'Is this where we are now …?'

The natural thing is to move closer to the map and sort of lean into the driver's side, supporting the leaning with the left hand towards the middle of the car on the inner side of the driver's seat. Then, a bit like Hannibal Lector, the handcuffs attached to the interior of the car at one end are easily applied to the non-suspecting with a chilling threat …

Lawrence, Stephen
Murdered by Gary Dobson and David Norris and others

Stephen Lawrence was a young lad from south-east London who was a noted athlete and hoped to eventually become an architect. He'd been with his friend Duwayne Brooks during the afternoon and evening of 22 April 1993. At 10.30 p.m., they were at a bus stop in Eltham. Stephen went to see if a bus was coming, and a group of five or six youths appeared.

Duwayne called out to Stephen about the bus and one of the gang shouted obscene abuse. The group came across the road and 'engulfed' Stephen: he was stabbed twice. Duwayne was a little distance away from the attack but turned to run and called Stephen to follow him.

Three eyewitnesses at the bus stop were unable to identify any of the attackers because the whole incident only took about fifteen to twenty seconds.

The gang ran off down a side road. Stephen somehow managed to get to his feet but only got about 100 yards or so before he collapsed.

He'd been stabbed on both sides of his trunk and his maxillary artery was severed; his clothing soaked up an enormous amount of blood. It's likely he died there rather than in the ambulance.

His murder, according to the first public enquiry, was 'simply and solely ... motivated by racism.'

But at the time, the police service was said to be rife with 'institutional racism'. And the Crown Prosecution Service wasn't entirely neutral. Like Kelso Cochrane forty years before, the decent in society expected justice but were to wait a long time for it. The incident helped prompt the government to legislate.

Back in February 1997, the *Daily Mail* showed the country who the killers were and told the country all their details – and also why they hadn't been prosecuted. The campaign wasn't going to stop.

Two of the gang were re-arrested and, with the double jeopardy rule now not applicable, they could face a re-trial. Now middle-aged, Gary Dobson and David Norris were convicted of the murder in 2012.

It was reported that the two convicted had committed a string of offences linked to violence and racism. Even though it's fairly certain who was there with them on that April evening, let's hope that one day they might decide to confirm it.

Leeson, Nick
Rogue Trader

Nick Leeson was born Nicholas William on 25 February 1967 in Watford, Hertforshire. He left school at eighteen and got a job in Coutts, a private bank with a few branches in the UK and quite a few more internationally. After this, Nick moved to Morgan Stanley – an American multi-national – in 1987. Then came a rather expensive paring with Barings Bank, where one of his first errors can be traced as he was denied a broker's licence due to an irregularity when applying.

This was brushed under the carpet in 1992, when he was sent to Singapore and applied for a broker's licence there – Barings were partly to blame for this non-disclosure. But that didn't seem to bother anyone, because he made some spectacular profits in his first year – something like £10 million, his bonus being just over two and a half times his salary!

His luck didn't last, though, and he started to conceal his misdemeanours in what was known as a Barings Error Account. His risks started then to get more and more ambitious and reckless as time went by. From the beginning of 1993 to the end of the following year he'd managed to clock up (or should that be clock down?) an additional loss of £206 million from the original £2 million.

It wasn't all pilot error, though, because a gamble that could easily have paid off was to bet that the Japanese stock market wouldn't move too much overnight. But at 4.46 a.m., 3,500 miles, away something did move – the earth! An earthquake measuring 7.2 on the Richter Scale hit Kobe, which is in south-central Japan.

This sent the markets he'd bet on to be stable haywire. His banking and brokering never looked likely to recover.

He left a note expressing his remorse, 'I'm sorry', and, as the losses passed the £825 million mark, he was on his way. Barings was declared as 'broke' on 26 February 1995.

They finally caught up with him in Frankfurt, where he was arrested and returned to Singapore. But he was authorized to trade by Barings Bank, so was it just that he'd not followed his employer's instructions? Whether it was criminal or civil, he went to prison for a few years.

While 'away', he was divorced, developed and recovered from cancer and wrote a book, *Rogue Trader*, later made into a film. Nick Leeson wasn't a bad lot, though his popularity within banking has never fully recovered. His cult status takes him to various places for after-dinner and conference speaking.

The trader's jackets of Barings were unique and distinct, and one Nick himself wore was sold later for £21,000. One worn by one of his colleagues, though, only sold for £4,000.

Lloyds Bank, Baker Street
Robbery

A most remarkable bank robbery took place in central London in September 1971. At Lloyds Bank in Baker Street, over a number of weekends, a gang tunnelled their way under neighbouring buildings and then up into the vault. No easy task; the ground was sloping and the streets of London stand on a maze of pipes, cables, sewers and even ancient burial sites.

But, like most criminal plans, it was simple. Find a secluded spot, dig down, dig along and dig up. A thermic lance was initially used to get through the reinforced concrete of the vault floor but this was soon stopped because of fumes, so explosives were used.

Once in the vault they opened as many boxes as time allowed. Folk would only store either illegal items or highly valuable items – jewellery, bearer bonds, securities, uncut gems and large amounts of cash, any of which may have had an illegitimate source.

Entry access for the public was through the vault door, but if this was locked there would be so many alarm features and access limitations, time-locks and such that illegal entry would be difficult to impossible. A bank vault is like an ordinary safe with an almost impregnable door, but with weaker sides, back, top and bottom. Not much weaker, though. So if the firm could get to the base of the vault then entry would be possible.

However, even in 1971 alarms were well advanced – the bank vault door had an alarm triggered by opening or by violence from a sledgehammer to a bazooka. The sides and top had vibration alarms so blasting in through the ceiling or restaurant next door wasn't feasible, but the gang discovered that the vibration alarm in the vault floor was switched off due to nearby road works. So that was the possibility that presented itself – entry through the ground.

It would take time and effort, but the firm knew where the tunnel would emerge, so they needed to assess where it could start and then how far underground before the horizontal became the vertical. They'd have to conceal the tunnel, which gave limitations, so for the ideal plot they needed access to a basement nearby; they soon found one two doors away. They obtained a lease for a vacant shop and in between was a takeaway restaurant, so a timetable for tunnelling could be devised, when the noise made would be less likely to be overheard.

Two of the gang posed as bank customers to gauge where the centre of the vault floor was, but they needed specialised knowledge of the building's construction. And it wasn't just the building, it was also the subterranean complexities of cables, sewers and other obstacles – without specialist help it might have been an impossible project.

Within three months, though, they'd obtained the building plans, assembled the expertise, gained additional digging muscle, and reached the bottom of the vault. Blasting up through the many feet of reinforced concrete would again need a specialist – too little explosive and they'd only scratch it and possibly affect the safety/structure of their tunnel. Too much explosive and the tunnel could well collapse, or they might inadvertently blow the foundations of the building up causing instability or collapse – this would bring all sorts of unwanted attention. So again, specialist help was needed, and viewing concrete doesn't expose its constitution nor its reinforcing. Those eventually convicted didn't have this knowledge.

But after three months a hole appeared in the floor of the vault, following a well-concealed explosion. It took three months because they could only tunnel at weekends and wanted to gauge their entry for after bank closing on the Friday afternoon, to maximise the time before the vault door was likely to be opened on the Monday morning.

Once in the vault they opened 268 boxes. The haul was estimated at between £150,000 and £3 million, which is a huge gap, but the police relied on what the owners of the boxes were willing to tell them. There were all sorts of rumours as to what was collected as 'extras', and even rumours that the crime was committed by the security services, neither of which have a ring of truth about them. Publicity wasn't banned but wasn't encouraged.

As to the customers owning the boxes, one was then head of the judiciary, Quintin Hogg. There was talk, never confirmed, that a member of the royal family had compromising photographs stolen. Another owner was reputed to keep his stash of child pornography there. But all the robbers wanted was cash and jewels – if anyone had a safety deposit box, it didn't follow necessarily they had things to hide; perhaps they just wanted security.

As for the robbers, it was claimed the gang of four later convicted dug the tunnel, set the charges and cut open the safety deposit boxes. But tunnelling was noisy and so not only did they confine their work to weekends, they also thought it wise to post a lookout with an overall view of the outside of the buildings to alert them to police activity through walkie-talkies. Ironically, it was this that alerted the police, but the police had limitations tracking the walkie-talkies. It was an amateur radio enthusiast who first overheard the robbers' conversations; he called the police, with little action being taken. Later he called them again and they advised he might record the conversations, which he did.

Radios were far inferior to what we have today and would have a limited range of only, say, about a mile or two, hampered by tall buildings, weather and electrical activity; it could mean the robbers weren't too far away from their amateur radio audience. In fact, he was in Wimpole Street, which is within two miles. Unfortunately, the two miles were from his home, and the police wouldn't know which direction the signal was coming from.

Eventually, the police did start to look but couldn't find the particular bank – if all looked well from the outside then they couldn't enter the bank without a warrant or evidence a crime was being committed. It wasn't until the Monday morning, when the manager opened the vault, that piles of rubble, a hole in the floor and hundreds of opened boxes were found.

Owners of the boxes had to be identified, informed and enquiries made as to what they kept there, and anything embarrassing or illegal would likely as not remain 'undisclosed'.

Once the tunnel was examined and the police could find its origins, almost at once they found a likely candidate for conspiracy, if not robbery. One of the firm had leased the building in his own name, Mr Wolfe, so the police had someone to hound. They rounded up his associates and alibis were not forthcoming. So with Benjamin Wolfe, Anthony Gavin, Thomas Stephens and

Reginald Tucker, were quickly placed under arrest and questioned. The police got no information from them.

In January 1973, the four men were convicted at the Old Bailey and received long sentences. Two other men accused of handling were acquitted. The police believed they knew who the mastermind was but he was never brought to book. Little of what was stolen was ever recovered.

Lockerbie Bombing
Pan-Am Flight 103

Flight PA103, from London Heathrow to New York, was in level cruising at 31,000 feet for about seven minutes when the last radar track was received. The radar then indicated a number of readings fanning out. Large parts of the aircraft fell on the town of Lockerbie and surrounding countryside. Within a few days, wreckage was forensically tested and scientists found clear evidence of an explosive. The explosion led directly to the destruction of the aircraft, killing all 259 souls on board and eleven residents of Lockerbie.

The Boeing 747 arrived at Heathrow from San Francisco, and many of the passengers for flight PA103 had travelled in from Frankfurt. They were transferred with their baggage for the onward flight to New York. Passengers from other flights also joined the flight at Heathrow. Flight PA103 pushed back at 6.04 p.m. and was cleared to taxi out to runway 27R.

It took off at 6.25 p.m. and was soon at 6,000 feet, approaching Burnham (between Slough and Maidenhead) before a right turn to head north over Bovingdon (Hemel Hempstead), and was cleared to climb to 12,000 and subsequently 31,000 feet, where it levelled off just north of Polehill (Between Bradford and Blackburn) at 6.56 p.m. Just over six minutes later, the Shanwick Oceanic

Control centre in Prestwick gave oceanic clearance, which wasn't acknowledged. PA103 disappeared from the radar and radar pick-ups then fanned out, indicating the aircraft had broken up.

Two huge parts of wreckage fell on Lockerbie; other parts, including the flight deck and forward fuselage section, were recovered east of the town. Residents reported a rumbling noise like thunder at just after 7.00 p.m., which increased in volume. Eyewitnesses described a meteor-like object, trailing flame, which hit earth to the north-east of the town. A larger, dark object, probably a wing, landed at about the same time in the Sherwood Crescent area of Lockerbie and ignited on impact. Lighter pieces of debris were carried by the wind over a large area.

Sixteen crew members, 243 passengers and eleven people on the ground were killed. Houses were set on fire.

A crew of three were flying the aircraft. The captain was male, fifty-five years old with nearly 11,000 flying hours, 4,000 on the 747. He was medically sound and his training schedule was all up to date. The first officer was also male, fifty-two, having done 11,800 odd hours with 5,500 on the 747. He too was medically sound with an up-to-date training record. The flight engineer was forty-six, with 8,000 flying hours, 500 of those on the 747. He too was medically sound and his training was up-to-date. None of the three had exceeded permitted flying hours over the last four weeks. The thirteen flight attendants were all medically sound and trained.

The Boeing 747 aircraft was a conventionally designed long-range aeroplane with most of the passenger accommodation in the main cabin, which extended the whole length of the aircraft. A separate upper deck was incorporated in the forward part of the aircraft.

Below the main deck were a number of compartments, the largest of which were the forward and aft freight holds for the storage of baggage in standard air-transport containers. The containers were loaded by a freight handling system on a system of rails about two feet above the outer hull of the aircraft. The forward compartment had a length of around forty feet and a depth of approximately six feet. Loading was through the forward hold through a door on the right side of the aircraft.

The aircraft was over 20,000 pounds less than maximum weight and had 240,000 pounds of fuel on board. The cargo didn't include any dangerous goods, perishable cargo, live animals or known security exceptions.

It was Pan-Am owned from construction in 1970, and had totalled 72,464 hours flying over 16,497 flight cycles. Its maintenance was up to date.

The weather was good with intermittent showers of rain, and at 31,000 feet they were well above the clouds; visibility was about twelve miles.

The cockpit voice recorder (CVR) noted the Shanwick oceanic clearance, but within a second or two a 'loud sound' was heard. This, together with the flight recorder, confirmed that the aircraft had performed satisfactorily up to that point. The CVR was functioning slightly below par and old recordings were faint in the background, but there was nothing untoward.

The hull or skin of the aircraft didn't suggest structural or material problems, and the settings of the controls and switches were consistent with the level of cruise.

About 90 per cent of the aircraft was recovered for investigation. A few skin panels were 'sooted' – forensic analysis of soot deposits identified explosive residues. Some debris identified as parts of baggage containers had damage consistent with detonated explosives and it became clear the explosion had occurred in the forward cargo hold. A radio cassette player was later identified as having been fitted with an 'improvised explosive device.'

There was characteristic 'petaling' of the area around where the explosive detonated. This led to a 'pressure blow' that destroyed the aircraft; no one was killed directly by the explosion but perished almost as soon as the aircraft disintegrated. Consideration of the seat allocation suggested the passengers in the forward part of the aircraft were first to be affected.

Dumfries Fire Brigade was in action by 7.07 p.m., and it soon became apparent that a major disaster had occurred. 'An explosive detonation within a fuselage, in reasonably close proximity to the skin, will produce a high intensity spherically propagating shock wave which will expand outwards from the centre of detonation,' was how the official report summed it up.

The separation of the major portions of the aircraft took something like two or three seconds, with major breaks occurring as it fell to 19,000 feet and then 9,000 feet.

So it was a bomb, and if the aircraft had left on time then it should have been over the Atlantic and very little could have been investigated.

Abdelbaset al-Megrahi has been convicted of the crime, but there's no conceivable possibility he was working alone. Iran, Libya and Malta have been mentioned, but the main problem for anyone is the confusion caused by political agendas and unreliable evidence.

What was established in Abdelbaset al-Megrahi's trial was that the bomb was placed on an aircraft that was heading for Frankfurt at Luga airport in Malta. It then was moved to Heathrow and on to PA103, but there was no evidence that Mr al-Megrahi put the bomb on the Air Malta flight at Luga.

A Heathrow baggage handler said that on the day of the bombing he saw a case on a cargo trolley that seemed to appear from nowhere while he was on a tea break; this was before the aircraft from Frankfurt arrived at Heathrow. Another strange incident was the discovery of a severed padlock on a baggage store. This is all very vague, and the Lockerbie Bombing may be one of those cases where each study asks more questions than it answers.

Lord, Alan

Attempted murder by his wife, Margaret Lord, and his step-father, John

The late Peter Cook gave time to Amnesty International for a comedy gig, *The Secret Policeman's Ball*, and as it was in the latter part of the 1970s he parodied the judge's summing-up in the then-recent trial of a leading politician who'd plotted a murder. The plot was futile and, as Mr (Justice) Cook explained, the defendants 'couldn't carry out a simple murder plot without cocking the whole thing up!'

Fact is stranger than fiction, but actually, Margaret Lord, a mother of two and thirty-one-years of age, and her husband's step-father tried, on numerous occasions, to murder her husband. The plot was undertaken in the most inept way. They used toadstools and then deadly nightshade in his food; they tried sleeping tablets and then ether; they tried electrocution and finally they tried putting a plastic bag over his head.

But according to counsel in court, they succeeded only in becoming 'the most incompetent assassins ever to appear before a court'.

The whole thing came about because they were 'swingers', as was the step-father on Alan's side, John Lord. On some occasions she'd have sex with both men, and this was claimed to have been at the instigation of her husband.

Birmingham Crown Court heard that the attempts were made over a number of months; altogether, they thought up six methods of killing him. Fortunately, none of the schemes worked – Alan was never even remotely aware of any attempts being made on his life and survived to see the trial!

In May 1974, Mrs Lord and John Lord were both given seven-year jail sentences for conspiracy to murder – they'd both pleaded not guilty to six charges of attempted murder, which, probably because of their bungling incompetence, was accepted by the prosecution.

The court heard that Mr and Mrs Lord had a stormy marriage and that Mrs Lord had indulged in sexual intercourse with other men, as well as them both taking part in group sex.

Mrs Lord had explained to police that she discussed her marital woes with her husband's step-father and said she'd been at the 'end of her tether'. They had discussed various ways that they could get rid of Alan. For the prosecution, Mr Frank Blennerhassett QC said the conspirators first tried to poison him with toadstools as he liked mushrooms with his meals, but this resulted in no ill-effects at all; Alan Lord appeared to carry on with life as though nothing had happened.

They then rethought their strategy and came up with the idea that they should try deadly nightshade as it was abundantly available. The story here gets a little confused, because they either gave him the wrong berries or the berries they wanted were out of season.

On a number of occasions Alan was the recipient of sleeping pills, but again, this didn't seem to take him anywhere near the Pearly Gates. They then decided that when he was asleep they could electrocute him. But when he was sound asleep, and although Alan's step-father bought the equipment they thought they'd need – bare wires from a plug to go directly into the mains – they never actually wired him up.

But they didn't give up on the sleeping tablets, and when Mrs Lord dissolved some in his food and he became stupefied, he was given ether but simply didn't die!

A plastic bag over his head made him give a loud shout and the plot was then abandoned. Mrs Lord said that when she heard Alan shout, it 'upset her', and his step-father confessed, 'I just couldn't go through with it. When (Alan) shouted it drained all the courage out of me'.

Then police uncovered the sordid details of Margaret Lord's stormy marriage and the group sex they'd indulged in.

She did say that Alan Lord was also a violent, jealous man; she could stand it no longer and turned to her father-in-law for help. Mrs Lord explained in a statement, 'Dad always had a crush on me. He was mad at the way Alan would treat me. That's why he agreed to help me to get rid of Alan. People all know I had good cause to do it after what I have been through. He has treated me in a shocking way.'

Not surprisingly, they blamed each other, but each was jailed for seven years.

Mr Lord collapsed at his wife's conviction and sentencing and was 'sobbing as his wife was led from the dock'.

Later, after seeing her in cells below the court, he said, 'She asked me to wait for her. I told her l will wait forever if necessary. I still love her very much despite everything. I shall never accept that she intended to kill me. I blame my stepfather. He was the instigator.'

Lord Lucan

Bingham, Richard John – vanished on Friday 8 November 1974

Lord Lucan married Veronica in 1963 and they had three children. When the marriage ended in 1972, he left the marital home. There followed a custody battle and Veronica gained custody, which invoked his displeasure.

On the evening of 7 November 1974, Sandra Rivett, the live-in nanny, was battered to death in the basement of the family home. Veronica was also attacked, and identified Lord Lucan as her assailant. Later that night he asked his mother to collect the children and borrowed a Ford Corsair to drive to a friend's house, after which he was never seen again. The car was found in Newhaven, its upholstery was stained with blood and with a piece of lead pipe similar to one found at the murder scene in the boot. A warrant was issued for his arrest.

Sandra Eleanor Rivett (née Hensby) was born on 16 September 1945. After she left school she was an apprentice hairdresser before working as a secretary; she then took a job as a children's nanny in Croydon. In March 1964 she had a son who lived with his grandparents; a second son was adopted. Sandra registered with a Belgravia domestic agency in summer 1974 and began to work for the Lucans.

Sandra would normally be out on Thursday nights, but had changed her night off. Veronica usually had tea at about 9 p.m., so Sandra went downstairs to make it. As she entered the kitchen, which was in the basement, she was beaten to death with a piece of bandaged lead pipe and placed in a mail sack. Veronica wondered what had delayed her, so went downstairs to look. She called out from the top of the ground-floor stairs and was suddenly attacked; she later said she recognised her husband's voice. The two fought; she bit him and squeezed his testicles and he gave up the fight. When she asked for Sandra he said he'd killed her. Lord Lucan walked upstairs and sent his eldest daughter to bed, then went into one of the bedrooms. When Veronica entered and saw him go into the bathroom, she just ran, down the stairs, out of the house and up the street to The Plumbers' Arms.

Lord Lucan called his mother later that evening about who'd look after the children, and spoke of a 'terrible catastrophe'. He said he'd been driving past the house and saw Veronica fighting with a man in the basement, so went to help.

Later that evening Lord Lucan drove to friends in East Sussex; Susan Maxwell-Scott was the last known person to see him.

Detective Chief Superintendent Roy Ranson was at work early the next morning; the doctor had pronounced Sandra dead so the forensic team moved in. There was no forced entry. The area around the top of the staircase leading to the ground floor was heavily blood-stained. A blood-stained lead pipe lay on the floor. The light bulb had been removed.

Also searched was Lord Lucan's new home in Eaton Row, but nothing was found. His wallet, car keys, money, driving licence and spectacles were on a bedside table. His passport was in a drawer. His car was outside and hadn't been driven – the battery was flat. DCS Ranson saw Veronica at St George's Hospital where she could describe events. Sandra's body was removed to the mortuary.

Pathologist Professor Keith Simpson said Sandra was dead before her body was put in the sack, and that the lead pipe found close by was the murder weapon. Sandra's ex-husband and boyfriend both had an alibi and other male friends were questioned and eliminated. Her parents thought she had a good working relationship with Veronica, and was fond of the children. Lord Lucan's description was circulated, but he was only wanted for questioning.

DCS Ranson discovered that he'd gone to see his friend Ian Maxwell-Scott, who said Lord Lucan had arrived a few hours after the incident and talked with his wife. Lord Lucan had written letters to his brother-in-law, Bill Shand-Kydd, and posted them. Mr Maxwell-Scott called Mr Shand-Kydd to tell him about the letters; on receipt, he took them to DCS Ranson.

The children were taken by their aunt to her home in Northamptonshire, where they stayed for several weeks.

The Ford Corsair was found in Newhaven. In its boot was a piece of lead pipe covered in surgical tape. Witnesses suggested it was parked sometime between 5.00 a.m. and 8.00 a.m. on Friday 8 November. Its owner, Michael Stoop, received a letter from Lord Lucan.

An arrest warrant for murdering Sandra Rivett and attempting to murder his wife was issued on Tuesday 12 November 1974.

The lead pipe found at the Lucans' house had traces of blood, which was of both Veronica's (group A) and Sandra's (B) blood. Some of Veronica's hair was also found on that pipe. Home Office scientists were unable to prove that both pipes were cut from the same pipe, although it seemed likely.

The position of the blood samples showed that Sandra was attacked in the kitchen, but Veronica was attacked at the top of the basement stairs.

The case made headlines around the world. In January 1975, Veronica gave an interview to the *Daily Express* and appeared in a reconstruction with posed photographs.

Sandra's inquest was opened on 13 November 1974 by Dr Gavin Thurston. Two witnesses were called: Roger Rivett, who'd identified his wife's body, and the pathologist, Professor Simpson, who confirmed Sandra had died after being hit on the head with a blunt instrument. The hearing was then adjourned pending police investigations.

Dr Thurston eventually heard from thirty-three witnesses at the full inquest, including Veronica. He questioned her on their marriage, her current relationship with him, her financial affairs, Sandra's employment and events on the night of the attack.

The landlord of The Plumbers' Arms described how Veronica was covered 'head to toe in blood' and in 'a state of shock'. She called out, 'Help me, help me, I've just escaped from being murdered.'

Professor Simpson discussed his post-mortem; death was due to 'head injuries' and 'inhalation of blood'. He confirmed that the lead pipe found was likely as not the murder weapon. He also described injuries that were probably due to punches from a fist.

Dr Thurston summarised the evidence and explained the options the jury had. They decided it was 'murder by Lord Lucan'.

Sandra was cremated at Croydon crematorium on 18 December 1974.

Some folk felt the inquest gave a one-sided view of events. Lord Lucan's fingerprints weren't found, there was no forced entry, and it wasn't possible to see into the kitchen from the street – and the kitchen was in darkness anyway. Veronica hadn't entered the basement either; blood splashes and stains confirmed this. There were no signs any intruder left by the front door, and the back door was locked.

In the forty years since, no sightings have been confirmed. He was 'presumed' dead in the early 1990s so the family could wind up his affairs and 'declared' dead in the late 1990s.

Manningham-Buller, Reginald QC; Viscount Dilhorne
Barrister and politician

Reginald Edward Manningham-Buller was born in 1905 and educated at Eton and Magdelen College, Oxford. He married Lady Mary Lindsay in 1930 and they had a son and three daughters. He will always be remembered for his inept prosecution of Dr John Bodkin Adams in 1957, when he should also be remembered for his astute dissection of the Profumo Affair a few years later. The tactics of the defence in Dr Adams' case rather threw him, because his great strength was cross-examination.

As a result of his powers of cross-examination he was given the nickname of Bullying-Manner; when he was elevated and became Baron Dilhorne then the name he was given was Baron Stillborn – far from unfair, this was downright rude. However, there was clear sparring between him and political commentator Bernard Levin.

He was called to the bar in 1927 and knighted in 1954. He acted as Attorney General in Sir Anthony Eden and Harold Macmillan's government until 1962, when he went to the House of Lords as Baron Dilhorne – he became Viscount Dilhorne after the Conservatives lost the next election.

In 1957, he prosecuted Dr John Bodkin Adams for the murder of Edith Morrell, but when Dr Adams was acquitted he entered a *nolle prosequi* against the indictment on the murder of Gertrude

Hullett. This was inappropriate, as it is usually in cases where the defendant is physically or mentally unfit and is likely to be permanently so. It stops a case, however, so isn't an acquittal; it's at the discretion of the Attorney General – a fitness to plead differs. Questions were later asked in the House of Commons and the leading investigating officer felt Dr Adams was let go – the case against Dr Adams for the murder of Mrs Hullett was far stronger than that against Edith Morrell.

It was Sir Reginald who wrote the first report on the Profumo affair but it was deemed top secret, so whereas Lord Denning's sold by the thousand, his was relatively unknown – but far more accurate and revealing. Sadly, though, his main objective, which leaps out of the page, is to protect the good name of the government, come what may. And what did come was a ruined political career for John (Jack) Profumo – Lord Astor didn't fare too well either. Christine Keeler and Mandy Rice-Davies attracted public hostility, and Steven Ward was ruined – he took his own life. Presently, there is a campaign to clear his name – one can only hope.

Viscount Dilhorne died in September 1980 and was survived by his wife of fifty years.

Manuel, Peter
Murder of Anna Kneilands, Marion Watt, her sister Margaret and daughter Vivienne, Sydney Dunn, Isabelle Cook and Peter, Doris and their son, Michael, Smart

Peter Manuel was born in March 1927 in New York, and when he was five his family returned to Scotland. He wasn't a great achiever and was bullied at school – he assaulted a number of girls and was sentenced to nine years at Peterhead Prison. He was a habitual petty thief. But it was when he used violence during the thefts that things became tragic – he seemed to shoot people without a second thought. It has been said his victim count may have been as high as fifteen, but it was for seven that he was convicted.

In September 1956 Mr Manuel was on bail, following a break-in at a local mine; he broke into a house by breaking a pane of glass in the kitchen door. In the morning, when Helen Collison, the cleaner, arrived, the house didn't seem to be right. Mr William Watt, the man of the house, was away, so it might have crossed her mind that his wife had stayed late in bed. Looking around the back of the house and finding the broken glass, Mrs Collison decided against going into the house alone. At that point Peter Collier, who was the postman, arrived, and he slipped his hand through the broken window pane and unlocked the door. Mrs Collison went in to investigate. What she found was horror. In the master bedroom Marion Watt, the forty-five year-old lady of the house, had been shot, together with her sister – shot at close range. Vivienne Watt was the sixteen-year-old daughter; she'd been shot too.

The police initially wondered if Mr Watt had created an alibi for himself. He had a number of shops in the Glasgow area, but one of the officers assigned to investigate another burglary in the area recognised Peter Manuel's handiwork. The police were soon on his tail but he wouldn't answer any questions when he was invited to 'help them with their enquiries'. Mr Watt re-entered the frame because a ferryman had been under the impression Mr Watt had travelled with his car on a ferry to the mainland – he was on a fishing holiday. He was incorrect and Mr Watt was exonerated; with the loss he'd had and then to be accused is unimaginable, but unfortunately routine.

Mr Manuel was given a three-year prison sentence for breaking into the mine I mentioned earlier. He left prison after a couple of years and headed for the Newcastle-upon-Tyne area. About twenty miles away, just past Consett in the small village of Edmundbyers, he murdered a taxi driver, Sydney Dunn. The motive appeared to be robbery, but he shot him as well as slitting his throat.

He wasn't long in the area before heading up to Glasgow, where, just after Christmas 1957, seventeen-year-old Isabelle Cook set off to meet her boyfriend and was never seen alive again – she was reported missing on 29 December.

Just over six miles south-east of Glasgow is the village of Uddingston. In Sheepburn Road, early in the morning of 4 January 1958, Mr John McMunn saw a stranger's face in his bedroom and shouted to his wife, asking, 'Where's the gun?' – the visitor was soon gone. But elsewhere in the street there was some anxiety: Peter and Doris Smart's house seemed deserted and the curtains had been closed for a day or two. Then Peter didn't show up for work on 6 January, so the police were alerted. His car was nowhere to be found either – the police forced in the back door and in the main bedroom was a lot of blood, but no bodies. Peter and Doris were in the second bedroom and ten-year-old Michael was in his own bed. All three had died of gunshot wounds.

And Mr Manuel was living it up. Usually broke, he was now flashing a good bit of money around and a couple of £1 notes were recovered from a pub – crisp new notes from a newly printed batch, and the bank could trace them. They had formed a batch for a cheque encashment for Mr Peter Smart. The net was closing and the police felt they had enough evidence to arrest Mr Manuel. On an identification parade he was positively identified by bar staff.

Even then it might have gone either way if he'd pleaded not guilty: he'd not been helpful to the police in the past. But when arrested and charged on 13 January 1958 he confessed to the murder of Peter, Doris and Michael Smart; he also told them he was guilty of the murder of Marion Watt, her daughter and her sister. He was also able to show the detectives where he'd buried Isabelle Cooke in a field.

At his trial in May 1958 he was found guilty on seven counts of murder, being found not guilty of the murder of Anne Knielands on the direction of the judge.

Peter Thomas Anthony Manuel was hanged at Barlinnie Prison in

Glasgow on 11 July 1958, one of the last to meet their fate there – he was aged thirty-one and there's little doubt he had psychopathic tendencies. However, it has been claimed that other health issues may also have been a contributing factor. He suffered from temporal lobe epilepsy – if this, as has been claimed, was withheld or suppressed at his trial then he may not have had a fair trial.

Mark, Sir Robert QPM
Police commissioner

With his tyre-safety adverts and his no-nonsense application to discipline there's no doubt he made the streets (and roads) safer. The same man said, 'A good police force is one that catches more criminals than it employs' – his main belief was that an effective police service needs public confidence to function. Robert Mark was born in Manchester in 1917, and although he didn't set the world alight with his academic prowess at school he did have hidden qualities of leadership. He worked selling carpets for a while before joining the police – not to his father's delight.

When war broke out he joined the Royal Armoured Corps; he stayed in for an extra couple of years after the war ended, and was demobbed as a major.

In 1957, he became the youngest chief constable in Britain when, at the age of forty, he was appointed to Leicester. He was praised when he cancelled an order for hundreds of parking meters and created a team of traffic wardens who were empowered to administer a fixed penalty fine system.

In 1967 the then Home Secretary, Roy Jenkins, brought him to London as assistant – and later deputy-commissioner of the Metropolitan Police. Mr Mark advised on policing in Northern Ireland and also worked closely with Lord Mountbatten, looking at prison conditions and security.

In April 1972 he took over as Commissioner of the Metropolitan Police, but morale in the force was low and there was evidence of corruption in Scotland Yard. A fight might be undesirable but sometimes necessary, and when he started looking at the CID in the capital he announced they'd be back in uniform if his clean-up was hampered. 450 officers left quite quickly!

As part of his strengthening of discipline, he intensified the investigation of complaints from the public and tried to improve police relations with racial and other minority groups. At the same time, he carried on an unrelenting war against crime, using new techniques and reorganising the expertise at his disposal to make them more effective.

He became Sir Robert in 1973 and, as he'd not come up through the ranks in the capital and nor had he been groomed by Hendon, he was often considered as an outsider.

'There are not going to be any no-go areas in London – we will police every street to uphold the law', was his reply to criticism of the manpower used (1,500 officers) for the Notting Hill Carnival. He was unrepentant in conflict with both politicians and lawyers when he voiced his worries about the jury system.

Sir Robert's autobiography, *In the Office of Constable*, was published in 1978 and he made lecture tours of America and Canada – in the latter, he helped streamline complaints procedures against the police.

He married Kathleen in 1941 and they had a son and a daughter. Sir Robert died in 2010.

Markov, Georgi
Murdered by Eastern Security Services

Some 'wars' might not see open conflict, as in armies attacking, but for some reason or other the 'conflict' is still described as a war. In the cold war, the conflict was more of a standoff between the Eastern Bloc – mainly the USSR and adjacent countries – and the Western European and North Atlantic Treaty (NATO) countries. The two distinct political ideals in evidence were seen as incompatible, but for some people on the street it was an exercise in control.

Some rebelled against this, though, and had the passion to risk their lives to speak out. Here in the west we heard little, with the exception perhaps of Kim Philby and George Blake, or our 'rebels' who defected to the east, but there was a good deal more publicity when their 'rebels' defected here. These people attracted labels, ranging from sympathiser to fanatic, and some were to meet their deaths in mysterious circumstances, but one person who was quite definitely murdered was the Bulgarian Georgi Markov.

He'd spoken out against the regime in Bulgaria, and from his adopted base in London he broadcast for the BBC World Service. There is more than a possibility, therefore, that he may have been a part of the agenda with our own 'cloak and dagger' people.

Initially Georgi went to his brother in Italy in 1969, before he came to London a couple of years later. But he'd bitterly attacked the regime in Bulgaria with his book (now hailed as a masterpiece in the east), *The Truth That Killed*. Georgi was married and had a daughter. When the Bulgarian secret police asked for help in 'dealing' with him, they received it. It may or may not have been through the KGB, but he was attacked with a weapon of such subtle sophistication there had to be some technological help in the background.

The story was that on his way to work one morning in September 1978, he felt a slight but noticeable sting to his leg, and he saw a man picking up an umbrella from the road before he disappeared into a taxi. Georgi's identity was well known. When he got to work he examined his leg and found a small pimple-like swelling where he'd felt the sting. The pain and discomfort lasted, and he confided his fears in a friend and colleague.

That evening he developed a severe sickness and fever, and so anxious was he that he was admitted to hospital. When he died four days later, owing to his background and his insistence he'd been the target of a deadly pellet, the Metropolitan Police ordered a post-mortem. There'd apparently been two previous attempts on his life.

Where he'd felt the sting earlier, a tiny pellet measuring about one-and-a-half millimetres across was found. Further analysis identified traces of ricin (a deadly chemical) and a gelatine coating which dissolved at body temperature. The pellet was hollow and had two drill holes through it to form a cavity in an X-shape. It was thought that this had been 'fired' from the umbrella hastily picked up on the morning of the start of this final illness.

There was no antidote, so his death was almost inevitable – but it took weeks to isolate ricin as the cause, so it was almost recorded as 'death by natural causes'.

It was later confirmed, in post-Cold-War discussions, that the USSR had collaborated with the Bulgarian secret police. Ricin was chosen because of the difficulty in its detection. Officially, forty-nine-year-old Georgi Markov's murder is an unsolved crime.

Mayes, Roderick
Murdered by his mother, Joy

It was 1995 when the tragedy was made public, and by that time, Roderick Mayes had lain in a shallow grave in his former home in the Boulevard in Weston-Super-Mare since 1972. By then, the two alleged perpetrators of the crime, his mother, Joy, and his grandfather, Thomas Thompson, were both dead. It was Roderick's brother Sean, away in Switzerland in early April 1972, who reported the tale twenty-three years later.

Sean's aunt had died, and he'd come home for her funeral when his mother explained that a few days previously, she'd killed Roderick. She told him she'd dissolved drugs in his cocoa before breaking his skull with a shoe scraper; she then slit his throat. Sean was told his brother's body was under a bed in the family home.

In February 1995 Sean walked in to Paddington Green Police Station in London and broke the twenty-odd year pact of silence.

If someone turns up out of the blue and tells police of a murder, he'll as likely as not be arrested. But the first thing is to establish that there's a body. So Sean was arrested and travelled to Weston-Super-Mare to what had been the family home in the 1970s in the Boulevard. The body was indeed found there, and was fairly well preserved because it had been wrapped in a candlewick bedspread and heavy plastic sheeting. Roderick's remains were examined by Home Office pathologist Dr Hugh White, who could confirm death was due to head injuries. Roderick's old medical records and his dental records confirmed his identity and his death was dated as 8 April 1972. At the inquest, the coroner said he was satisfied that Roderick Mayes was unlawfully killed.

The brothers' grandfather, who'd been instrumental in the overall plot, had died on the third anniversary of Roderick's death. His diary gave some clue that what Sean said had some truth in it. His daughter and their mother, Margaret Joy, had married Charles when in Cairo serving with the forces at the end of the war. They parted in 1950 and Charles seemed to leave the scene completely. Joy Mayes died on 23 September 1991. That left Sean carrying the can, but if his story was true then the only offence he committed was conspiring to prevent a lawful and decent burial; there were, however, good reasons why the police didn't press charges.

Back in the seventies, Roderick had drifted into a life of drugs and was heavily into the LSD scene. His mother felt the only way she could prevent her son from destroying himself was by killing him.

Sean had fared rather better and made a good career for himself as a musician with the band Fumble. He'd toured with others too, playing keyboards for stars such as David Bowie and Chuck Berry. Also, he was an accomplished writer, publishing a biography of Joan Armatrading; he also co-wrote on Kate Bush.

Roderick did pursue higher education at Taunton but was a solitary character, though 'very nice' and 'intelligent'. His old friend Jane Raven said she used to call him Oscar, and was told he'd 'done a bunk' when he disappeared.

After Roderick's disappearance, Mrs Mayes left Weston and moved to Twickenham.

By 1995, it was only Sean who was still around to try and get his brother a decent burial. This he did. But there was an inquest, and even though there had been a good bit of police input, it was Detective Sergeant Mike Robinson of the Avon and Somerset Police who gave evidence.

'Rather than see him suffer, the mother decided to end his life. She gave him sleeping pills in his cocoa and when he fell asleep she hit him over the head with a heavy metal scraper until she felt the skull give way. That did not kill him and she took a knife from the kitchen and cut his throat.'

DS Robinson added that the story was that Roderick's drug abuse was heavy and long-standing. He also explained why it was at this point, that is in 1995, that Sean had reported the matter, saying, 'He had disclosed through counselling that his mother had killed his brother and that he and his grandfather had assisted in the burial.'

After the inquest DS Robinson explained, 'It has been decided that no proceedings will be taken against the only surviving person, Sean Mayes.'

Sean Mayes wasn't expected to live beyond the end of 1995, and he died from an AIDS-related illness in July of that year.

Miles, PC Sydney
Was not murdered by Derek Bentley, and probably not by Christopher Craig either

After looking at the National Archive files and reading a couple of books on that dreadful night in Croydon in November 1952, I'm left with the question of not who shot PC Miles, but who didn't shoot him.

The background of the story is that two teenagers – Derek Bentley, who was nineteen, and sixteen-year-old Christopher Craig – were attempting a burglary at a confectioner's warehouse. They'd made it on to the roof when they were seen by a resident in a nearby property, who phoned the police. The police attended and when the officers got on to the roof, or at any rate were at the door of the stairs leading to the roof, Christopher Craig produced a gun and started shooting. One of the officers Detective Constable Frederick Fairfax had told Chris to hand over his gun, but DC Fairfax was invited to come and get it. Shortly after, a shot or two rang out and DC Fairfax was hit in the shoulder, though the bullet didn't penetrate his skin, it merely knocked him off his feet – but it was a shock. Derek Bentley apparently went to his aid and was then taken as a sort of shield back to the top of the stairs twenty or so feet away. It was later claimed Derek said to Chris, 'You bloody fool,' but the words 'let him have it, Chris' are now universally accepted as what was put into Derek's mouth – he never said it! DC Fairfax took Derek back to the stairs and armed reinforcements were called.

So, on a flat rooftop with four skylights with a height of two feet six inches to four feet six inches at their peak, were Chris, holed up beyond a lift-head, and DC Fairfax and other officers at the stair-head, where Derek Bentley had been taken. Whether he was under arrest at this point is academic.

Derek hadn't been armed with a gun. Chris had a .455 calibre gun. He'd sawn part of the barrel off so it would fit into his pocket, but this would adversely affect the aim of the gun and the path of a discharged bullet.

The distance between the lift-head and the stair-head was thirty-nine feet – that's from the wall nearest the lift-head where Chris was holed up, so it was a few inches more, but we'll stick with thirty-nine feet.

In his modified gun Chris had a mixture of undersized and correctly sized bullets.

It was dark. When Police Constable Sydney Miles goes through the stair-head door, Chris peeped around from behind the lift-head thirty-nine feet away and fired, without perhaps taking proper aim, with a modified gun in the dark. At the trial, the jury were told that the chances of hitting him were a 'million to one'.

However, PC Miles fell down dead. Chris had appeared, shot, and then gone back behind the lift-head so didn't know what had happened; officers later said they heard two shots fired in quick succession, but this doesn't necessarily mean Chris fired both shots.

A bullet passed through PC Miles' head, but it was never found.

The layout of the roof of the warehouse is such that the stair-top, at the point PC Miles came out of it, was just under a right angle from the firing position of Chris when he appeared behind the lift-head to shoot. The view would be to the left of PC Miles' head unless he turned sharply to his left, which was the direction the police knew Chris was in.

At trial, defence counsels John Parris, for Chris, and Frank Cassalls, for Derek, didn't ask any questions of the pathologist who examined PC Miles, Dr David Haler. He suggested at a later date that the calibre .32 to .38 was most likely the size of bullet that caused the wound that killed PC Miles; Chris' gun didn't take such a calibre, and a ballistics expert later told David Yallop, whose book about the case appeared in 1971, that the gun Chris had wouldn't fire such a bullet. The standard police-issue firearm at that time was a .32.

To sum up: there was a modified, inaccurate gun; a wrong sized bullet wound (not proven but highly likely); and conditions were dark.

Chris was under cover, so appeared, shot and concealed himself; in that split second PC Miles was not facing the gun to give the entry and exit wounds, and Chris' gun would not discharge the likely size of the bullet. When PC Miles fell mortally wounded there were two shots fired/heard in quick succession, and a police standard-issue gun fired a bullet that might fit the wound.

Later in David Yallop's book, he quotes Chris as saying, 'What I've never been able to understand is how I shot him between the eyes when he was facing away from me and was going the other way.'

Of all the police officers on the roof that night in earshot of Derek Bentley, some said he didn't say, 'Let him have it, Chris.' One of these was Police Constable Claude Pain, whose evidence wasn't called at trial because 'he hadn't gone along with the others'.

Both Chris and Derek were convicted of the murder of PC Miles, and for years after Chris thought he'd fired the bullet. Derek was hanged, but his trial was not conducted fairly; his conviction was later quashed and he received a free pardon.

But taking into account the above, at the trial in 1952 one might say there was a reasonable doubt – but more accurately a huge doubt – that Chris Craig fired the lethal bullet.

Mnilk, Heidi
Murdered by person unknown

In the summer of 1973, two seventeen-year-old girls had come to England from Kassal in Germany. They stayed in West Wickham and were on their way back there after a day's sight-seeing in

London. They caught the 4.57 p.m. train from Charing Cross, but sat in separate carriages – one of the girls, Doris Thurau, wanted to smoke, but her friend, Heidi Mnilk, didn't.

So Heidi settled down to the journey as the train called at Waterloo and London Bridge. Then, just after the train departed from London Bridge, Andrew Lee and Steve Arnold, who were sat in the next carriage, heard a scream and then saw something fall onto the track: when they looked closer as the train accelerated they could see it was the body of a girl. Heidi had been attacked, stabbed in the throat and thrown from the train.

When the train pulled into New Cross station the lads saw a man alight the next carriage, and move rapidly towards the ticket barrier – they tried to alert the station staff but were unable to.

Andrew and Steve would later work with detectives to create a photofit image of the man they'd both seen; they could even describe a squint. Detective Chief Inspector Tom Parry who led the search in the early stages explained that the photofit picture went out to all stations.

The attacker was between thirty-seven and forty-five years old, and about 5' 7" tall. He had short, brown hair and a tanned, or red, spotty complexion with a slightly pointed chin and thin lips, and was clean shaven. He wore a black or dark-grey jacket, baggy trousers, and a red or blue check shirt.

'He looked straight at Steve in our compartment; he must have known we saw him,' Andrew added. 'I said to one of the station staff, "Did you see that man?" but by that time he'd disappeared.'

Police reconstructed Heidi's murder with a policewoman dressed in similar clothes as Heidi. Police officers travelled in the next compartment to make a record of where the train passed and when, and when the attack occurred, as well as precisely when the body was thrown from the train. The whole exercise was recorded on cine-film.

A five-inch bladed 'bowie'-type knife was found near the body and this was examined as a possible murder weapon.

Also found was a gold neck chain, and crucially, Heidi's camera with thirty-six exposures, which it was hoped would provide more clues; it was thought her attacker might have followed her.

When the train got into New Cross station, Mr William Harris, who was a porter, had been approached about the attacker. 'I was busy seeing the train out and the boys were telling me something but I did not understand at first. I didn't see a man get off the train.'

However, police thought that the publicity from the reconstruction would jog a few memories to add to the leads from Andrew and Steve.

Detective Superintendent Bob Ramsey had taken over the investigation and he was encouraged by the public response. The police wanted to trace a couple who were seen entering the coach just after a man dashed from the train, and could have passed quite close to him. They wanted to find Heidi's coat, which had a distinctive blue and white checked pattern.

The WPC who'd portrayed her worked with her colleagues at Charing Cross Station and distributed a fifteen-point questionnaire for people who'd travelled on that train on the fateful afternoon.

Detectives were given a lead by an unnamed lady who recognised the photofit; she'd travelled on the train when it stopped at New Cross, where, on this occasion, a man had joined the train.

He pulled a knife and asked, 'Are you a German?'

'No, do I look like one?' she asked.

'Yes,' he said. 'I hate Germans, especially German women.'

This had happened about six months previously, but she could also give the police details of the knife, which corresponded with the knife found near Heidi's body.

DCS Ramsey thought this was a vital lead, but time passed.

Around a year later, a woman gave police information about a

Deptford resident who worked in Covent Garden; when arrested he managed to bolt, but was soon caught, and although interviewed under caution it didn't lead anywhere. The enquiry was running out of leads.

An inquest at Southwark recorded a verdict of murder by persons unknown. The coroner said there was a 'remarkable' resemblance between the Identikit pictures of the man who pulled a knife on the woman who said he hated German women, and a man seen leaving the train by two schoolboys.

Heidi's murder enquiry had stretched to fifteen months.

By the summer of 1975 the trail had gone cold, but in early August there was a frightening attack on a young lady. Wendy Hall had boarded a train at Holborn Viaduct, and a man got on when the train stopped at Tulse Hill. Almost at once he closed the windows in the carriage, and when the train travelled through a tunnel he pounced on Wendy. 'The compartment was completely dark. He forced his fingers into my mouth and I bit him. But I never felt him stab me.'

He'd actually stabbed her four times, which became apparent as the train came out of the tunnel. At Tooting station he left the train, as did Wendy – but whereas he was quickly away from the scene, she collapsed in the ticket hall.

Again, a full reconstruction took place, but the main question was whether he stayed on the train and had got into a different compartment or not. It did bear many of the hallmarks of the attack on Heidi, but this was now two years on.

One has to ask how many times he set out from home intent on another attack, but the circumstances were against it.

Any theory that the man attacked in the heat of summer hadn't proved the case, and when 1977 was in its first week he may have struck again. This was the eighth attack that seemed to bear his hallmarks – whether he was actually imprisoned after this for other crimes or was otherwise occupied has never really been explained.

Twenty-four-year-old Kim Taylor was stabbed three times in the shoulder and the chest – she was alone in a carriage with a man. The train was the 4.08 p.m. service from Norwood to London Bridge and the man suddenly struck as the train passed Bermondsey Station – Kim managed to pull the communications cord and he fled the scene. She made a full recovery, though the shock would have affected her for much longer.

'This motiveless attack seems to tie in with six others. But so far we have not been able to link the stabbing with the murder of Heidi Mnilk. We believe the same maniac is responsible for them all.'

The attacks stopped, but the murder of Heidi Mnilk remains unsolved.

Moonlighting Mums

Tales of armed robbery, cannabis farming and people trafficking

Running a home is a job that deserves all the credit it's due, and more. A lot of mums also juggle a career as well as a family, but it's beyond me what keeps them going the twenty-five hours a day they need to put in. Some mums, though, don't follow a career, so there are times when the going can get tough in a different way. A little ingenuity might be needed to deal with a temporary dip in good fortunes; two ladies from quite differing walks of life came up with vastly differing solutions. As there were kids involved I'll use initials rather than names.

HW had a teenaged daughter and her husband commuted to London each day, where he worked in a bank. So when money got a bit tight she decided to become an armed robber. She learned the finer points of stealing a car for the getaway before she went into a sub-post office in Orpington, Kent. She'd carefully laid her plans to drive around a bit first to pluck up the courage. When she approached the targeted post office, she bided her time so that other customers would be served and leave the shop. She said that she 'did not want to frighten anybody.'

She presented a parcel which the sub-postmaster had to open a counter hatch to receive, but he found himself looking down the barrel of a gun. HW demanded money and made her escape with just over £200.

The police were on to it and traced her to another Kent town. When they paid her a visit, with the euphemistic 'could you please help us with our enquiries', they found £16,000 worth of cannabis for sale. She had been busy.

Her husband knew nothing of her moonlighting escapades. HW was charged with robbery, possessing a firearm, stealing a car and possessing cannabis with intent to supply. She pleaded guilty at the Old Bailey in 1988 and was given five years.

Her daughter was fairly philosophical, but could understand her dad's shock at it all. She said, 'I am shocked at my Mum going inside but there is nothing I can do. Dad is not as strong as me and he will be very upset.'

Their marriage survived; at any rate, HW and husband still shared the same house after the millennium.

In the second instance, £50 was the price a 'lonely old man' paid to adopt the daughter of his niece. He'd never married, but now he had someone to care for. He bought her clothes and gave her money to buy sweets; he'd take her on outings, and then he'd sexually assault her. He had convictions five or six years previously, for which he'd been fined.

He got probation for the latter offence, and died a couple of years later.

The mother was given a two-year conditional discharge when she appeared in court just before Christmas, 1972. She admitted agreeing to receive the payment for the adoption of the child. The magistrates considered social and psychiatric reports; her solicitor explained that she had no knowledge of the motives of her uncle in the arrangement, nor of his past record. Furthermore, she didn't realise that the arrangement constituted an offence.

The mother married shortly after and so her anonymity was ensured.

Morris, Raymond
Murdered Christine Darby
The only suspect in the murder of Margaret Reynolds, Diane Tift and Jane Taylor

'They'll never catch the fellow they are after, he's too clever for them' Raymond Morris said, to which his wife replied, 'I hope they do catch him, whoever he is'. His wife was fifteen years his junior, and as the police were departing from the police station just opposite their flat, little did she realise that her husband was the guilty man. The murders all came after rape.

Seven-year-old Christine Darby had been murdered in one of the most beautiful and scenic parts of England, Cannock Chase. This is an area to the south of the town of Stafford and of Cannock, stretching as far as Rougeley in the east. It covers about 3,000 acres.

In February 1969, Carol Morris showed no emotion as her husband Raymond Leslie was given two life sentences, stumbling as he left the dock at Stafford Assizes. He'd been held on remand at Winson Green prison in Birmingham and had been attacked by inmates several times already – he was now heading for Durham and isolation for his own safety.

And although he was almost certainly guilty of the rape and murder of three other little girls earlier, he was only tried for the murder of Christine Darby. Following the first two murders, that of six-year-old Margaret Reynolds in September 1965 and five-year-old Diane Tift in December that year, whose bodies were found together on Cannock Chase in mid-January 1966, Mr Kenneth Braine-Hartnell Coroner said, 'While such a repugnant pervert is still at large no child is safe.'

Ten-year-old Jane Taylor went missing in the Cannock Chase area in August 1966, and so far no trace has been found.

But either the police's luck changed or a ten-year-old-girl in Wallsall had the luckiest escape of her life – he tried to abduct her but she escaped. Now there was a description, of both him and his car. Mr Morris was arrested on 4 November 1967. He was questioned very closely about the murder of Christine Darby. His wife said they were out shopping at the time of the killing and so the police had to back off. But when the police found Mr Morris's interest in photography included pornographic shots of his young niece, things changed.

Carol made the decision to help Detective Superintendent Ian Forbes from Scotland Yard trap the killer. DSupt Forbes was the second senior Scotland Yard detective asked to help, and had worked with Carol to help her through the terror of facing the fact that her husband was guilty of such a depraved crime.

For eighteen months the police sought this killer, and for eighteen months he'd stayed one step ahead. DSupt Forbes knew he was a cool character. He was an engineer and was a foreman at his workshop. Carol was his second wife; he'd married Muriel and had two sons by her before he simply told her she wasn't a part of his future plans. According to other family members, he was quite charming but his emotions were never shown.

It took the one breakthrough to nail him and it's worth thinking about just how hard the police worked on this case. An 'army' of detectives interviewed 40,000 suspects – every man in the Walsall area between the ages of twenty-one and fifty. They took over 14,200 statements and once they knew he had a grey car then they checked these too – 1,375,000 of them! They had managed to get an identikit picture and DSupt Forbes said, 'Put a name to this face and we will have our man.'

The shape of the face, mouth and chin, the lined forehead and even the dimple were all correct. Four people gave similar descriptions. Mr Morris was coldly arrogant and contemptuous of police efforts, but he underestimated DSupt Forbes, who always appeared kindly and cheerful but who knew the killer would strike again. Could he catch him before it happened? Television can never portray the pressure real detectives are under.

In November 1968 Mr Morris tried again, but the little girl escaped – and a young married lady, Wendy Land, witnessed the incident and took his car registration number: 492 LOP. On November 15, the hand of Detective Chief Inspector Pat Molloy felt his collar. Mr Molloy later wrote his own book about the case.

His family never suspected a thing. His first wife, Muriel, was stunningly beautiful, wooed by his sweet talk; he actually wrote her poems. Then he calmly and coldly dropped her. 'I thought the world of my husband. Nobody knew him better than I did. With his charm he could talk his way out of anything. I nearly went through the floor though when I read about his arrest. Now I've had time to think about it, everything fits.'

His second wife, Carol, had known him for most of her life as their parents lived next door to each other. They married in 1963 and things were good, but when she discovered the truth ... She saw him once more, when he was on remand, just to show her disgust and threw her wedding ring at him. But not once throughout the police chase did she suspect him, and thought nothing of confirming his alibi that they'd been shopping. However, she knew she was protecting him once DSupt Forbes had shown her the evidence.

Thereafter, she was a key prosecution witness and much as he stared at her and did all he could to intimidate her, it didn't work

– she destroyed his alibi. She said later that she wished to move away from the area. I hope Muriel and Carol recovered; I know the mothers of the little girls didn't.

Mothers are strong characters. It was only Mrs Morris senior who'd have any contact with her son. Mr Morris had three brothers and a sister. Peter Morris, his brother, suspected something. 'He was always a ladies' man with a very glib tongue and he had stacks of girlfriends in his youth. But he had no emotions. He could laugh with his face but never with his eyes. He was never physically cruel as far as I know, but he always wanted to be the star. I think he wanted to go down in history as the man who could spit in the face of the police and get away with it.'

His employer said, 'The thing I remember about him is that he was always cool and logical. You could never make him angry.' He had an IQ of 120.

The night he was arrested there were celebrations in Walsall – some pubs were drunk dry.

Raymond Morris continued to protest his innocence. On 2 March 2014 he died in HMP Preston, having been in prison for forty-five years.

Neilson, Donald – The Black Panther
Murdered Donald Skepper, Derek Astin, Sidney Grayland and Leslie Whittle

Donald Neilson was born as Donald Nappey on 1 August 1936. He was only eleven when his mother died, but precious little is known about him until the crimes of the Black Panther hit the headlines in the 1970s. Three sub-postmasters were murdered and a seventeen-year-old college student was kidnapped and murdered.

He married Irene in 1955 and they had a daughter in 1960; his wife persuaded him to leave the army, where he functioned very well. He worked hard in civvy street, but the businesses he started, building and taxi driving, for instance, were not a success. As a result, he turned to crime. It has been suggested he was successful at this, and his Walter Mitty commando persona was probably what helped him disappear into the night after a crime.

The chilling side is that he wouldn't hesitate if he had to shoot his way out of a tight corner; in fact, he did so on at least three occasions. This resulted in three fatalities; he was also guilty of an attempted murder – he shot a security guard, who lived for a year and a day before dying and was not therefore a murder victim.

But the thing that probably sickened the jury more than anything was the kidnap and murder of the seventeen-year-old Leslie Whittle. The girl was found hanging in a drainage shaft. On post-mortem it was found that her digestive system was empty, though Mr Neilson claimed he'd given her sustenance. He also claimed he hadn't pushed her to her death, but that she'd fallen – one has to ask how long would it have been before she died of starvation.

One theory is that she died when she fell from the ledge to which he'd tethered her and was strangled. The post-mortem examination suggested her heart stopped beating because of the shock of the fall – she may have fainted in weakness and fallen, with Mr Neilson not even in attendance.

It was said the police left a bungling trail, but this is unfair. There was no guarantee she would have been released even if the ransom money demanded was actually handed over.

The Leslie Whittle case made Mr Neilson Britain's most wanted man. It was the forensic evidence that linked the kidnapper to the sub-postmaster killings. The wife of one of his victims said he was lightning-quick, like a panther, and always dressed in black. He could also enter a building silently, though he'd avoid any property where there was a dog.

Like many criminals, he was caught by accident and it was by two coppers on patrol, PC Tony White and PC Stuart Mackenzie, who only wanted to ask him where he was going at a late hour. They didn't think this slight-statured man was a criminal but he seemed to try and conceal his face. When they did challenge him, he produced a sawn-off shotgun and forced one of the officers into the back of the car while he got in the front. The driving officer had the shotgun placed in his armpit.

Mr Neilson gave instruction of where to drive to, but it was in the opposite direction. They turned around, but during the journey PC White was instructed to look for rope and as a junction loomed, PC Mackenzie swerved the car right and left, asking which direction he should take. The gun loosened as he looked up at the road and PC White pushed the barrel away from his colleague, who braked violently. The gun was fired and PC Mackenzie was propelled from the car; he made for a nearby fish'n'chip shop for help. In the event, it took four men to subdue Mr Neilson enough to handcuff him.

They called for back-up and looked in the carrier bag. There were two of the hoods the Black Panther was said to wear. They'd got him. Forensics and fingerprints supported the charge.

Some people were convinced Mr Neilson told the truth when he claimed that he didn't murder Lesley Whittle, but his plea that the other deaths from gun fire were accidental were dismissed. His legal team wondered if his conviction for the murder of Leslie was a reflection of the public backlash at the publicity.

He was given five life sentences, twenty-one years for kidnapping, ten years for blackmail and further ten year stretches for burglary and possessing a shotgun with intent to endanger life.

Mrs Neilson was convicted of cashing stolen postal orders and said she was forced to; she was jailed for twelve months. Gilbert Gray QC was retained for her appeal and Mr Neilson gave evidence. Being the Black Panther's wife had made her conviction almost a foregone conclusion; she served eight months.

Donald Neilson's crimes were still considered so horrific that even in 2008, when he was debilitated by motor neurone disease, an application to leave prison and die in a nursing home or hospital was rejected. The reason given was the evilness of his crimes. The illness was terminal, and he died in December 2011; he'd been in prison for thirty-five years.

Nelson, Revd James
Murdered Mrs Nelson, whose Christian name and details are often overlooked

James Nelson was twenty-four when he beat his mother to death at their home in Garrowhill, Lanarkshire; he was sentenced to life imprisonment. By the time he was thirty-four, it was 1979 and he'd served ten years. His parole was enacted and he applied to enter the ministry of the Church of Scotland and that year began a course of studies at St Mary's College, St Andrews, in Fife.

Only a handful of people knew of his background, and it wasn't until he'd nearly finished his studies that it became public knowledge that a paroled murderer was about to become a minister. There were people with reservations and they'd said Mr Nelson had shown little remorse for his crime. But he did have some support: Revd James Whyte, who later became Moderator of the General Assembly, discussed the matter with Rev William Henney and he agreed to take him on.

Within the church itself, some felt he shouldn't be admitted and at the General Assembly in 1984 there was a debate; some clergymen voted against his admission. This was where Revd Whyte, who was the Professor of Theology at the university, offered the argument that if one accepted the belief in forgiveness, then this shouldn't prevent anyone following a minister's path, following whatever crime, into the ministry. Revd James Mathieson also gave his support with a strong speech.

Mr Nelson was ordained and served the parish of Chapelhall and Calderbank in Lanarkshire. Again, the matter wasn't made public, and when it did break some of the congregation left the church.

But, going back to consider the crime itself, it was an extreme use of violence. He claimed that the provocation was that his mother had been 'very rude' about a girlfriend whom he'd intended to marry. He described how it had put him into a 'cold rage', and explained, 'There was a police baton hanging in the hallway ... I just lost my temper.' The baton had belonged to his grandfather.

His sister, Anne, had strong views on the entire affair and there was a prolonged estrangement between them; she only learned of his wedding from a newspaper. She'd tried to address her feelings while he was in prison but was never really able to. 'Jim seems intent on constantly exonerating himself but I can never come to terms with the fact he forgives himself.'

The two didn't have a happy upbringing. Their father subjected them to physical and emotional abuse, and the household was constantly tense. Anne described their father as a 'church saint and a house devil'. As they grew up, brother and sister were close, but later drifted.

It was Anne and her father who discovered their mother's body, as Mr Nelson had dragged her out to the garage: they'd been to a church function, but when they got home they found blood splashes and so followed the trail of blood. Her father was unable to deal with the situation, but Anne dialled 999 and checked for any signs of life – although the body was warm she knew her mother had died. 'Her head was to one side and I could see her brain.'

During her visits to her brother in prison, the event wasn't discussed, and he even became disrespectful to their mother's memory. Anne felt she should break contact with him.

His father did visit him in prison but the relationship never looked likely to sort itself out, and he didn't attend Mr Nelson's wedding.

It seems very odd that even though Revd Nelson said the murder was not excusable, he did seem to think that the actions were explicable – one wonders how he dealt with his feelings.

The sixty-year-old Revd James Nelson died in hospital on 1 August 2005.

Olive, Clive
Murdered by Brian Moore and Albert Dorn

It hadn't been long since Detective Chief Superintendant Jim Marshall had seen a twenty-two year-old man receive a life sentence for the murder of a schoolgirl in Bexhill-on-Sea in East Sussex. A quite contrasting case came up, though no less sickening, but the first question was one of where to start.

In January 1973 a body was discovered in Shoreham Harbour between Bexhill and Brighton. It was a young male, probably in his late teens. The decimal coins in his pocket gave some idea of when he died and forensic pathologist Dr Hugh Johnson found diatoms (a single cell organism) in his vital organs, so he was alive when he'd entered the water. Still alive but unlikely to survive: he'd been beaten and had concrete slabs attached to his ankles and his wrists were bound. Whoever put him into the harbour was guilty of murder.

He was a local lad who'd been reported missing some weeks previously, and had a police record for minor crimes. He lived with his mother and brother but his father had left some years previously. Clive Olive was a bit of a loner, but liked girls – the attraction was mutual. He frequented coffee bars throughout Brighton and it was here the police could start to build up a picture of his life.

Clive, or Ollie, as he was known, did have a crude tattoo that was identified and related to a group of Hell's Angels called the

Mad Dogs of Sussex. However, Ollie didn't own a motorcycle, as did those usually associated with such groups. There was plenty of evidence from his contacts that something was worrying him in late February. Others described fear – and in the Gondola Coffee Bar, the bizarre double life of Clive Olive began to unravel.

DSupt Marshall was to write a book on the case and he called one of the ladies 'Karen', so I'll stick with that. Ollie had a 'friendship' with her, though it might not have been seen like that by the girl, her later boyfriend or the police, and later in court the word 'rape' was used. This occurred in September 1972, and Karen had sworn she'd never have anything to do with Ollie again. But it's never as simple as that, and the effect such an event can have can sour future relationships.

Brighton is popular as a resort, but this was the Brighton of shabby terraced streets and coffee bars. 'Thugs and dropouts' were fairly common fixtures, but the police thought the murder had been well planned. They were looking for more than one person. The profile of Karen's later boyfriend, Brian Moore, cropped up. He was a member of the Mad Dogs, as were his sister Christine and her husband Albert.

They had a grubby flat whose walls were festooned with swastikas, a portrait of Hitler and Hell's Angels posters. There were around twenty other members of the group, mainly teenagers, and their initiation ceremonies were quite repugnant. Mr Moore joined at the suggestion of Christine and Mr Dorn.

To other young folk their alternative lifestyle and beliefs might hold some appeal, and Karen had sort of strung along with them. When she got together with Mr Moore, she persuaded him to leave the group and hoped they'd settle down. He was besotted with her and when the story came out about what Ollie had done, he became tormented.

When Mr Moore got the name from Karen, he started to discover a bit more about Ollie. The Mad Dogs were prone to violence; it didn't take too long for DSupt Marshall's team to put the pieces of the jigsaw together.

When the case came to Lewes Crown Court, Mr Michael Eastham QC could describe how Ollie was beaten up, bound hand and foot, had concrete slabs attached to his ankles and was thrown into the harbour. He died from drowning.

Brian Moore, Christine Dorn and Albert Dorn all entered pleas of not guilty to murder.

Mr Eastham told the court, 'Moore became obsessed and worried by a half-belief that Olive had raped her. When Moore asked her if she had ever had sexual relations with a man, she replied, "No, not willingly." The information preyed on Moore's mind.'

He went on to say that Mr Moore traced Ollie to the Gondola coffee bar and arranged a meeting, but they'd already stolen concrete blocks, rope and a plastic bag from a building site. All three were in the van when they picked up Ollie; Mr Moore started to punch and strike him with a truncheon. Ollie fell unconscious, they tied him up and attached the concrete blocks to his ankles.

With Albert Dorn, he dumped Ollie in the harbour. 'They believed his body would never come to the surface again.'

In court, Karen corroborated the story that she'd been raped. Barely above a whisper, she told the court that Mr Moore became jealous, tracked down Ollie and killed him. 'We sat on the floor talking and then he put his arm round me and pulled me over. He had sexual intercourse with me. I did not consent. I struggled quite a bit. When it was over I got dressed and left. I never went out with him again.'

Later, when she'd formed a bond with Mr Moore, she said, 'He asked me if I had ever experienced sex. I told him the circumstances and the name of the boy. He was very angry and said he wanted to kill him.'

Karen explained that when she was on her way to school one morning Mr Moore had met her. 'He told me they had found Clive and killed him,' she said. 'He said Clive was being rather boastful. He was cocky about it.'

Mr Moore initially denied the murder, but later stated that he thought Ollie was dead when he went into the harbour, but he 'bobbed about and a lot of bubbles came to the surface'.

He was to say, 'I do not feel I have done anything wrong. He raped my girl and I thought I should put him out of the way so that he wouldn't rape any other girls. I know it was against the law but what he did was against the law as well. I went completely berserk. I was shocked to find he was dead.'

Two consultant psychiatrists gave their assessment of Mr Moore. To one, he was in a state 'where he was either killing Ollie or committing suicide', but the alternative view was that he was dangerous. 'He looked upon killing as other people look upon illegally parking a car.'

Was he then guilty of manslaughter because of diminished responsibility?

The jury were out for over six hours. The verdicts were unanimous: Brian More and Albert Dorn were guilty of murder. Both were given life sentences.

Christine Dorn was guilty of manslaughter and jailed for ten years.

Mr Justice Thesiger said of Brian Moore, 'I doubt whether the Secretary of State would ever feel justified in releasing him.'

In November 1974, Christine Dorn's appeal against her conviction was upheld. Neither of the men were given leave to appeal.

O'Nione, Paddy, AKA Paddy Onions

Underworld execution

James Davey was born James Bowen and changed his name when his brother was murdered. He was well known to the police – and word on the street was that he'd shot Paddy Onions. Paddy was also under an assumed name, but his real name was O'Nione and he was quite a character in the London Underworld. He did a couple of jobs with Frankie Fraser, so his reputation preceded him.

In 1951 he found himself in court accused of being a decoy in a robbery, but the jury acquitted him, which was quite a surprise when the law wasn't 'beyond reasonable doubt'; in practice it was sort of 'near enough'. In 1963 he was in the police's sights again for smuggling watches, which was a common crime in those days – walking through customs with a dozen Rolex watches strapped to each leg.

But the tie-in with James Davey (Bowen) was that he executed Paddy for a £5,000 bounty put up by an underworld figure. Well, Paddy was definitely shot, and the police said they had evidence. But the question remained as to why he was shot – a policeman did witness the event, but when he gave chase to the gunman he got away. It has been suggested Paddy was a police informer and that a drug deal he was fixing up fell through with disastrous consequences – or was he involved in a protection racket? But the more popular theory is that it was a revenge shooting for the killing of one Peter Hennessy who died in a knife fight at a charity event at a Kensington Hotel. The Hennessy Brothers were heavily involved in the underworld, and Peter Hennessy was also 'second best' in a fight with Eddie Richardson. Did Paddy kill Peter and later pay the price?

James Davey (Bowen) was well known to both sides of the law and there are two versions of what happened when he was arrested. One story says he lunged at a police officer and was restrained – the other story is that the police tied his legs together with his trousers and handcuffed him, as well as holding him down on the floor. He went a ghastly shade of blue. Whatever is the truth, a couple of weeks later the family decided his life support machine should be switched off.

There was some question at the inquest as to whether the police had used 'unreasonable force', but a verdict of accidental death was returned. As a result, we don't know about Peter Hennessy, we don't know about Paddy Onions and we don't know about James Davey; perhaps it's far better that we don't know about these things.

Operation Eagle
Police investigation

The police have called the case 'Operation Eagle', which is far better than the name of 'Batman Rapist'. Whatever the name, it's been going on since the early 1990s.

On a May evening in 1991, as a thirty-six-year-old woman was parking her car, a man produced a knife and forced her to drive to a secluded spot. In the autumn of that year an eighteen-year-old girl was grabbed, dragged into a field and assaulted. After this, though, there was a three-year gap before he struck again in 1994. Was he away somewhere? Abroad, a different part of the country or in prison? There was then a two year gap, but in 1996 three women were attacked, and then another three in 1997.

He seemed to have an intimate knowledge of Bath and its surrounding areas, and only once is it reported that he went to Kingswood, in Bristol (which is about eleven miles), where he raped a nineteen-year-old girl in 1996.

One recurrent theme was an apparent satisfaction that he gained from his victims wearing tights. He'd force them to remove their underwear and then put their tights back on – he would rip his way through them. On one occasion one of the girls wasn't wearing tights but he had a pair in his pocket he forced her to put on.

In all that time, though, the police have only built up a vague picture of him: white, probably in his thirties, and between five foot eight inches and five foot ten inches tall. Two of his victims spoke out on a *Crimewatch* programme, encouraging other victims who were attacked to come forward. On one occasion a woman was able to scream out – often victims are paralysed with fear, especially when a knife is produced – and the attacker ran off, but dropped his fading grey baseball cap. It had 'Batman Forever' embroidered on it in green.

A good few names had come up in the enquiry but even with DNA testing his identity remains elusive. However, the police won't give up – it's a crime of 'diminishing returns', which means the level of violence could escalate, and he's been linked to murder victims.

There was a substantial reward for information leading to a conviction.

Operation Julie
The first multi-force operation

Operation Julie was a police investigation into the production of LSD. The operation involved eleven police forces for two and a half years, and broke up one of the largest LSD operations in the world. In 1977, raw material to make 6.5 million 'tabs' (with a street value of £6.5 million) was seized.

Two manufacturing bases were born of one, with David Solomon and Richard Kemp, who was a chemist. However, they needed a sales distributor and Henry Todd joined them at their base in Cambridge. Leif Fielder then joined them as their tablet maker – the role of tablet maker is a difficult role as the doses needed to be even but with a tablet large enough to handle.

By 1973 the system ground to a standstill as tensions were showing: Messrs Soloman and Kemp went to mid-Wales and Henry Todd recruited Andy Munro with a base in West London – the two were independent from each other. Messrs Todd and Fielding's organisation grew from then on and supplied 'wholesale' dealers.

Detective Inspector Richard (Dick) Lee of the Thames Valley Drug Squad heard of the activities of Mr Kemp and an accident necessitating Mr Kemps car being examined by police gave them a breakthrough – a scribbled and torn up note listing an ingredient needed for top-quality LSD. They now knew the operation was active in Wales, and this led to a meeting in Brecon and the establishment of an operation that drew officers from a number of forces – the genesis of Operation Julie was at hand.

In fact, ten police services seconded officers and they were to be based in Wiltshire's main police HQ in Devizes. They observed Mr Kemp's movements and his visitors. One regular contact was an American, Paul Arnaboldi – when the police mounted a clandestine break-in to Mr Arnaboldi's house they took samples of, among other things, the water drains; these contained LSD traces. Twenty-four-hour surveillance was commenced and his phone was tapped.

Meanwhile, Messrs Todd and Munro were still in the picture in West London.

Information started to come in, mainly about the huge amounts of tablets available, so after just over a year the officers – with help from the uniformed branch – swooped on eighty-seven separate properties in England and Wales. There were 120 arrests. The French and Swiss police were also mobilised, as Europe was a major distribution target. With legitimate search warrants, they found enough raw material to make 6.5 million tablets, with a street value of about £1 each. (This would be worth about £47.5 million today.)

It was a record 'bust', but the trial was also mammoth – it took over four weeks for the prosecution to present their case. Messrs Kemp and Todd got thirteen years, and Messrs Fielding and Hughes eight years. 120 years were shared by the lesser conspirators.

The Operation Julie team was disbanded in 1978. Another 1

million tablets were destroyed and it was estimated that over 100 countries were supplied by the two firms.

Otterburn: The Mystery of Evelyn Foster

Brown, Ernest, the murder of Frederick Morton

Frederick Morton was a cattle farmer; he was married to Dorothy and they lived near Tadcaster, Yorkshire. One of Mr Morton's employees was a chap called Ernest Brown and he started an affair with Dorothy. But it wasn't all a bed of roses because early in September 1933 Mr Brown struck Dorothy, and later, armed with a shotgun, he explained that he was off to shoot some rats.

Dorothy was concerned, and more so when she discovered the phone was dead. At 3.30 a.m. there was an explosion, and the garage was on fire. The fire raged and, even though the fire brigade did a sterling job, the police couldn't investigate until the following morning. When they did, they found the two cars and Frederick Morton sat in one – he'd been shot in the chest.

Tom Pierrepoint hanged Ernest Brown at Armley Prison, in Leeds, on 6 February 1934. Just before Tom pulled the lever, the prison chaplain pleaded with Mr Brown, 'Confess your sins and make your peace with God.' All present thought Mr Brown uttered a single word: 'Otterburn.'

Otterburn is a small village fifteen or so miles from the Scottish Border and just over thirty miles north of Newcastle-on-Tyne. The Cheviot Hills are part of a breath-taking landscape. But why would he say this? *Did* he say this?

Assuming he did, then one needs to find links.

Otterburn had the usual things like pubs, hotels, a post office and a garage. The garage owner had a daughter named Evelyn, who even in those early days, drove a motor car. 'I gave a lift in my car to a man who was smartly dressed, wore a bowler hat and had a Tyneside accent. He wanted to go to Ponteland, about 25 miles away, to catch a Newcastle bus.'

She said this from a hospital bed where she was being treated for severe burns. The conclusion of the coroner's jury was that the stranger had set her car on fire.

It transpired that after she'd picked him up he started touching her inappropriately. She was upset and pulled onto a grass verge, and he punched her unconscious. When she regained her senses, she realised he'd poured petrol over her and the car and then set it on fire.

Before she died she could tell the police her assailant was a natty dresser, he wore a bowler hat and spoke with a Tyneside accent – just like Ernest Brown. He liked the ladies but would hit them if he felt some twisted justification, just like Ernest Brown. He also raised fire indiscriminately and he was indifferent if a life might be in danger.

The coroner's jury decided Evelyn Foster from Otterburn was murdered, and it's widely believed now that, as Ernest Brown uttered the word 'Otterburn' just as he was about to be executed, that is where the guilt for Evelyn's murder belonged.

Paisnel, Edward John Louis

Committed multiple sexual assaults as the Beast of Jersey

On 6 March 1960, a twenty-five-year-old girl waited for a bus to St Helier. A car, a pre-war Rover, stopped beside her. 'Would you like a lift into town?'

In the easy-going Channel Islands then, such offers weren't suspicious. She got in and he accelerated, fast; she held on to the arm-rest. Suddenly, he braked, and then turned into a field.

'What do you think you're doing?' she asked.

He got out of the car and ran round to drag her out. She fought back, but was overcome; her wrists were tied behind her back and a noose slipped around her neck. She could see a sinister mask.

'I'll kill you,' he told her. 'I've killed before.'

She was raped.

Afterwards, he picked her up and threw her into the back seat, backed out of the field and set off. She feared for her life, but managed to loosen the cord and reached out to pull the door handle; the door was hinged at the rear and flew open. He tried to grab her but lost control of the car: his mask fell off and she saw his face. She fell into the road, rolled over, staggered to her feet, and ran towards the lights of a bungalow, from where help soon came. Later the police found the car – it'd been stolen before the attack but contained no clues.

Three weeks later, a housewife woke to a strange sound from the telephone. Alone in the house with her fifteen-year-old daughter, she tiptoed downstairs and clicked on the light switch, but could see nothing. There was a shadowy figure, a masked man holding a small torch. Powerful hands gripped her and a soft voice demanded money. Speaking in a whisper, fearful her daughter would hear, she said she had no cash and begged him to leave. He pushed her into a chair, tying her wrists together behind her back. She heard movement upstairs so shouted to warn her daughter, but the girl kept coming. He moved to the bottom of the stairs and she pushed herself up and ran out and towards a neighbour's house, kicked on the door and hammered on windows. However, the man and her daughter weren't there. Her daughter had been led with a noose around her neck, so tight that her eyes bulged and turned deep red. She was raped.

The description matched that given by the first victim, and they noticed the man's clothes had a 'musty smell'. More attacks followed.

On 30 July, an eight-year-old boy was abducted and assaulted.

On 18 February 1961, a twelve-year-old boy was led from his bedroom by a noose, but not harmed.

On 4 March, an eleven-year-old boy woke as a man tightened a belt around his neck. He shouted and the intruder escaped.

In April an eleven-year-old girl was carried from her bed to a field and assaulted. She spoke of the musty smell.

Each had the same *modus operandi* and brought panic to the island; reports came in of other attacks dating back to 1957.

Detective Inspector George Shutler vowed to catch the Beast of Jersey. He painstakingly scrutinised all the evidence. When would he kill? His height was five foot six inches to five foot eight inches, aged forty to fifty, very familiar with the east of the island. He spoke good English and Jersey's French patois. He wore a beret/ hat and mask and coat with a 'musty smell'.

On 25 April 1961, Detective Superintendent Jack Manning of Scotland Yard went to Jersey. He organised foot patrols and observations, and for almost a year there were no more attacks.

Then a nine-year-old boy was taken from his bed to a sports field on 19 April 1962. He was assaulted; his attacker had a long overcoat 'with a funny smell'.

On 19 November 1963, an eleven-year-old boy was the victim, and the following July a ten-year-old girl.

Nineteen cases. Scotland Yard returned. Mass fingerprinting was carried out and 20,000 people were interviewed.

In the latter part of 1964 a sixteen-year-old boy was led from his house with a noose around his neck. Then there was a two-year lull until the beginning of August, 1966.

However, mid-way through that lull eleven-year-old Joy Norton was assaulted, strangled and stabbed over thirty times. She was found in a field. A letter was sent admitting the crime, but not until after a twenty-two-year-old man with an alibi, who didn't have the right coat or a mask and whose clothes didn't smell, was convicted of murder and went to prison.

In August 1966, a fifteen-year-old girl was raped with the Beast's usual *modus operandi*.

Police and volunteers spent three years watching every road junction, path and hedgerow. No Beast, no assaults – was there inside information getting to him?

Then, in August 1970, a young boy was taken from his bedroom to a field and assaulted.

On 10 July 1971, a car jumped a red light. The police routinely pursued, but there followed a terrifying car chase before reaching a dead end. The driver escaped on foot, but Police Constable John Riseborough brought him down with a rugby tackle. The man wore wristbands with nails sticking out and nails protruded from his lapels.

They searched him and found a face mask, a spiky black wig, a small torch masked with black tape, a trouser belt carrying a knife sheath, two lengths of sash cord, a pyjama cord, and a woollen hat. He was forty-six-year-old Edward John Louis Paisnel, of Grouville, in the eastern part of Jersey. He fitted the description.

He was a well-respected builder, from one of the island's oldest families; he was a pillar of respectability, called 'Uncle Ted' by the children in the foster home his wife ran.

DI Shutler was called.

His home was searched. His wife, Joan, was questioned but couldn't help; they didn't live as man and wife. He lived in his office, which doubled as a bed-sitting room. The police searched it, and found that on one wall was a decorative tapestry, which concealed an alcove. Hanging on the wall, pointed downwards towards a glass bowl, was a wooden dagger. Below was a china toad and a chalice with a glass container of cloves.

They found a hidden room, with a musty smell and a peculiar, eerie atmosphere. Everything fell into place – the clothing and the nails sewn into the jacket pointed to the world of witchcraft.

Among his books they found *The Black Baron*, written about the French nobleman Gilles de Rais, who'd slaughtered more than

300 children in frenzies of blood-lust. The similarities between them were great, and Mr Paisnel claimed to be a descendant.

During the interview, he was shown the raffia cross found in the stolen car he'd driven just prior to his arrest.

'Is this yours?'

Mr Paisnel flung himself backwards and raised his hands in front of his face. His cheeks turned deep red and his eyes bulged. A bizarre sound echoed through the room. In a strange voice, he said, 'My Master would laugh very long and loud at this.'

On Monday 13 December 1971, Edward Paisnel was found guilty of thirteen offences against six people; there were many other offences that the police didn't pursue.

He was sentenced to thirty years.

Poulson, John

Corruption in government

John Llewellyn Poulson was an architect of some repute, but his business ethics were far from what might be considered proper. He operated a scheme of bribery and corruption that went as far up as the Home Secretary of the day, Reginald Maudling.

It was in the late 1960s and early 1970s that his business empire came crashing down, and one has to wonder who else was involved whose profile was never made public. It all came out in a bankruptcy hearing at Wakefield, in Yorkshire, where it was claimed he'd been told to 'turn off the taps' if he were to avoid starvation; this advice from a solicitor was greeted by Mr Poulson with a raspberry!

The point was that people were kept in the dark about his and his firm's activities, and at the time Mr Maudling was a chairman of one of his companies.

The bankruptcy hearing was told of Christmas gifts of drinks, turkeys and flowers to councillors, officials and their wives. Cars were supplied to a magistrate, a bank manager and an officer of what was then called the Ministry of Social Security. The total value of this was said to be around £300,000 at the time and would be equivalent to about £4 million now.

Mr Poulson was quoted to have said, 'I have been a fool, surrounded by a pack of leeches. I took on the world on its own terms, and no one can deny I once had it in my fist.'

When convicted, the major charge was fraud and he was given a five-year jail sentence; this was later increased to seven.

Mr Poulson's contacts included Newcastle's council leader, T. Dan Smith, who was given a six-year jail term. George Pottinger also went down – he'd been put in charge of a £3 million redevelopment of Aviemore as a winter sports complex.

There were also three serving MPs but they found a legal loophole to slither out of trouble which prompted the House of Commons to institute a register for members' business interests.

Mr Poulson served his time in Armley Prison, in Leeds; he was in Wakefield and Oakham prison before finishing up at Lincoln, from where he was freed on 13 May 1977. He was discharged from his bankruptcy in 1980, with his creditors receiving about 10 per cent of what they should, but he did promise more when his autobiography – *The Price* – was published. This book was to give Mr Poulson's side of the bribery and corruption scandal and demonstrate his innocence. However, the publishers feared libel and most copies were destroyed.

At the trial, his lawyer outlined Mr Poulson's anxiety that he might die before the end of his sentence, but he lived until January 1993, when he died aged eighty-three.

Journalist Paul Foot said of him, 'In many ways he was a model for the "enlightened self interest capitalism", which became known as Thatcherism.'

Prison Escape

There have been dozens of examples of this from George Blake the spy to Ronnie Biggs. Some quite spectacular escapes have been planned and failed.

There was a breakout of four prisoners from Blundeston Prison, in Suffolk – now closed – in 1969, which would give a good example. The prisoners hijacked a prison officer's wife's car, and with it, her handbag, containing £15. This was a frightening ordeal for the lady, but thankfully they didn't have hostage-taking on their agenda. The men were all serving substantial sentences and their crimes involved violence and theft. The police issued their usual warning for the public not to approach them.

The car was later found in Gorleston, over the border in Norfolk, and it was noted that a Morris 1100 was missing from fairly nearby; this turned up in Great Yarmouth, and inside it was prison-issue clothing. Police scoured the area but found little in the way of clues.

Meantime, of course, questions were asked about their absconding from what was a fairly modern maximum-security prison, with up-to-the-minute technology such as closed-circuit TV. The men worked in a tailoring workshop and they managed to get into an adjoining room, from where they could get onto the roof. From here they jumped down into the yard, surrounded by a twelve-foot fence, which they cut through.

The prison governor explained that the prison officer's wife was stopped and the men just jumped into her car and pushed her out.

William Bright was thirty-four, serving seven years for rape and theft.

James Sims was thirty-seven, serving seven years for robbery with violence.

Peter Packham was the oldest at forty-three, serving ten years for shop- and office-breaking and firearms offences.

Herbert Coster had been inside for seven years; the thirty-four-year-old had been convicted of armed assault with intent to rob.

The Flying Squad started to consult their grapevine. Some clothing belonging to Mr Bright was found at an address in Brixton, in London, and they felt he was being helped by some of his underworld contacts, one of whom was arrested for harbouring him. Police intelligence also suggested the other three escapees were also in the capital.

It was James Sims who was the first to be traced, and at Mile End Underground Station he was apprehended by two detectives; he'd been on the run for eighteen days. Less than a week later, police raided a house in Ashford, in Middlesex, which led to William Bright rejoining prison life. Three others at the address Mr Bright was taken from were also charged with assaulting police officers as well as assisting his escape and harbouring. It's pretty clear that a prison escapee is reliant on his connections on the outside to remain at large. By mid-August it was only Peter Packham who remained unaccounted for, but he was picked up in Newquay.

The Railway Rapists – John Duffy and David Mulcahy
Also convicted of the murder of Alison Day, Maartje Tanboezer, Anne Lock and others

Sometimes the crimes a suspect is convicted of are only the tip of the iceberg, and the crime of rape, sadly, is one of the crimes which often goes unreported. This can be for a number of reasons and one reason for women can be 'self-blame', which is slowly being eroded. As we learn more about it, then it seems one of those crimes that are frequently planned in advance; most rapists choose to act the way they do. But what can start as an unpleasant lunge and grope at a girl begins a process of diminishing return – the thrill gets more only if the crime gets worse. One man in the early 1980s in London committed something like twenty-six rapes and three murders: the question of what the full extent of his campaign was is enough to make one shudder.

And there are the occasions when a crime that the police and courts are sure can be attributed has to be left open, as there isn't sufficient evidence to prove the guilt. John Duffy is currently serving a life sentence for rape and murder: when convicted, the police were sure he'd committed a third murder, but there wasn't enough proof to satisfy the criminal law. Over a decade later, his partner in crime was convicted of the same catalogue of rape and the two murders, and he was also convicted of the third murder. It's highly unlikely these two will ever be released, so that third verdict might have helped the family move on – but not much.

The minimum tariff for Mr Duffy was set to thirty years, but that's simply the earliest point that he can apply for parole – the parole board will assess the level of dangerousness as a part of its deliberations.

In the original trial of just Mr Duffy, the judge directed a verdict of not guilty of murdering the thirty-year-old Anne Lock, but Detective Chief Superintendent John Hurst, who led the murder hunt, said, 'Duffy killed Anne Lock. We are not looking for anyone else. We have closed the file on the case. Duffy was our man.'

The police revealed then that although he was given seven life sentences for two murders and five rapes, he was probably responsible for up to thirty further rapes. Women lived in terror for over four years. Almost all of the attacks took place in close proximity to railway lines.

In December 1985, when one of earlier victims was giving evidence in court against him, she may have blocked him out of her mind – this is denial, and is quite common – so was unable to identify him. But it was a failing by the police that even though this happened, they should have had some idea about what happens to a victim's mind.

Mr Duffy's wife was getting far past the end of her tether with his erratic behaviour, and he spent three weeks in prison after he savagely attacked her. Police objected to bail, but he got it; within weeks, the first murder took place – that of Alison Day.

Alison was on her way to meet her boyfriend Paul Tidiman just after Christmas in 1985 – he lived in East London. As she stepped down from the train at Hackney Wick station, Mr Duffy was there, ready to grab her. Not far away was the River Lea, where she was taken; the knife in Mr Duffy's hand could be felt in her back. She was found on a secluded piece of ground over two weeks later.

Maartje Tamboezer was from the Netherlands, and she was raped and murdered in April 1986. She was due to go on a school outing and had been to a shop to buy some sweets; she took a shortcut along a railway line and Mr Duffy was there to rape and strangle her.

One major difficulty is that in any case, the accused has a right to face their accuser, which can be terrifying. These days evidence can be given by video link, so it's not quite as bad, but still, the accused is innocent until proven guilty, and some may be outraged they are accused of such a crime. One of the most intimidating ploys Mr Duffy used in court was his hard, cold stare. One can imagine the effect this might have on an innocent teenage girl.

So, unsurprisingly, he entered a plea of not guilty and sat in the dock, where he 'gloated'. It was likely this gave him a further thrill.

The police thought they knew his accomplice, but would have to wait for thirteen years before they could see him convicted, which came about because Mr Duffy helped them along with the evidence.

In the meantime, in February 1988, Mr Duffy received his sentence.

Mr Justice Farquharson told him, 'The two murders are ... as appalling as I've come across. The wickedness and beastliness on two very young girls hardly bears description. I was not surprised to see the effect it had on the jury. Quite apart from cutting short these two young lives, you have blighted the lives of the two girls' families.'

John Duffy Senior, his father, his mother, Philomena, his sister Susan and brother Jimmy were in court.

The jury of six men and six women took over nineteen hours over two days to convict, but were unable to reach a verdict on two rapes and three assault charges.

David Mulcahy was convicted in 2001 as his partner.

The Home Secretary increased both men to a whole life sentence, but it's for a judge to decide sentence. It's unclear whether this will make any difference to the time served and it's likely they'll both die in prison.

Randall, Amanda
Murdered by Graham Bowen

It sounded as though life was far from irksome for fourteen-year-old Amanda Randall. She was well liked, from a pleasant, hard-working family, and she would often help out in the family corner shop ran by her father, Dewi, in Llanelli, South Wales. Just around the corner was a pickling factory, where she worked for a few hours in the evenings to earn a bit extra. Her brother also worked there, and Amanda may have just given him the slip, as she was seen going into a small shed within the factory precinct. As Colin, her brother, left the factory very soon after her, one has to wonder if she intended to go to the shed; there are no reports of anyone being seen with her at that stage.

Detective Superintendent Pat Molloy, who was then head of the CID for Dyfed-Powys police, was to later say, 'We have no idea why she should want to go in there.'

At first, though, she was merely a missing teenager and with the dark of mid-November, the police could only do a limited search before the following day. These were anxious times for her parents. The following morning, a lady walking her dog discovered her body. Amanda was partly clothed and it didn't seem as though she'd been sexually assaulted, but the injuries to her face were appalling – so much did the facial injuries feature that the police initially thought a machine at the factory had inflicted her injuries – and she was then removed. This was quickly discounted by forensic experts searching the factory; some of the factory had fallen into disuse.

But DSupt Molloy was vastly experienced and looking at the facts he must have wondered why, if her brother Colin had left the factory so soon after her, didn't he either catch up with her or at least see her ahead of him. So the theory then developed that a motorist had been parked close to the factory gates and he lured her into his car. Off he drove, and the battered body was found the next day. But why would she get into a stranger's car?

Home Office pathologist Dr Glyn Williams had liaised with the other forensic staff and the detectives. There was a sexual element to the crime, though not to the point of assault or rape; the word 'element' was attributed to DSupt Molloy. He knew, as did his team, that they were looking for someone particularly vicious and dangerous.

It shocked the town to its core. Her uncle Bernard said she was a home-loving girl. A neighbour who'd helped in the search said, 'She was such a sweet child, who was always playing happily in the street. A quiet, refined girl and very hard-working.'

But few clues were forthcoming from the factory staff. To get from the factory to where she was found there must have been a car involved, and she either got into the car voluntarily or she was forced in. There was no evidence at the factory that the attack had happened there, but the police combed every inch of the place;

unfortunately, it was hosed down daily. But there was also the shed.

The murder weapon was 'sharp and unusual', and a team of police frogmen searched a reservoir near to where Amanda was found.

Her father had said, 'She would never have gone with anyone she did not know.' He was also quoted to have said, 'She would never go near a stranger.'

But the story began to clarify itself to DSupt Molloy. He said, 'I believe I know the sequence of events, but I'm not going to discuss these for obvious reasons.'

The case came to court in Swansea in June 1979. Acting for the prosecution, Mr Aubrey Myerson QC said that although Amanda was aware of her attractiveness she was very strict about her boundaries. A thirty-one-year-old married man, Graham Bowen, pleaded not guilty to her murder.

Mr Bowen was employed as a fitter at the factory. He had 'expressed his desire' for the girl and some activities were witnessed, though it is unclear if this was against Amanda's will. What was described as 'horseplay' also occurred between them.

However, Mr Bowen had lied about his relationship with her and also lied about his movements on the night of the murder. No murder weapon had been found, but it was thought to be an axe. It became very clear in Swansea Crown Court that Mr Bowen knew a lot more than he'd let on.

As he was employed in the factory he could bring his car into the factory precincts, but there was never any satisfactory answer of whether Amanda had gone into the shed in the grounds. What became clear, though, was that he was 'besotted' with her. She'd found herself in his car, and at some stage he 'half-strangled' her. Then he drove Amanda away from the factory to where she was later found, though it sounds as though he butchered her where he dumped her body, in the lonely lane in a neighbouring village.

The court recognized the 'sexual element' DSupt Molloy had described as a sexual assault. It was claimed Mr Bowen had a sexual obsession with her.

'This is one of the most foul deeds that I have ever had to deal with', Mr Justice Tasker-Watkins said, as he sentenced Mr Bowen to life imprisonment.

Regan, (O'Rourke) Mrs Florence

Murdered by her bigamist double-killer husband, Anthony Regan (O'Rourke)

He was described as a vicious killer – and that's exactly what he was. Even at the end of his third murder trial he waited nonchalantly for the three and a half hours the jury took in their deliberations. But this time they found him guilty of murder, guilty of killing the wife who'd stood by him – 'the wife' he'd married bigamously, who waited while he served a prison sentence for the bigamous marriage. The only time he seemed shaken in the whole of the third murder trial was when the foreman of the jury announced 'guilty'. Anthony Regan, otherwise known as O'Rourke, was now going to prison for life.

The trial had lasted for three days, under Mr Justice Roskill, and he could barely conceal his contempt. 'The jury, who knew nothing of your record, have arrived at a just and true verdict in this case. They did not know that ten years ago you were sent to prison for ten years for manslaughter, and that this is the second human being whose death you have brought about by violence.'

His first murder resulted in an acquittal, but he'd said quite frankly in a magazine article that he was actually guilty.

This third murder was in late 1962 when he killed his wife with a potato knife following a row. He actually hid her body in a wardrobe in a spare bedroom for a while – some reports refer to twelve weeks. Police and welfare officers called to the house, but Mr Regan always had an excuse for his wife's absence.

His wife, Florence, was thirty-nine at the time of her death and together they'd had three children. There was also a daughter, Joan, from Florrie's previous marriage. They all lived together in Long Readings Lane in Burnham, which is not far from Slough, though just over the border in Buckinghamshire. They lived in what sounds like a pleasant three-bedroomed semi.

It had been the fresh start Florrie Regan had wanted. After Mr Regan's ten years in prison the family moved from Walworth, in London, to settle in Burnham. They also changed their name from O'Rourke, but it made little difference to his lifestyle and he returned to petty crime – of all jobs, he became a night security guard, and promptly stole what he was supposed to be guarding. Another twelve months inside, and still Florrie was there waiting for him when he came out.

But he admitted he'd developed feelings for Joan, his step-daughter, and this seemed to lead to tense rows as she began to retreat from him; the rows increased in ferocity until the one that cost Florrie her life.

It was Joan who finally set the wheels in motion to solve the mystery of her missing mum. Joan had left home to live with friends, and she became increasingly anxious and suspicious when little information about her mother was forthcoming. She managed to get a key and opened one of the bedrooms. She called the police, and Florrie Regan's body was found.

The police searched the room inch by inch and Mr Regan's handwriting was discovered in a diary close to the body. 'Dear Sir, I killed my wife on Saturday. It was in our bedroom at the foot of the bed. I killed her with a knife in the chest. I love my wife but also love her daughter Joan. After killing my wife I put her in the wardrobe for a few weeks.'

His defence was quite futile; he told the police his wife was seeing another man and when he confronted her, an argument ensued and things escalated.

Florrie Regan had known he'd kill again. He'd boast that murder was easy, murder was thrilling, and that he had the urge to kill again.

Florrie's best friend said, 'They were always afraid ... never free from worry and dread ... He used to sneer at the law, and say how simple it was to outwit the police ... He was a frail and harmless-looking little man, but he was a devil and a monster. Flo's big worry – the worry that drove her almost insane – was that her daughter Joan might be his next victim.

'And she blamed herself because, in the past, she had lied to save him from the gallows. She admitted to me that she lied in the witness-box.'

It led to his first acquittal, in 1950, of the murder of Thomas Pickering, who was thought to be a friend of the family. Old Tom, it was said, was his friend – but the story was that Mr Regan thought he liked his wife a little too much, so he attacked him with a poker. At any rate that was the story fed to Leeds Assizes, but one has to think that as Mrs Regan said this in the witness box, was she coerced into doing so by her husband? The jury felt it hadn't been murder. It appears, though, that manslaughter wasn't an alternative conviction they could consider.

A year after this acquittal he strangled fifty-six-year-old Rose Harper, but it's a mystery as to why. He was convicted for manslaughter and sentenced to ten years. Mr Regan later told a magazine that he'd murdered two people, and scoffed at the way his lies deceived two juries. 'I wanted to find out what it was like to kill. And I had to kill again to show it wasn't a fluke.'

Reprieves

Was there ever a reason for His or Her Majesty to interfere with the due course of the law? In practice, this was a task carried out by the Home Office and, until capital punishment was abolished in England and Wales, nearly half were reprieved: 1,485 were convicted, of whom 755 were executed – only about one in ten women sentenced were hanged.

This might suggest that the Home Office bent over backwards to reprieve, but this is a matter for debate when one thinks of folk such as Ruth Ellis and Derek Bentley. There was never an explanation given for a reprieve. One read in a newspaper that prisoner 'A' had been reprieved, or prisoner 'B' had his appeal denied – as to why remained a mystery. It was never stated. Looking back now, it all seems a bit of a lottery.

People such as Ruth Ellis were hanged despite a huge public outcry, but the majority of murderers just get caught up in a domestic issue which spiral out of control. There have been calls to return to capital punishment, but generation after generation of politicians of all political complexions have resisted it. The main reason is that too many mistakes were made in the past. Stefan Kiszko, for instance, would have been hanged for a sexually motivated child murder – yet he was innocent. The Birmingham Six would have been executed – in both these cases they served far more time than was the average for a murder. Averages, of course, conceal truths, but is there any suggestion or implication that the politicians might have thought of the voting public? Did the civil servants or the Home Secretary know what happened to the attitude of Joe Public? It's a mystery.

Donald Thomas murdered a police officer in London in 1948 and served almost half of what Freddie Sewell served for shooting a police officer in 1970. It has now come about that politicians should not slap a mandatory 'whole life' tariff on a prisoner – judges are charged with that job – but the American model of life without parole seems a hopeless plight for someone. However, this doesn't address the question of why one killer was reprieved and another hanged. The answer would seem to be that it would depend on many factors – like the mood of the country, Home Secretary or Home Office. I wonder if there was any correlation between the 'nasty' murders and those that were 'softer', and an election where a hanging might sway voters feelings. Politicians are, after all, doing a job, and it's better to be in power than in opposition.

Nevertheless, a trial judge asking for mercy on behalf of a jury would rarely be ignored. The judge had no option but to pass the death sentence for murder. In a Royal Commission just after the war, it was found that in the century up to that time, only six killers went to the gallows where a plea for mercy was taken from the court to the Home Office.

The Appeal Court was set up in the first decade of the century, but that was to appeal against conviction and not sentence. However, this has changed and with the coming of the European Court of Human Rights and the Criminal Cases Review Commission (CCRC) there are plenty of safeguards against an erroneous conviction – providing the two bodies work as they should. There is evidence to suggest the CCRC will find any excuse not to send a case back to the Court of Appeal. And in the case of Sion Jenkins wanting compensation for false imprisonment (a child killer, again, would have been hanged), he was told he wasn't innocent enough.

As for criteria for reprieves, this is impossible to assess as for one thing, each case is unique, and there are factors which might sway the decision – child killers, poisoners and gun crimes – but loose sexual morals in the case of women also seem to have been considered. Age might be a factor, as could medical conditions. Epilepsy, definitely, and severe mental illness. But at least two convicted murderers were reprieved because they'd slit their own throats and a bloody mess in the 'lower' execution chamber was undesirable.

If the prisoner was considered 'fit', then the rather euphemistic 'the law must take its course' was recorded. But as all decisions were subjected to the Official Secrets Act then suggestions of an unbalanced system can't be resisted.

Children whose lives are ended by their mothers have been taken out of the equation. It's long since been recognised there are medical reasons. Recent advances have made it all the more understandable that these tragedies happen. Apart from the odious calculation of odds by one particular paediatrician, the mums haven't come through the court system. Women are no longer stigmatised for unmarried status – it does take two to make a baby, after all.

Sadly, there have been murderers reprieved who have gone on to commit further murders, but there were convictions for murders where there was a clear and obvious bias towards the victim – who did fire the shot that killed PC Miles?

If the whole system of reprieve was a lottery, then the Homicide Act of 1957 made it a charade. Men who strangled when they raped were spared the noose, yet a robber who murdered would hang. This didn't happen in practice, but it could have. Murder in the furtherance of theft would bring out the noose. In 1962 George Riley was hanged for such a murder, yet he didn't steal anything. The less said about this Act the better, but one wonders if the government intentionally made the Act unworkable as a means to an end – the final abolition of capital punishment.

Eventually, capital punishment was abolished. It's been voted on since and in some countries, the vote was put to the entire electorate. If this happens in the UK there should be provision for erroneous conviction, though how this might work out in practice I don't know. Perhaps the right question hasn't been asked. If a system of reprieves was so inconsistent, then was sentencing policy equally as inconsistent in using a blanket death sentence? One has to finally ask about erroneous convictions, though, and just how many reprieves were granted where someone in authority noticed an error or that evidence was withheld. This was all done in entire secrecy, but slowly the truth will emerge as the files at the National Archive are opened.

Reyn-Bardt, Malika
Murdered by husband, Peter

It came to its conclusion at Chester Crown Court on 13 December 1983; a twenty-three-year mystery turned into a conviction for murder. It might not have, but the whole thing blew up because a skull was discovered at around about the place an airline executive had buried the body of his wife, twenty-three long years before.

He'd told detectives that they'd had a blazing row and he'd strangled her before he cut the body up and buried the pieces. They'd had a whirlwind romance and married literally within days of meeting. Malika Reyn-Hardt was a petite, dark-haired and stunningly beautiful lady, but her agenda didn't seem to fit with marital bliss, a couple of kids in a semi-detached house in commuter land. She realised that in 1960, anyone who was homosexual would be in danger of losing their job, if not a lot more. The court heard that she tried to blackmail him and the negotiations didn't quite go to plan.

Of course, by 1983 the law had been changed and people didn't take as much notice of sexual orientation as they had twenty-three years before, so his motive for the killing may not have seemed as desperate.

But no trace of Malika's body was discovered, which I'll discuss shortly, and it's unclear what steps – if any – he took to report her missing. In court it was acknowledged little was known about her; the only thing known for sure was that she'd worked in a coffee bar and was a portrait artist. She loved to travel, and as Mr Reyn-Bardt could procure cheap flights and she could bring some 'normality' to his life, despite his orientation, the two seemed to have fallen into what he later described as a 'business agreement'.

Due to the fact that they married within four days of meeting, a lot of publicity was attracted, even with a picture and a write-up in one of the 'dailies'. The proposal had come within only a couple of hours of meeting!

By the time it came to court, Mr Reyn-Bardt lived in Knightsbridge, in London, and he denied murdering Malika, who was around thirty-two at the time of her death; this was estimated to have occurred between October 1960 and the end of June 1961 at his home, which was then in Wilmslow, in Cheshire.

When the case came to court, Mr Martin Thomas QC explained to the jury that it was a marriage of convenience and described what was thought to be the rationale behind it, but it wasn't long before she left him; the marriage wasn't consummated. Then in October 1960 she visited him at his cottage, near Wilmslow, which he shared with his male partner. They had a row about money and he claimed she wanted more money than he could give her, so, after a heated exchange, he lost his sense and strangled her – she'd tried to claw him with her long nails. He said, 'She wanted money – more than I could give her. She threatened to expose my homosexuality, blackmail me and disgrace me. She got more and more angry. She came at me like a vixen, clawing at my face. I boiled up inside, I was in a frenzy. I grabbed her shoulders then around her neck. I don't remember what happened next until she was lying at my feet. I realised I had killed her. I had to get rid of her body. I dragged it out of the lounge on to the patio. In desperation and panic, I severed her. I hacked off her legs, her arms and her head. It's like a nightmare. I was covered in blood.'

He'd tried to burn his wife's body on a bonfire but was afraid of the smell, and decided he should bury her in a ditch; this, he estimated, was a couple of hundred yards from the cottage. 'I am glad it's all over. It haunted me for more than twenty years.'

The conviction attracted a life sentence. Little was said in mitigation by Victor Durand QC, defending.

The skull that led to this episode was discovered when an excavator digging for peat 300 yards from Mr Reyn-Bardt's former home uncovered it.

The police had made a thorough search for the rest of her body but didn't recover any further remains; it was thought that over the years foxes had taken the bones away.

But was the skull that of his wife? Experts from Oxford University examined it and concluded it belonged to a woman who'd died in about AD 400; other experts disagree.

Richardson, Superintendent Gerry GC
Murdered by Freddie Sewell

In a popular seaside resort, and only a few yards from the seafront, Police Superintendent Gerry Richardson was shot at point-blank range and died on his way to hospital. Supt Richardson was born in Blackpool in 1932 and grew up to be a dedicated copper and first-rate sportsman. He was respected as a 'hands-on officer'. In 1978, a trust fund was set up in his memory to help youngsters with their sporting dreams.

The murderous gang were jailed for a total of over ninety years. Frederick Sewell, who had 'sprayed the street with bullets', received thirty years for Gerry's killing. As a gang of robbers, they were incompetent, and when they attacked the jewellers' shop in the Strand, in Blackpool, the owner had pressed the silent alarm button. PC Carl Walker, who managed to trudge on with his career and reach the rank of inspector, responded, along with Gerry and Kenneth Mackay, awarded the George Cross for the bravery they showed. When a police officer puts on his uniform or picks up his warrant card he, or she, increases the risk of violence against them – the risk is real.

Frederick Sewell was sentenced to life imprisonment at Manchester Crown Court for the murder and the judge recommended he should serve thirty years. There was again a call for the return of hanging for the murder of police officers.

Mr Sewell and his gang had travelled up from London to do the raid, which would have yielded a haul of just over £106,000.

The other four men who comprised the gang were jailed for terms ranging from ten to twenty-five years, with the heavier sentences falling for the violence. The trial judge, Mr Justice Kilner Brown, told Mr Sewell, 'I do not sentence you in any spirit of revenge. I do not sentence you in any spirit of prejudice or emotional involvement. It is necessary not only to sentence you in relation to your own part and on your own character but also as a warning that any man who shoots down a police officer in the course of his duty must expect the severest punishment which is permitted in the courts.'

Mrs Maureen Richardson, Gerry's widow, was in court to hear the sentences. She said, 'I wanted to see justice was done, but certainly did not go to gloat over the fate of these men. This thing happened to me. It has altered my whole life and I felt entitled to be there.'

Both Mrs Richardson and her husband were brought up in the area where he served and lost his life, and as the decades passed, that day stood vivid in her memory. She never remarried and finally returned to her job in teaching.

When news came of an armed raid, Gerry would be out with his men and had a reputation of 'leading from the front'; that spurred on his colleagues to liaise with the Metropolitan Police to catch the men. Mr Sewell was arrested within a few weeks in a dingy bed-sit in Holloway – the other gang members were also soon rounded up.

Mr Sewell had managed to get into the boot of a get-away car, but with rewards offered by newspapers it was little wonder the police knew where he was.

A man and two women were later convicted of aiding and abetting, so all the gang and their helpers were convicted. In 2001 Mr Sewell left prison, apparently a wealthy man owing to some property deals done while he was 'away'. A wealthy man – it doesn't seem fair.

The Richardson Gang
Violent gang leaders

Charlie Richardson was born in January 1934, and his brother Eddie in January 1936; they were South London lads and there was a younger brother, Alan. The two elder brothers were brought up during the war – dad was in the Merchant Navy so was frequently away. Charlie became street-wise and Eddie was just as shrewd.

They did work hard and had considerable intelligence, but their way of dealing with business associates who let them down wasn't considered as appropriate; their reputation changed into one of a sadistic torture gang. They were said to pull teeth using pliers, cut off toes with bolt cutters, nail victims' feet to the floor with long nails, use whipping and inflict cigarette burns; electric shocks were usually administered in a cold bath to give an extra kick. This would follow what was called a mock trial, where Charlie Richardson would officiate. They knew a couple of doctors who'd been struck off who could treat their victims thereafter. When the torture was finished the victim would be given a clean shirt, so woe betide anyone who heard they were to be 'taking a shirt from Charlie'.

There must have been some truth to this, but just how much was exaggerated is unclear. Some of their victims have issued statements saying their testimony at the trial was untrue; Lucien Harris was one who'd said he'd had the electric shock electrodes attached to his genitalia. He later said he hadn't.

Whether the trial was fair is again open to question, and one of their associates, who I'll discuss in a moment, later challenged the judge at a London station but never faced any 'punishment'. He said the judge was biased. There was also a family link from the lawyers to a juryman.

Their associates, though, were selected from mixed pedigrees. George Cornell was a drug dealer who'd often sample the merchandise himself. He'd started off his career with the rival Kray gang but defected. Mr Cornell was unstable and unpredictable and thought he could call Ronnie Kray a 'fat poof' and get away with it. This nearly brought about a gangland war. George Cornell was later shot dead as he drank in the Blind Beggar pub in March 1966, by Ronnie Kray.

Frankie Fraser joined in the action in the mid-1960s. He'd had a very good war, stealing just about anything he could get his hands on – 'The best thieving time ever.'

In the 1950s he'd been with Billy Hill and his gang, so was of 'sound' pedigree. He was called 'an enforcer' and would often 'rough people up'. He denies ever pulling teeth out of people with a pair of pliers.

They claimed they were legitimate businessmen: Charlie a scrap dealer and Eddie a trader of fruit machines. It's plausible, but so is the assertion they used this to give an honest front to less honest lines: fraud, racketeering, usury (loan sharking), theft and stolen goods. The so-called 'Long Firm' was a speciality where they would build up a lot of trust with suppliers, place a huge order and then vanish. Charlie regularly donated to a 'Police Fund'.

But police evidence was mounting and one of the gang turned Queen's Evidence.

Charlie was arrested 30 July 1966; Eddie was already inside

for affray. The 'Torture Trial' was held at the Old Bailey early in April 1967. They were found guilty of fraud, extortion, assault and grievous bodily harm. Charlie got twenty-five years and Eddie had ten years added to his five-year sentence. Eddie left prison after about eleven years and Charlie was freed after eighteen.

Charlie Richardson died of peritonitis in September 2012. Eddie lives abroad.

Rosenthal, Daniel
The murder of Milton Rosenthal, his father, and Leah Rosenthal, his mother, whose body was never recovered

Daniel Rosenthal lived in Hedge End, Southampton, a nice area of bungalows and not quite the place that a 'mad scientist' would be expected to be found. There were overgrown bushes all around his bungalow and he shunned the outside world. His lounge was like a laboratory and each week he cut up several dozen chicks and experimented on their brains and embryos. He'd dig strange holes in his garden at all hours, usually with a desert spoon. He was described as a 'mad scientist', and clearly he was in urgent need of treatment. But with the Mental Health Act he would either have to go into a hospital on his own volition, or be taken in – as he appeared to pose no danger to anyone, the latter wasn't an option. To him, no doubt his behaviour was normal.

In August of 1981 he went to Paris to see his father – his parents lived apart, and it has been suggested he was looking for more money to fund his bizarre life. He'd written letters describing his parents as psychotic, but as far as records show, they seemed quite in touch with the real world. But his father at any rate may have thought Mr Rosenthal may not be quite well, and it's thought that he wouldn't give his son any money.

Milton Rosenthal vanished. Mr Rosenthal's mother visited him soon after and said that his father seemed to have gone missing – she'd rung him to see how her son's visit had gone – and Milton Rosenthal's maid said he wasn't at the flat and she didn't know where he was.

Soon after, his mother's whereabouts also began to raise concerns. Her friend rang Mr Rosenthal and he said his mother had left for London – but there was no sign of her. After further phone calls to him, Leah Rosenthal's friend couldn't get any sensible information. Eventually, she went to the police.

Mr Rosenthal told them the same story, in that his mother had left and, as she had multiple sclerosis, had got a taxi. The police officers' suspicions were aroused when they couldn't find evidence that any local taxi firms had taken her, and none of the neighbours remembered seeing a taxi at the bungalow.

Detective Inspector Mike Southwell contacted the Paris flat of Mr Rosenthal, and the maid told him, through her tears, that she believed her boss had been murdered by his son. So far, there were only two missing people – there were no bodies.

It wasn't too difficult to get a search warrant for his house in Hedge End, and in went the forensic team.

The house was filthy and squalid, but one room seemed to have been recently cleaned – dried blood was found in minute traces in the floor tiles. Other samples were found on a pair of shoes – the blood group was the same as Leah Rosenthal; she'd been a donor when she'd lived in Southampton. So if he had killed her and cut up the body, then what did he do it with? A clean and new-looking hacksaw was examined by Mr Mike Sayes, a forensic scientist – where the blade was attached to the main body of the saw, there was a bolt, under which was 'connective tissue, probably skin'.

So had he cut her into pieces after killing her?

There followed a widespread sea, air and land search, but no trace of his mother was found. The detectives believed Mr Rosenthal had killed his mother, dismembered her body and dumped her.

Over four intense days of interview, Mr Rosenthal gave the police no indication that he'd harmed either of his parents. He did tell them that a lot of the blood they'd found came from the baby chicks he experimented with; he mainly disposed of the remains of these in black bags he'd bought from Wisebuys in Bitterne, not far from his home in Hedge End.

DI Southall and his team got very little from him. 'He was the most difficult and unusual person I've ever dealt with. He was in another world – he wasn't listening to us. He wasn't interested in our questions, he was actually looking down at us as if to say, "You peasants, you're never going to catch me."'

They felt sure they had enough scientific evidence to charge him. But with no bodies and no confession, would a jury feel this proved guilt beyond reasonable doubt?

As the trial approached, though, they got the breakthrough they needed. On a French farm, about eighty miles from Paris, the headless remains of a man were found. The remains were in a black bag, and still affixed to the bag was the price tag – from 'Wisebuys Bitterne'.

The forensic scientist Mr Sayes was able to examine the body parts, and he found the distinct pattern the saw made on bones when the body was cut up. In Milton Rosenthal's flat in Paris, the police found a hacksaw whose blade made an identical pattern. The maid had reported that Mr Rosenthal was locked in the bathroom of the flat for three and a half hours during his stay with his father, and this corresponded with the last time she'd seen his father. With this evidence the police formed the theory that he'd smashed his father's head in and then simply cut up the body, before bagging it up and driving into the countryside.

The police thought at trial that Mr Rosenthal's lawyers would challenge the evidence – although circumstantial, all the pieces linked – but there was no challenge; he merely stated that his parents had been killed by the CIA or the FBI. The trial was soon over and he was convicted of murder; he was an in-patient at Ashworth Special Hospital for a number of years.

This was unusual, because the murder of his father almost certainly took place on French soil, and the case against him for his mother was left on file: no trace of her remains were ever found. One theory was he'd dissolved her in acid, but this was disproved when the police examined the drains around the bungalow. The discovery of a frog prompted one police officer to form a very strong theory! However, the frog wouldn't have survived if acid had gone down the drain.

Ruxton, Dr Buck

AKA Bukhtyar Rustomji Ratanji Hakim – murder of Isabella Kerr (partner) and Mary Jane Robertson (housemaid)

Buck Ruxton came to the UK in 1930, having trained in medicine in Bombay. He went to Lancaster, the county town of Lancashire, where he set up in general practice. He was well received and was a hard-working and bright GP. His patients liked him, and if they fell on hard times he wouldn't charge them.

He didn't marry, but acquired a 'common-law' wife, Isabella Kerr, with whom he had three children. She was an outgoing, gregarious sort of soul and would often be in the company of the well-to-do about Lancaster; she was a popular socialite, but Dr Ruxton wasn't happy. To his great discredit, he had a jealous streak, which would always cloud his judgement.

But Bella, as she was known, couldn't convince him that she was faithful – there is no evidence she wasn't. Things went from bad to worse and eventually he strangled her, but he couldn't get rid of the body and his crime was discovered by their housemaid, Mary Jane Rogerson. It's thought that he strangled her too.

He was trained in medicine, so dismembering the bodies

presented few problems, and he wrapped the body parts in old newspapers – but where he would take them from there was another problem.

He travelled north to Dumfriesshire to a small town called Moffat, where, just north of the town on the main Edinburgh road, a bridge crossed a stream. It was here that he dumped the body parts, close to a set of hills known as The Devil's Beef Tub, and locally the area is now known as Ruxton's Dump. It's over 100 miles from Lancaster.

The significance of the body parts' wrappings is that one of them, the *Sunday Graphic*, was only sold in that particular edition in the Lancashire area. This was the first break for Detective Inspector Jeremiah Lynch, who'd come up from Scotland Yard to assist the investigation. As the paper was delivered to his house, Dr Ruxton's name was on a subscription list but, when asked, he said he'd never been to Scotland. However, his car registration number was noted in a police officer's pocket book, as he was in collision with a cyclist when returning from Dumfriesshire.

He was arrested. The forensic evidence was unique; firstly, the scientists could extract fingerprints from the fingers of Mary Jane, which they matched up to the house. Secondly, the X-ray of one of the skulls fitted perfectly to a picture of Bella from some while back. So convincing were forensic experts Professor John Glaister and Professor James Brash, from Glasgow and Edinburgh respectively, that the jury were only out for about an hour. On Friday 13 March 1936, Dr Ruxton was sentenced to death.

His patients and other Lancaster folk rallied and a petition of over 10,000 signatures was delivered to the Home Office after the Court of Appeal had dismissed his appeal. That didn't cut any ice. On Shakespeare's birthday, 27 April, Dr Buck Ruxton was hanged at Strangeways Prison in Manchester.

Saunders, Ernest et al.

The Guinness Affair

The so-called Guinness Affair of 1990 saw four business tycoons criticised, tried and convicted, and three men were sent to jail. Eleven years later, the Department of Trade and Industry finally got around to reporting and roundly branded one of the 'four' a as having a 'dubious attitude to the truth'. Ernest Saunders was attacked for awarding himself a £3 million bonus in the take-over scandal.

In 1990 Mr Saunders, together with Anthony Parnes, Gerald Ronson and Sir Jack Lyons, were all found guilty of illegal share manipulation involving £2.7 billion. Guinness was to take over Distillers – the Johnny Walker & Gordons Gin Group. Sir Jack Lyons was stripped of his knighthood and fined, and the others received prison sentences.

It wasn't a simple rip-off. They were convicted of a number of offences, including theft, conspiracy to defraud and false accounting. They used a share operation that suggested the value of Guinness shares was higher than they actually were. This told Distillers' shareholders that the take-over was more attractive than perhaps they might have thought.

Of course, Mr Saunders had a good record with Guinness and had helped the company steer themselves to a high position, a record of which he was justly proud. And as for the Distillers take-over, he claimed he'd done nothing wrong. The 'rules' of take-over weren't clear cut and he felt he was merely a scapegoat.

He may have been, but charges such as theft, conspiracy to defraud and false accounting are serious – and if money was lost by shareholders as a result, then they can quite reasonably expect the law will protect them.

Mr Saunders was originally sentenced to five years in jail, though this was reduced to half that on appeal. In the event, he served ten months before presenting with symptoms of early-onset dementia. Miraculously, he recovered, which means he didn't have the disease. One wonders how doctors were convinced.

It was said that one of the enduring images of the Guinness trial and the long-winded aftermath was Mr Saunders 'shambling figure', often supported by one of his grown-up children. By the last decade of the millennium, Mr Saunders had three homes in England and Switzerland and enjoyed an affluent lifestyle. Not bad for someone who at about the time of his trial was 'unable to recall three numbers backwards'.

Saville, Derek
Disappeared without trace, December 1954

Derek Saville, a twenty-three-year-old bus driver, kissed his girlfriend goodnight and vanished on 7 December 1954. He hasn't been seen or heard of since.

It was nearly midnight in the village of Canon Pyon, about seven miles from Hereford, when he left eighteen-year-old Ivy Wood at her home near the village hall. The following day his bicycle was seen propped up against the hall. Police searched ditches, woods, and streams, but found nothing.

Ivy said, a day or so later, 'I'm sure some harm has come to Derek. He was so level-headed and well-liked. The night he disappeared he called for me at 8.30 and we had a couple of drinks at the Plough Inn. Just before midnight he said, "I have to be up early, so I'll say goodnight." We kissed and he said we'd meet again next day. He was happy the whole evening. He had nothing on his mind, no money troubles. In fact, he was due to pick up his wages the next day, and also £10 that he had saved in the village thrift club during the year.'

But the previous October of 1953, Derek had been attacked by a mystery man; he'd been on his way home and turned round just as a man was about to strike him; the man ran off. Some time later, a bus inspector wearing a uniform like Derek's was attacked on the village common.

Derek's landlady, fifty-year-old Miss Ethel Thomas, said, 'He had a good breakfast last Tuesday, and when he left said he intended to visit his mother in Gloucester.'

Soon hundreds of soldiers and airmen joined the search. Police were aware it could become a murder hunt. Detective Inspector Reginald Weaver, head of Herefordshire CID, was quoted to have said, 'Do not exclude the possibility that this man may have been the victim of foul play.'

The village had a population of around 600 at the time, and Derek only lived just under a mile away from Ivy, with whom he'd been going out with for about three months. In the pub, he was a popular figure and a valued member of the darts team. At first, Ivy thought he'd been called into work for a different shift, but as time passed she thought he might have lost his memory some way or another and wandered off. But she knew he'd soon come to light somewhere. She observed, 'It doesn't look as though he has gone willingly.'

He was a frequent visitor to his mum, who lived in Dymock, in Gloucestershire, but he wouldn't have just taken off without a word. The police increased the scope of their search over the countryside towards the Welsh border.

Eighteen-year-old local lad Edward Williams had been friendly with Ivy, though it hadn't come to anything – she went her way, with Derek, and he went his. There were no hard feelings, but he felt the entire village were considering him a likely candidate to answer the question of the whereabouts of Derek Saville. However, the police soon realised that Edward didn't know the answer; he'd been at home with his parents in nearby Tillington.

There had been a few incidents were Canon Pyon's residents saw a strange man late at night, and the police had started to think they had a murder enquiry on their hands. They tracked down all the former lady friends of Derek's but again drew a blank. By Christmas week he'd been missing for a fortnight and the local CID now definitely considered the matter a murder enquiry – they were convinced it had something to do with his love-life. 'This was murder, we now feel sure,' said DI Weaver. The search continued along the local Wye and Lugg rivers.

One has to ask if, when the police tracked his lady friends down, they missed someone from the list. Perhaps it had been a married lady? Most of the girls said Derek was irresistible. DI Weaver also suggested a young man who had less success with women – these days, one can ask the relevant question outright.

Scotland Yard were to be called in if a body was found.

Come the new year of 1955, and still there was no news. The village darts team, with Ivy's father, Reginald, led one search team and Alfred Probert, the captain, led another.

A private detective was hired who thought he had the answers, and vital new evidence was brought forward about two men seen in a car on the road from which Derek was thought to have disappeared – this sighting was on the night of his disappearance. A shallow 'grave' had been found, but was empty – the private detective thought this grave was only temporary. He sent a ten-page dossier to Scotland Yard who didn't feel it took the enquiry anywhere.

The August after Derek vanished, some woodland was dug up, but again no clue was found, though the information from a lady who saw two men carrying something large near the wood on the night of the disappearance had seemed worth following up.

Years passed, and even though the case was never closed, activity declined. Early in the new millennium, a man came forward. He lived in Perth in Australia and said he knew of some digging at the time in Canon Pyon; he hadn't come forward for fear from the men who were digging, one of whom was thought to be his own father. Despite much activity, no clue was found as to the fate of Derek Saville.

Seston, Jackie
Murdered by person unknown

The weather was bitterly cold on 2 October 1973, and bitterly cold weather can have the most unusual effect on things. Upon arriving at about 2 p.m. at his girlfriend's house, Albert Taylor had a huge shock; his girlfriend's sister had been stabbed – the sight of the blood upset him and he left the house. This made the police suspicious, as did the fact that when he got to the house the dog hadn't made a sound – a dog he was friendly with. So the police built up the case that Albert had gone to the house and found Jackie alone; he had decided to rape her. She resisted, so he stabbed her to death.

It was crucial he had an alibi for the time of death, and he said he didn't get to the house until 2 p.m. and he'd been on Peterborough Station at 1.15 p.m. He was sure of this because he'd looked up at the clock and it had shown the time – he thought the clock had an odd 'tick', and it stuck in his mind.

The police were far from convinced, and the jury at Leicester Crown Court were told that it was an electric clock and made no ticking sound at all. They found him guilty, and off he went to start his life sentence.

He wasn't prepared to accept that the court didn't believe him, and he 'bombarded' the Home Office with complaints that he did hear the clock tick. Eventually, his case arrived at Justice, which, in the days before the Criminal Cases Review Commission, took up cases where they thought there'd been a problem with a conviction.

The Home Office therefore asked for an independent police investigation, and this fell to Detective Chief Superintendent Peter

Crust of Essex CID. DCS Crust may be forgiven for thinking Albert's alibi was bizarre, but he applied what he called 'good old-fashioned detective work'. And he was thorough; he decided he should find that clock and examine it. However, in the interim, the station at Peterborough had gone through a bit of a facelift and the clock was gone – but DCS Crust found it. Did it make a noise? According to reports, he didn't at first think so. But it wasn't 2 October, and it wasn't bitterly cold.

DCS Crust spoke to a maintenance engineer who worked at Peterborough station. Mr William Brennan said, 'That old clock was always giving us bother. It used to make a terrible clicking sound.'

And this was worse the colder the weather became. DCS Crust took the clock to the manufacturer, who tested it and confirmed the clock did make a clicking sound in cold weather.

Albert Taylor was therefore to hear Lord Lawton at the Court of Appeal quash his conviction for Jackie's murder, saying there was a 'lurking doubt'.

So after five years, he was out, and a free man. He said he hadn't heard from his former girlfriend, who'd subsequently married, and thought it would be 'unfair' to contact the family.

Jackie Seston's murder remains unsolved.

Sheffield Pub Massacre

Michael McFarlane, Thomas Owen, George Morris; murdered by Mohammad Ishmail

It was on New Year's Day 1960 that the jolly sing-song at the East House pub in Sheffield was disturbed by a series of gunshots. Three men were killed and two injured, and it transpired that the killer wanted to die but his religion forbade suicide. His rationale therefore was to commit murder and be hanged. It didn't quite work out that way.

Mohammed Ishmail was a thirty-year-old whose history prior to the shooting is sketchy. All I could dig out was that he was an unemployed labourer. He originally hailed from Somalia.

It was twenty-one-year-old Michael McFarlane, twenty-nine-year-old Thomas Owen and thirty-two-year-old George 'Fred' Morris who took the fatal shots, but two other men were wounded, one seriously enough to put him in a coma for a while and a wheelchair for life; the other victim caught a bullet in the wrist. I have read that Mr Ishmail opened fire indiscriminately, but would he have hit five different people, or would some of the bullets have gone into furniture, masonry and the like? He was diagnosed with schizophrenia and had suffered from paranoia. While this isn't uncommon, it's very uncommon for someone to let go with a fire arm. I have written of another similar case in London in 1913, and although there may be others, it might show how rare this sort of tragedy is.

Mr Ishmail was found unfit to plead at trial and therefore was sent to Broadmoor, but it wouldn't have been at her Majesty's Pleasure. It would have been under the Mental Health Act, which had just been introduced (it 'repealed', or replaced, others) in 1959, and the difference between this and subsequent Acts was that under this Act a patient could, under exceptional circumstances, be held indefinitely.

Mr Ishmail was a Muslim, a religion that forbids suicide, but it also forbids murder, so this, again, shows how disordered his thoughts were. It's unlikely he was discharged from Broadmoor after twenty-two months, but more likely he was discharged from his section (of Mental Health Act) purely for deportation purposes. It is unlikely he'd be deemed to be no longer a threat. It would be almost certain that, even if his psychosis was under control, defaulting on medication would soon have him disturbed again.

This seems to have happened, because a while later he shot at a judge in a court in Somalia, and after a few years in jail went on a shooting rampage again, taking lives in the process. He was gunned down himself in this later event.

Shipman, Frederick Harold

Numerous murders

On 13 January 2004, the most evil Englishman God ever put breath into was pronounced dead in Wakefield, in Yorkshire. I expect, and would hope, he was grieved by his family, but his passing wasn't grieved by many. One question I still ask is whether he hanged himself or whether person, or persons, unknown got into his cell. The 'powers that be' will always say it was suicide. His name was Frederick Harold Shipman.

Most of us have got some sort of stereotypical idea of what a murderer looks like, and we're proved wrong time after time. However, even the police and Dr Shipman's peers thought that a doctor couldn't possibly be behind 'unnecessary deaths'. He's been listed together with Dr John Bodkin Adams, but I think, of the two, it was Dr Shipman who murdered for either pleasure or to satisfy some desire for ultimate power.

Life started off quite well for him, and his intelligence showed he was an above-average pupil, but at seventeen his mother died and this was mooted as being part of the reason his life went the way it did. He went to Leeds University and although his girlfriend Primrose fell pregnant, her parents were apparently quite understanding. Primrose and Fred (as he was called) later married and had more children.

In the mid-seventies, his career as a doctor was progressing, though he got himself into difficulty with a drug called pethidine, which was addictive. He forged prescriptions and was asked to leave his job as a GP in Todmorden. He seemed to overcome the problem. By the late 1970s, he'd established himself in practice in Hyde, Greater Manchester, and by the early 1990s he had set up on his own – his practice attracted many patients.

One of these was Kathleen Grundy, and when she died suddenly and her daughter found a dubious will in favour of Dr Shipman, the process started. On 7 September 1998, he was arrested for Mrs Grundy's murder. The can of worms exploded.

He denied everything, even treating the police investigation as a bit of a game – a competition – but they are too world-wary for that. It was soon found that some of his fellow GPs in Hyde were uncomfortable with the sheer number of deaths of patients on his surgery list. Local undertaking firms were equally as puzzled.

He was convicted of fifteen murders, but his total may have been over 200.

Silverman, Sydney, MP
Solicitor and politician

Sydney Silverman was born in Liverpool in 1895 and educated at Liverpool University. He went to Finland, where he lectured in English, and on his return trained as a solicitor, again at Liverpool University. He sat on various Liverpool Committees before he became a Labour politician for Nelson and Colne. He was a vociferous opponent of capital punishment and was probably the most influential politician to seek its abolition.

He was a pacifist by nature, and opposed war – he only reluctantly supported Britain's entry to the war in 1939, and it was opposition to the rife anti-Semitism in Europe that seemed to be his driving force. In the Great War, he was imprisoned for his conscientious objection to military service.

He entered local politics in 1932 in Liverpool, and unsuccessfully ran as MP before he was elected as the Member for Colne and Nelson (Lancashire) in 1935. He was to hold this seat until his death in 1968.

Although he wasn't ever appointed to cabinet, his influence was wide. He was a founding member of the Campaign for Nuclear Disarmament and had earlier opposed Germany's rearmament. He also worked hard with the unemployed. His main victory, however, was in the abolition of capital punishment.

He wrote widely on the subject of miscarriage of justice in the 1940s and helped highlight the perjury of John Christie in the hanging of Timothy Evans in the late 1940s and 1950s. One detraction was his seeming desire for solo performance; he seldom, if ever, worked in groups.

The House of Lords defeated his private member's bill on the abolition of the death penalty, which had received its third reading in the House of Commons in June 1956. As Mr Silverman had steered the bill through the Commons, he was to say, 'If the Lords reject it I don't think it will alter the opinion of a single MP. The most that can happen will be the possibility of deferring the amendment of the law.'

The 1957 Homicide Act was all but an open farce. It introduced the idea of capital murder, which was either where a gun was used or where a murder was carried out in the furtherance of theft. Under this Act, for murder in the pursuance of robbing a bank with a gun, one would hang – but for murder after rape at knifepoint one wouldn't.

Mr Silverman was an astute man and just sat back while this madness took its course, before he took the Murder (Abolition of Death Penalty) Bill through the House in 1965. This abolished capital punishment for a period of five years, and effectively the punishment was over for good; the bill became law in 1969, after his death.

His death saw another lawyer become an MP in the Nelson and

Colne constituency: Mr David Waddington, who defended Stafan Kiszko on a murder charge. It was a good job they didn't hang Kiszko, as he was eventually cleared of the murder.

Sims, Edwin

The murder of Lillian Edmeades and Malcolm Johnson

Lillian Edmeades and her boyfriend Malcolm Johnson were both sixteen, and attended church regularly. It was in their church that they were last seen alive – after the service they went for a walk.

It was unusual, but not unheard of, for a member of the public to turn up at a newspaper office with a story, and in September 1961 Edwin Sims asked to speak to Tom Tullet at the *Daily Mirror* offices. He said it was a confidential matter, and as soon as Tom was with him he confessed to a murder.

In court, it was claimed that if Mr Sims hadn't confessed to the crime it would have been difficult to detect him, as he'd taken steps to conceal the crime and suspicion wouldn't have been aroused. When he went to Tom Tullet, he said, 'I have killed a man and a woman – teenagers, I think.'

To support his story, Mr Sims had brought a ladies and gentleman's watch. He'd mutilated the girl, and now also produced her severed breasts, which were wrapped in paper. Mr Tullet immediately sent for the police and the search for the victims was quickly underway.

The crime happened near Gravesend, in Kent, in an area known as the Dinton Marshes. He'd attacked the youngsters as they walked together, tied them up and strangled them; he was also in possession of a shotgun. Tristram Beresford QC, prosecuting, told the court that he'd stripped the bodies and put them both in a dyke.

In court, Mr Sims pleaded not guilty to 'murder in the course or furtherance of theft', which in 1961 still carried the death penalty, and the all-male jury soon returned a verdict of guilty to manslaughter on the grounds of diminished responsibility.

He was given a sentence of twenty-one years by Mr Justice Finnemore, who described the crime as a 'wicked, cruel and ruthless killing of two innocent young people'.

It was claimed Mr Sims was a 'grossly perverted sexual psychopath'. Dr Francis Brisby, medical officer at Brixton Prison, explained that sex had moved away from being a morbid fantasy and had developed into a pathological obsession. Mr Sims underwent treatment at Broadmoor Special Hospital.

Spilsbury, Sir Bernard Henry
The Father of Pathology

Bernard Spilsbury was one of four children, and he had four children himself – three sons and a daughter. Two of his sons died: Peter in the blitz, and Alan just after the war. It was suggested the demise of his sons was a deciding factor in his decision to end his life with gas at his laboratory in 1947.

He's been criticised more and more as the years have passed, but he was one of the leading pathologists of his day. Mr Spilsbury became qualified in medicine in 1905, and later that year started as an assistant pathologist, but it was the case of Crippen in 1910 that gave him a reputation that may have been too big. In a path lab, everything depends on skill and knowledge, in a witness box it depends on how persuasive evidence is given.

He did make a huge contribution to the development of pathology as a science. His observations in the Brides in the Bath case convicted a murderer (George Joseph Smith), and he discovered that a solicitor in Herefordshire (Herbert Rowse Armstrong) seemed to be distributing arsenic in chocolates. He also maintained that Tony Mancini was guilty after his acquittal, and finally, Mr Mancini admitted he was. In 1930, a hosiery salesman with a high sex drive had a string of women and risked a string of child maintenance orders; he bumped off a complete stranger and set fire to his own car – the good pathologist could tell the court how the victim died and that it wasn't one hosiery salesman, who had been faking his own suicide, and that led to a conviction.

By the mid-1920s, forensic pathology was well established, and Dr Bernard Spilsbury was knighted in 1923.

The question for historians now is whether he wanted celebrity status or just to be a good pathologist. His 'invincibility' in court gave some concern to lawyers and he could be dogmatic.

It's worrying that he always insisted on working alone, but it's only in more recent times that openness has been an issue. A refusal to work with students was a failing, but he did lecture and his input to training, therefore, is sound – but what of the budding pathologists who wanted to work with someone of Sir Bernard's reputation?

Another problem was his inflexibility, and therefore questions have to be raised as to his objectivity. However, none of the cases he was involved in have been shown to be a miscarriage of justice, though there are some loud questions. In the fullness of time, more will be said of Sir Bernard, but in some cases there can be no doubt.

Spriggs, John

Sentenced to death for the murder of Harold Cunningham in 1957.

It's sometimes difficult to understand what makes people do what they do. Halfway through November 1957, a pub customer got into an argument over a pub tap clip. So much did this escalate that the man was asked to leave the pub, although it was getting on for closing time. Most people, after a moment's reflection, would put the matter behind them, perhaps with a little embarrassment. The pub worker was a chap called Harold Cunningham, who was forty-two and married to Nellie; they had six children. The customer – and there were no reports of excessive drinking – was one John Spriggs, who was twenty-nine, married to June, with four children. Mr Spriggs was a factory worker who'd been in the RAF for his national service, though he was discharged for being 'abnormal'.

At about 10.40 p.m., three shots went out of Mr Spriggs' gun and into Harold Cunningham's body; by the time Nellie could get to him, he was dead. The murder took place in the College Arms Hotel in Erdington, which is in the northern half of Birmingham, and it would have taken Mr Spriggs about fifteen minutes to walk to his home, pick up the gun and return to the pub. He left the pub still carrying the gun and at 10.45 p.m., the police were at the scene of the crime – they cordoned off two square miles and the description was quite good: 'gunman is aged twenty-five to thirty, 5' 9". tall, slim, sallow round face, dark brown hair. He sported a blue double-breasted blazer with light grey trousers which were creased. He had a light coloured shirt and tie. He had black shoes and was flat-footed.' Not surprisingly, he was described as 'dangerous'; the gun was a revolver so might have had three more bullets.

Road blocks were set up covering all roads leading out of the Erdington area, and tracker dogs were sent to the pub to try to pick up the scent. Not too far away was Sutton Park, where the police thought he might try to hide out.

About twelve hours later, June Spriggs sent out for brandy, as her husband seemed to have fallen into a desperate illness. Their friend went to the College Arms Pub, where CID officers were interviewing potential witnesses, and only a few minutes later armed police and detectives rushed to the house in Brackenbury Road, where they found the man and he was taken to hospital. Mr

Spriggs was now more or less in custody, and when he recovered he was charged with murder. His illness was the result of a large overdose of drugs.

In only six weeks the trial had taken place. Mr Spriggs was found guilty of Harold's murder and sentenced to death. Had he stabbed Harold, the new Homicide Act would have given him a life sentence. As it was, he was to be the first man sentenced under the new Act to be given a reprieve, as there was some anxiety as to his mental health. It was at the end of January that news from the Home Office reached the prison, and the governor gave June Spriggs an extra visit so they could share the news.

It was a supervised visit, and Mr Spriggs was in the prison hospital. He would have recovered from the overdose by now as that had been well over two months ago. One has to assume it was his mental health the staff were looking after. June hugged him and said, 'Darling, I shall be waiting for you, no matter how long it is.'

More detail of the crime was reported. Apparently, Mr Spriggs had removed the clip from the beer pump handle and Harold Cunningham had taken it from him and told him to leave. At the trial, it was felt that Mr Justice Jones had misdirected the jury as to the definition of 'abnormality of mind' and 'mental responsibility', but this had initially been rejected. The Home Office took the case up and a reprieve from the death penalty was given – he was now sentenced to life imprisonment.

June Spriggs later told reporters, 'I had given up hope. Then came this wonderful news – and I was allowed actually to kiss my husband. We were too overcome to discuss the future.'

But the future has a habit of coming, and when Mr Spriggs was released in 1978, nineteen years after the murder, he didn't return to Birmingham but eventually settled in Cardiff. Backtracking four years, June had remarried, so their divorce can be tracked earlier than that.

By now, of course, their children had grown up, but life did settle a bit again and he met and formed a relationship with a divorcee of similar age. They'd met soon after his release. In the autumn of 1984, his new partner was battered to death with a steam iron. John Spriggs took a huge overdose of painkillers, and died upstairs in the bedroom.

Stonehouse, John MP
Conspiracy, fraud, theft and forgery

John Stonehouse was a Labour MP for Walsall, in the West Midlands, and in November 1974 the news broke that he'd drowned, as his clothing was found on a beach in Miami and there was no sign of him. However, things were not quite as they seemed.

He was born in Southampton in 1925 and educated at the then all-boys Taunton College in Southampton, and later at the London School of Economics. Mr Stonehouse entered Parliament in the 1950s and his talent, and therefore his rise, were never in doubt. He became Post-Master General and managed to avoid, with the help of Prime Minister Harold Wilson, any serious allegations that he was a spy for one of the Eastern Bloc nations. But who knows.

In those days a lot of leeway was given to MPs and their business interests, and for that matter, the status of those businesses. It must have raised eyebrows when it was claimed that the Mafia were involved in his disappearance. When official papers were declassified under the Freedom of Information Act, it would appear some parts of what had been claimed about his activities were true.

Going back to his disappearance, little attention was paid as to whether he was a spy or not, but there were some questions about some of the accounts with charities he was involved with. This was all rumour, to begin with, but as the questions got a bit louder then he may well have considered his options. An obituary was actually published even though his (dead) body hadn't been found.

He was found alive and apparently quite well on Christmas Eve, 1974, in Australia. The police thought he was Lord Lucan. He'd taken an assumed name of Mr Markham, and he was in the company of his secretary, Sheila Buckley. It took a while, but eventually he was returned to the UK, where he faced over twenty criminal charges for conspiracy, fraud, theft and forgery; Ms Buckley faced lesser charges.

His reception committee rushed him straight off to Brixton Prison. As he was still alive and there hadn't been a by-election, he was still an MP, so he made an appearance at the House of Commons after he'd been granted bail.

Finally, he came to trial and was convicted: he was sentenced to seven years imprisonment and Ms Buckley received a suspended sentence, as Mr Justice Eveleigh felt Mr Stonehouse was the master planner.

He was released on parole in August 1979 after three years of HM Blundeston, but later, Sheila said the toll on his health was considerable. Barbara Stonehouse had divorced him, so when he came home he and Sheila married – they later had a son.

Ms Buckley returned to her job as a secretary and Mr Stonehouse wrote a couple of novels. He died aged sixty-four in 1988.

Straffen, John
Murder of Brenda Goddard, Cecily Batstone, and Linda Bowyer

John Thomas Straffen was born in Borden in Hampshire, and he was to become the longest-serving prisoner when, at his death in November 2007, he'd clocked up fifty-five years. He strangled two girls in Bath in August 1951, for which he was found 'unfit to plead', and was detained at Broadmoor. But from there he escaped and while out, he strangled another little girl. He was sentenced to death, but the Home Secretary, David Maxwell-Fyfe, suggested to the new Queen Elizabeth II that his sentence should be commuted to life imprisonment.

He wasn't returned to Broadmoor – as he'd escaped it, it was deemed not secure enough to hold him, so he spent fifty-odd years in different prisons.

His father had been in the army, so the family had travelled widely. He had encephalitis in India when he was a six-year-old, which affected his mental development, and, when assessed (he had many assessments in his life) at age twenty-one, his mental age was ten.

Mr Straffen was said to have an intense dislike of the police and he seemed to make a bizarre link of the police to the murder of little girls. I understand Mr Straffen rationalised it as an annoyance to the police when he murdered a little girl, though this must be considered a gross over-simplification. It's sometimes difficult to understand the behaviour, good or bad, of someone with this level of learning disability, and there are times they might form an idea which cannot be reasoned out. This is really quite different to delusional or paranoid states as they are often temporary and can be treated. Management of someone who has the belief that the police are annoyed in this way isn't easy, and assessing their dangerousness presents difficulties.

In the late 1960s, secure units within prisons were developed and Mr Straffen was one of the first prisoners to go to Parkhurst on the Isle of Wight. But, to give some measure of how difficult he was to place for his own rehabilitation and to protect the public, the next six prisoners were thieves and not child killers. With his arrested development, Mr Straffen was a placement problem for the authorities.

It's common to find many reports of other inmates and their violence targeted to child killers and rapists, but it's rare to find any reports of violence towards Mr Straffen, so it may be that the prison population might have a better understanding of some things than others. No Home Secretary would release him, but if his feelings of hatred for the police and his thought that he'd kill children to annoy them persisted then his level of dangerousness would always be high. Therefore, one has to conclude it would have been dangerous to allow him the freedom. It's all very well to make the argument that whole life tariffs are not desirable, but the case of John Straffen is an argument in their favour.

The story of five-year-old Brenda Goddard, nine-year-old Cicely Batstone and five-year-old Linda Goddard is a great tragedy, a tragedy one hopes will never repeat itself.

Britain's longest-serving prisoner died after fifty-five years of incarceration on 19 November 2007.

Sutcliffe, Peter William
The Yorkshire Ripper

There are a couple of suggested reasons why Peter Sutcliffe started his reign of terror. Either he was cheated by a prostitute or he was hearing the voice of God, telling him to murder prostitutes. The latter reason suggests a severe mental illness, but the illness itself is quite common and violence is rare. It's more likely we'll never know his real reasons, and in this short piece I don't intend to explore them.

He was born in June 1946 and grew up in the West Riding of Yorkshire; he eventually became a lorry driver, got married and lived with his wife in Bradford.

Ms Wilma McCann was thought to be his first victim, in 1975, but by that time he was twenty-nine – one has to ask if he was violent before this. It has been asserted that the police were aware of him since 1969, so perhaps he was active earlier than first thought.

I don't suggest anything, but Mr Sutcliffe might have changed his methods. Some people wish to 'disappear'; for example, a girl disappears from Town A, with or without some kind of substance problem – she goes to London and then to Town B, in Yorkshire – she is murdered and then buried. Who's to say that any of the girls reported missing in the early seventies didn't meet their end in this way, and still occupy 'graves'. In fact, there were a couple of reports where he'd attacked a prostitute in Bradford with a baton of some description, and he was arrested in a red-light district carrying a hammer – he was charged with being 'equipped for stealing'. Subsequently, a number of people's deaths have been linked to him.

It was from 1975 that his activities made the headlines – thirteen women were killed. At least two, if not more, were not involved in prostitution. He was also to attempt to kill seven other women. The major Yorkshire towns became 'no-go' areas for women of all ages and fear was strong. He was called a number of things, and the old-fashioned word 'evil' was one of them.

In January 1981 he was driving a car with false number plates and arrested. He confessed to being the man shortly after. At his trial, he was convicted of thirteen murders and seven attempted murders. His tariff on life sentence was thirty years, but it's very doubtful that he'll ever be released.

Thirkettle, George
The Murder of Florence Collins

London was enjoying a bit of a heat-wave in July 1904. Twenty-year-old Florence Collins had recently broken off her engagement, so she wanted to enjoy life, dress, go to the theatre and enjoy her freedom. She'd been engaged to Mr George Thirkettle for four years.

Florence lived with her mother, father and two lodgers in Ridley Street, Dalston. It was here that Mr Thirkettle murdered her.

A report from the Coroners Court quoted her mother, saying he was jealous, possessive and frightening. About eighteen months before the murder he'd struck her son, Frederick. There was another incident when Mr Thirkettle had taken Florence by the throat and threatened her, and on another occasion he'd threatened her life.

On 27 July, a coroner's jury returned a verdict of wilful murder against George Thirkettle, which wasn't uncommon in those days.

At the time of the murder, he'd cut his own throat. He was soon in the German Hospital in Dalston, and the police started piecing together events of the night.

Florence had written to him to say she didn't wish to see him anymore, and though he went to her house on two occasions, she refused to have anything to do with him. She later told him there was pressure from her parents; they'd told him not to come to their house.

The investigation soon recreated the events of the night of the murder. In the early hours, when the family were all in bed, Mrs Collins heard the sound of breaking glass at the back of the house. Florence slept alone, but adjacent to her bedroom was a Mr William Tregonning, a lodger. He'd heard what he described as a 'crash of glass', and then a few seconds later the sound of footsteps on the stairs. Mr Tregonning opened his door just as Florence's was closed – he said he heard it being 'shut and locked'. Soon after, he heard screams of 'Mother! Mother!' and knew something was very wrong. Without wasting a second, he left his room and passed Mrs Collins coming up the stairs.

Mrs Collins' description of the night was more-or-less the same, but she did scream out when she'd heard the sound of glass breaking and footsteps, 'Who's that! Who's that!'

She was alert, so when she heard her daughter cry out for her, she went straight up the stairs to her room. But it was locked, and soon she heard her daughter scream, 'Murder!'

Police Constables George Rouse and Rufus Haywood were

soon present, and when they discovered Florence's door locked the didn't hesitate to break it down. The room was in darkness but by the light of a constable's lantern Florence was seen standing near the door: blood was pouring from a wound in her neck and had soaked her nightdress. Her death was timed at about 2.30 a.m.

Police Inspector Henry Grove and Police Sergeant Edwin Sly came to the house with Mr Tregonning, and with the two PCs they just about controlled Mr Thirkettle. He'd been standing at the foot of the bed and had a cut to his throat from which blood was pouring.

Dr Bernard Goiten attended, and could confirm that the wound on Florence's neck, which was about four inches long and about one inch deep, had led her to bleed to death. The wound wasn't self-inflicted.

Mr Thirkettle, who was bleeding from the cut in his throat, was then taken to the German Hospital. On the way to hospital he said he just wanted to live long enough to repent his sins.

He'd entered the house through the kitchen window, which he'd broken. His coat, hat and boots were found in an outbuilding.

It seemed an open and closed case. Florence hadn't wanted to give him up, but his behaviour had become more and more erratic and eventually she had to finish the relationship. This may have caused bitter resentment and she did fear what he'd do; he'd threatened violence in the past.

Mr Thirkettle's sister said they'd been quite close. She told the court of her brother being away with the army and how he'd been wounded fighting in Africa. He'd also suffered from a fever. Since his return to England he'd become a blacksmith, and his work record seemed okay.

Interestingly, she explained that Florence Collins had come to see her when Mr Thirkettle had been in the house – they were told it was the pressures at home that were the main reason for her decision. They arranged to meet later that day, but Florence's father came instead.

She later described her brother as 'fretting', and he'd told her that it was the break-up of the engagement that had upset him. As he talked, he became distressed, and he decided he'd go for a walk, though she thought he'd be better off in bed.

She did add that since he'd come back from Africa he was 'strange', but didn't elaborate on this. She also thought there seemed to be some parental disapproval.

On remand in Brixton Prison, Mr Thirkettle was assessed by Dr James Scott, who could see no sign of insanity; therefore, he was fit to plead.

George Thirkettle was found guilty of murder and sentenced to death.

In hospital, his progress to recovery from the wound in his neck was slow, and it was felt by the executioner that the wound might break open if he was hanged. As a result of this, he was reprieved.

Waddington, Yolande
Murdered by David Burgess

The pub where Yolande was last seen alive is still there and would rather not be reminded of the events – pubs are places for socialising and merriment, and today it is a good eating house. Nevertheless, when Yolande left there on Friday evening, 28 October 1966, she was only seen alive by one more person. In the summer of 2012, David Burgess was given a life sentence with a minimum of twenty-seven years for her murder.

In April 1967, as nine-year-olds, Jeanette Wigmore and Jacqueline Williams went off on their bicycles to look for primroses. Their friend Janice asked one of the girls' sisters to stay and play with her, and that saved her from the clutches of a child killer, because David Burgess was convicted in July 1967 of Jeanette and Jacqueline's murders.

At trial Mr Burgess tried to make out that another local lad, whom he only knew as 'Mac', had carried out the murders – he hadn't seen him, but had seen him running off. He had to explain, though, how a speck of blood from a rare blood group – which wasn't his own – had got on his boot. Jeanette Wigmore had been stabbed to death, so blood would have dripped from the wound. Mr Burgess said he'd approached her body and lifted it up after he'd seen 'Mac' running off. The problem was that 'Mac' couldn't be traced; no one in the village of Beenham, in Berkshire, where the tragedies unfolded, knew 'Mac'.

He didn't please the jury with his callous attitude, and with the forensic evidence it only took just over two hours to convict. David Burgess was given two life sentences and the following year, in Durham Prison, he confessed to Yolande's murder to prison officers but denied it to police, taunting them to find proof.

The two girls' families moved away from Beenham, and so did Mr Burgess's family. All three were well-established before the tragedy struck. Years later, as police kept Yolande's file open, one of the villagers remarked, 'My late husband knew him and said he was horrible, even at school … he used to pull the wings off insects.' He also had a glass eye following an air-gun accident, which added to his look of menace.

In 1995, he absconded from an open prison and one of the girls' fathers said it was a scandal – not the only one in that institution. Mr Burgess didn't do himself any favours, though, as parole might have been on the agenda.

Forensic science had progressed, and he found himself charged with Yolande's murder; he stood trial forty–five years after the crime. His attitude in court was nonchalant and he seemed bored, as one reporter put it. He was found guilty.

David Burgess was nineteen when he was sent to prison in 1967. His further conviction in 2012 means he can apply for parole in 2039, when he'll be ninety-two.

Wallace, Julia
The Man from the Pru

William Wallace was much travelled by the time he settled down to married life with Julia, whom he'd married in March 1914. Some sources say she was a good bit older than him, but they were said to be very happy together. Julia was a Yorkshire lass, and when William's job in Harrogate finished they moved to Liverpool, where his father helped him secure a position as a collecting agent with the Prudential Assurance Company.

They settled in Wolverton Street in the Anfield district, and were reasonably affluent, though he found the job dull. He did some part-time teaching and took up the violin so that he could accompany Julia, who was an accomplished pianist. William was also keen on botany and was a committed chess player.

On Monday 19 January 1931, he was at the Liverpool Central Chess Club, where he was to play that evening. However, before his arrival a telephone call had been made to the club, inviting him to visit a Mr R. M. Qualtrough at 27 Menlove Gardens East the following evening, regarding some insurance.

The following evening, he set off and crossed Liverpool by tram. But he couldn't find Menlove Gardens East. Nor could he discover if Mr Qualtrough lived at Menlove Gardens North, South or West. He returned home, but he'd spent three quarters of an hour looking.

As he neared his house his neighbours said they hadn't been able to get into his house, but he got in easily enough and found Julia battered to death in the sitting room.

When the police started to investigate, they found it hard to believe his story about this mysterious customer and he was arrested. He protested his innocence and the evidence was circumstantial. Nevertheless, he was charged with murder and was put on trial at Liverpool Assizes.

When someone is battered to death, blood and tissue will fly everywhere, but this didn't seem to be an issue at his trial – or rather, the lack of it on his clothing didn't. He was convicted and sentenced to death.

Luckily, the Court of Criminal Appeal quashed the conviction as the verdict was 'not supported by the weight of the evidence'. In other words, the jury had got it wrong!

William Wallace went back to his job in insurance, but left the house they'd shared as gossip made life uncomfortable; there were even threats made against him. He took a job at head office and moved to Bromborough.

However, his health deteriorated – he had a kidney removed some years before he died in 1933.

The murder of Julia Wallace remains unsolved.

Ward, Stephen
Not a criminal ...

Stephen Ward was the son of Arthur and Eileen, a vicar and his wife, and was born in Hertfordshire in 1912. At school, he wasn't a particularly distinguished scholar but ambled through, and after a few dead-end jobs his mother convinced him to travel across to America, where he could train as an osteopath. He loved America, but returned and set up practice in Devon, where his father had been moved to. In the war he was with the Royal Armoured Corps, based at Bovington, in Dorset.

Stephen was also a skilled portrait artist, and with the two skills – osteopathy and art – he went to London. His practice took off in popularity, and many people high on the social ladder became clients; he also sketched many of them. As a result, his social status also climbed and with the coming of the late 1950s and early 1960s he was a regular attendee at parties and functions of the wealthy.

He was also a close friend of Lord Astor, the conservative politician, whom he'd successfully treated; accordingly he was given access to a rather comfortable lodge on Lord Astor's estate. At his mews flat in London, he'd often hold parties where some very attractive ladies would make themselves known. One of them was a special friend whom he took to Lord Astor's estate at Clivedon, Buckinghamshire, where she met another conservative politician and had a brief relationship with him – her name was Christine Keeler, and the politician was John (Jack) Profumo.

The problem was two-fold. Firstly, Jack was a married man whose political career could come crashing down with a sex scandal, and secondly, Christine was also having a bit of a fling with a Russian Naval Attaché. Christine's close friend Mandy Rice-Davies may or may not have been having a fling with Lord Astor, although he denied it – well, he would deny it, wouldn't he?

The political time-bomb went off, and Jack Profumo resigned as an MP and member of the cabinet. Harold Macmillan's government had never had it so bad. The Home Secretary, Henry Brooke, who had the most amazing track record for blunders, roped in MI5, Scotland Yard and God knows who else to find a scapegoat. It fell to Chief Inspector Samuel Herbert and Detective Sergeant John Burrows to find some dirt. Normally, a crime is committed, discovered, reported and investigated. Here, a crime was assumed, but not actually committed, and through some wrangling got into court.

It was decided that Christine Keeler was a prostitute, because Jack Profumo had given her a gift. She then gave Stephen £20 or so towards his phone bill – she'd been staying in the flat rent free. £20 for a phone bill is *not* living off immoral earnings – but a very twisted trial said it was. It would certainly have been questioned on appeal.

In their 'investigation', the detectives had acted in a way to destroy Stephen's practice – his wealthy and influential friends deserted him. He took an overdose of barbiturates and died.

The whole story of Stephen Ward must go down as one of the most obscene chapters in British History.

West (*née* Letts), Rosemary and Fred West
Serial killers

Cromwell Street in Gloucester has become synonymous with Fred and Rose West, who, between them, murdered at least ten young women; this may well have been just the tip of the iceberg. Their victims were often dismembered, and often a finger or toe was missing.

It was also likely that Fred murdered at Much Marcle, where he grew up, and Rose murdered at their former address in Midland Road. Solo killings were about even – Fred murdered both his first wife and Anna, a former lover; Rose killed Fred's step-daughter, Charmaine, explaining to a neighbour she'd gone to live with her mother.

It was a sick joke that finally put the police on to Mr and Mrs West. Heather Ann, who was born to the Wests in 1970, disappeared, and often their other children would joke about the patio. When the police finally turned the place over, they found ten bodies.

Rosemary Letts was born on 29 November 1953 in Devon. Her home life was far from satisfactory. When her mother was pregnant with her she went through a course of electro-convulsive therapy, and while this was unlikely to have harmed the pregnancy, the anaesthetic might have done so; the risks were quite high.

Rose grew up and achieved little at school. Her father was having regular sexual intercourse with her; her own sexual appetite was ferocious and she grew to prefer older men. Her mother left the marital home, mainly because of Mr Letts' violence, but did return – things were as turbulent as ever.

When Rose met Fred, her father actually disapproved of the

relationship, but no sooner had he voiced his disapproval than Rose fell pregnant with Heather, who was born in October 1970. Rose had only been fifteen when they met; when she was sixteen, she and Fred moved in together in a caravan before moving on to Midland Road.

From here, Fred went to prison for a while, which was when Charmaine 'disappeared', though it's been suggested she waited for Fred to come home before they buried the girl's body. It's possible that this wait was for Fred to remove some fingers and toes. Her natural mother, Rena (who had moved back to Scotland), came looking for Charmaine and was strangled for her trouble – she had fingers and toes removed too.

In January 1972, Fred and Rose married; Mae was born in June of that year. By now, Rose was helping out with their finances working as a prostitute. Fred liked bondage and violent sex with young girls, and so they converted their cellar at their new house in Cromwell Street into a torture chamber. It has been said that the first 'client' was their eight-year-old daughter, Anne-Marie, who was raped by Fred while Rose held her. The threats to keep quiet were, not surprisingly, obeyed.

They met the stunningly beautiful seventeen-year-old Caroline Owens in 1972, and she agreed to move into Cromwell Street as a nanny. She was tied up and raped repeatedly, told that if she were to breathe a word she'd be murdered and buried in the cellar. She got away and reported them to the police, but Fred got off with only a fine – the main charges weren't pursued.

Stephen West was born in August 1973, and four more children were born in the next ten years. Fred was father of some, but not all.

People often disappear, but they usually turn up. Longer disappearances are unusual, but not unheard of. Lynda Gough, Lucy Partington, Juanita Mott, Therese Siegenthaler, Alison Chambers, Shirley Robinson and fifteen-year-old Carol Ann Cooper and Shirley Hubbard all vanished. They were all found in Cromwell

Street, bricked up in the cellar or buried in the garden. Most were dismembered, with fingers or toes missing.

Fred West was supposedly obsessed with sex, needing it several times a day. Anne-Marie left Cromwell Street to live with her boyfriend, so Fred moved on to Heather – she resisted and discussed things with her friend. This sealed her fate, and she finished up dismembered; Fred built a patio where her body was buried. Fred and Rose put out the story that she was a lesbian and had moved out of home.

Finally the police moved in and started to dig around the back garden and in the cellar. The warrant to search had been obtained after Detective Constable Hazel Savage had reported back to her fellow officers what had been said of Heathers disappearance. Professor Bernard Knight was on site, and could tell officers when a second femur was found that there was more than one body. Orthodontic Professor David Whittaker provided almost miraculous identifications.

Detective Superintendent John Bennett led the investigation. Fred West was charged with twelve counts of murder, but hanged himself while on remand at Winson Green Prison in Birmingham.

Rose West went on trial at Winchester Crown Court on 3 October 1995. The jury returned guilty verdicts on ten separate counts of murder on 22 November. She was given a life sentence and is unlikely ever to be released.

The so-called House of Horrors, 25 Cromwell Street, was demolished. A garden and pathway now stand in its place.

White, Lady Alice Jane
Murdered by Henry Jacoby

Nearly 100 years later, the hotel is still in existence and it retains a balcony running the length of the first floor. It was on the door of one of the first-floor rooms that Sarah Pocock knocked to say good morning to a guest. At first, she thought Lady Alice White was wearing a red nightdress, but she'd actually had her head mashed in by a hammer. Amazingly, she was still alive, and so the doctor was called. In fact, one was telephoned and another was summoned. They both thought it would only hasten matters to move her, and so, making her as comfortable as they could, they let nature take its course.

The police attended and Detective Superintendent George Cornish led the enquiry. The first peculiarity was that there was no sign of a forced entry into the room, but another lady (some were long-term residents rather than guests) advised that Lady White often left her door unlocked. However, Alf Platt, who was the night porter, said that no one he either didn't know or know of had entered the hotel. All other possible means of entry were discounted, so DSupt Cornish arrived at the conclusion that the killer was in the hotel.

All staff were closely questioned and it emerged that Henry Jacoby, a pantry boy, hadn't been at the hotel for long. However, he was popular and worked hard; he was eighteen years old.

Late at night, Alf Platt heard his name being called. Mr Jacoby was in the main hall and suggested there was an intruder in the hotel, but they searched the hotel and didn't find anyone. When questioned, Mr Jacoby said he'd been going to the toilet when he'd heard something – but although there was a toilet adjacent to his room, which was to the rear of the building, the toilet he was heading for was towards the front. Mr Jacoby said he didn't know a toilet was that close to his room, but one of the housemaids said she'd seen him looking at her from the toilet.

When he finally admitted the crime, he said he'd gone up a back set of stairs, found Lady White's room unlocked and went in to steal from her. She awoke and screamed, so he hit her with the hammer he was carrying. In court, the jury seemed to believe that he'd gone to Lady White's room, possibly to steal, but had attacked her.

On 7 June 1922 he was hanged at Pentonville prison, despite the jury recommending mercy for such a young man. Thomas Ellis, the hangman, later said how casual Henry had been about the whole thing; he had even thanked the prison governor and his staff for their kindness.

Whybrow, Christopher, QC

The attempted murder of by his wife, Susan, and her lover Dennis Saunders

Fortunately for all concerned, the murder plot failed. But it was bound to hit the headlines because of the prestige of the intended victim: Christopher Whybrow QC was an experienced barrister in London, and his wife wanted to inherit a valuable country house with over ten acres of land – it was worth £400,000 in 1991.

Fifty-year-old Susan Whybrow had taken flying lessons, provided by Mr Dennis Saunders, who was in the process of divorcing his wife. He was four years older than her and they fell madly in love. The solution was to dispose of Mr Whybrow.

Norwich Crown Court heard them enter a plea of not guilty to attempted murder. They admitted kidnapping Mr Whybrow and conspiring to cause him actual bodily harm; Mrs Whybrow said she merely wanted her husband 'duffed up', and there was a vague suggestion of domestic violence, which didn't materialise into any solid allegation.

The event unfolded on 18 October 1989. A few weeks before, Mr Whybrow had related a tragic story of a man who'd fallen off his sit-on lawn mower and finished up dead in a pond, which 'planted the seeds of the conspiracy', explained Charles Kellet, prosecuting. The lovers plotted that Mrs Whybrow would lure her husband into a room for sex after a walk in the garden; Mr Saunders waited in the barn and was to pretend to be a burglar. When Mrs Whybrow took her husband out into the garden, he was attacked; he was tied up with a car towrope, blindfolded and gagged. Mr Saunders led him to the side of their pond, where he heard the sound of an engine and realised it wasn't a burglary – his life was actually in danger. A big struggle then ensued, and he called on his wife to help, but she didn't. Mr Whybrow managed to loosen the rope and the blindfold as he fell into the pond, and he managed to escape the couple.

He arrived at his neighbours drenched and covered in pond weed, and the police were subsequently called. Mr Kellett concluded his case against Mrs Whybrow and Mr Saunders by explaining that the police investigation revealed that the ride-on lawn mower and ear protectors were all at hand in order to 'make it look as if Mr Whybrow had fallen off and been killed in an accidental drowning … the ear muffs would have to be at the scene.'

The loving couple fled. They took the car ferry to France and on to Italy, where, after a week, Mr Saunders telephoned his wife. They returned and were arrested at Folkestone on arrival.

The jury at Norwich Crown Court took about two-and-a-quarter hours to find them guilty of conspiring to murder Mr Whybrow. Mrs Whybrow was jailed for eight years and Dennis Saunders was given a ten-year sentence.

Williams, Dr Ivy
Lady barrister and academic

Ivy Williams was born on 7 September 1877 in Newton Abbot in Devon. Her parents were George and Emma; her father was a solicitor. She had a brother, Winter, who was two years older than her. He had been educated at Corpus Christi in Oxford and became a barrister – he was killed in the Great War.

Early on, Ivy and Winter were educated privately, studying Latin, Greek, Italian and Russian; Ivy was also fluent in French and German. She travelled Europe extensively. In the years before 1920, women weren't admitted to universities, so she studied with the Oxford Home Students; she took a second-class degree in Jurisprudence and then later took a Bachelor of Civil Law degree and was awarded a doctorate. None of this, however, was officially recognised. Academic regulations were to see a reform in 1920, although it sounds as though she had to sit further examinations, but at forty years old she could join the Inner Temple and could train as a barrister.

In May 1922, she was called to the bar. Sir Henry Dickens KC, son of Charles Dickens, was delighted at this move forward. The Law Journal reported the occasion as 'one of the most memorable days in … [the] legal profession'. Dr Ivy Williams had broken through a barrier that had stood for over five centuries.

Dr Williams, as she was now known, didn't practice but went back to her academic work as a tutor and lecturer in law at Oxford, being elected an honorary fellow of St Anne's College, Oxford, in 1956.

Going back to 1922, the 'calling' is a bit of a ceremony and is usually accompanied by a dinner and speeches. Dr Williams was, of course, the centre of attention, but her dress for the evening seemed as important as her achievements. She didn't trouble too much, but, as tradition dictated, she thanked Sir Henry and the Treasurer. It was reported that she'd impressed with her quiet manner.

She spoke of her own and her father's dream that she would become a barrister, but she didn't intend to practice: she was satisfied. She'd paved the way for others.

It was further noted that, as the wine waiters passed among those present, Dr Ivy Williams celebrated with water!

She died in February 1966, aged eighty-eight.

Young, Graham Frederick

Poisoner of his own family and other victims

Graham Frederick Young was a poisoner. He killed three of his victims, but others suffered long-term effects. He was born in Neasdon in North London and has been known as the St Alban's Poisoner and the Teacup Poisoner.

His killing came in two distinct phases: as an adolescent, in 1962, and then again in 1971. The reason for the cessation was his first conviction for murder, when he was sent to Broadmoor. On his release in 1971, he lived with his father and step-mother, to whom he promptly started administering doses of thalium.

After the second lot of slayings, he was sent to Parkhurst Prison on the Isle of Wight. He died there in 1990, and officially it was of natural causes – a myocardial infarction (a heart attack). But was his death natural? His knowledge of poisons was encyclopaedic and if he'd decided to take his own life with something or other, then he might well have fooled the authorities.

Shortly after Mr Young was born his mother died; she'd had pleurisy in pregnancy and a history of tuberculosis. Mr Young went to live with his aunt and uncle, Winnie and Jack, to whom he became very close: he did have a sister, Winifred, who was eight years older, but she went to live with her grandparents. Life settled for the junior members of the family, but his father remarried and once they'd set up their home then Mr Young and his sister went to live with them. There were times when members of the family became violently ill with mainly gastric disorders, which was Mr Young experimenting with various poisons; this was the early 1960s and, although he was only in his early teens, he knew what he was doing.

By fourteen, he was administering antimony to his family, which causes violent gastric upsets (and is also cardiotoxic, which is why there might be some doubt as to his own death). He did have a large reserve of the compound or element, which he bought from pharmacists, claiming they were for school experiments – he'd lie about his age to obtain them.

When all of his family members – his step-mother, his father and his sister, as well as a friend – went down with the mystery illnesses, his aunt Winnie started to wonder. It's hard to entertain the idea that he was deliberately poisoning his relatives, but he chose them as his victims so that he could keep a detailed diary of the effects. On Easter Saturday 1962, Molly, his step-mother, died, and his Aunt Winnie again wondered; she'd known of his fascination with poisons and chemicals. Then she realised that he too suffered the same, or seemingly the same, symptoms as the rest of them. Part of the reason for this may have been that he'd forgotten which of the family foods he'd laced, though this is doubtful, because he was a good record-keeper; perhaps he thought he might escape detection and otherwise cover his tracks if he too had a mild dose of the symptoms.

Either way, he saw a psychiatrist, who was alarmed enough to contact the police. He was arrested, and was quite animated in confessing to the poisoning of his sister, father and his friend at school. However, the charge was attempted murder because his step-mother, whom he'd almost certainly poisoned, was cremated, so any forensic evidence went with her.

After the police investigation uncovered the possibility that there might be a mental illness, Mr Young was assessed by two psychiatrists, who deemed him to be suffering with a personality disorder. He was sent to Broadmoor hospital under the Mental Health Act 1959. There is some suggestion that he was also autistic.

Under the 1959 Mental Health Act, a patient could be detained without limit of time, and it was for the Home Secretary to decide periods of leave, discharge and the like. He was discharged after nine years, deemed as 'fully recovered', but as a personality disorder isn't curable, only manageable, then this raises its own questions. In hospital, he'd studied to improve his knowledge of poisons, so 'fully recovered' were meaningless words written on a piece of paper rather than an assessment of his mental state. It was stated he'd extracted some poison from plants in the grounds with which he murdered another patient, but this was never proved; he also told a member of the nursing staff he would kill a person for every year he'd been in.

Mr Young was discharged from Broadmoor in February 1971 and moved up to the Hertfordshire area, specifically Bovingdon, where he'd been found a job in John Hadland's Laboratories. His new employers were told of his mental health, but not in detail, and his probation officer didn't contact them. By now his sister Winifred had married and settled in Hemel Hempstead, so she wasn't too far away. Also not too far away was London, where he would go to build up his stock of poisons from chemists.

His new colleagues were friendly. Soon after he started, one of them, Bob Egle, became ill with a strange tummy bug, but there'd been a few cases with local school children so the symptoms were written off as a local bug. Bob improved and went back to work, but got ill again. Meanwhile, Mr Young was well settled and showed kindness to his colleagues – he'd often make them tea and coffee. Bob Engle became ill again, and this time things were more severe; he was admitted to hospital and died in severe discomfort on 7 July 1971. The official cause was pneumonia.

Another colleague, Fred Biggs, became the next in a long line of people becoming ill at Hadland's – he was admitted to the National Hospital for Nervous Diseases, where he died after a few weeks of agony.

Finally, alarm bells started to ring. Amazingly, Mr Young asked the company doctor if it was possible Bob Engle and Fred Biggs had died of thallium poisoning; he'd also told other folk that his hobby was toxicity and poisons. The police became involved and someone, somewhere, finally decided to ask about his time in 'hospital'.

He was arrested on 21 November 1971, and in his pocket he had thallium. When his flat was searched, the police found a poisoner's lair and a stock of antimony, thallium and aconitine. There was a chilling diary, detailing doses he'd administered, their effects and a decision about whether his victims should live or die.

His trial commenced in mid-June 1972 at St Albans Crown Court. He faced two counts of murder, two of attempted murder and numerous counts of administering poison. He pleaded not guilty as the notoriety seemed an attraction. He was found guilty and given four life sentences. His defence of the diary was that it was a fantasy for a novel!

Graham Young died in Parkhurst prison on 1 August 1990; myocardial infarction was written on his death certificate. He was only forty-two.

INDEX

Adams, Dr John Bodkin 9–12, 67, 163–4, 210–1, 282

Allitt, Beverley 12–6

Andrews, Ronald 75, 78

Aram, Colette 16–9, 86

Archer, Baron Jeffrey 19–20

Armstrong, Herbert Rowse and Katherine 20–22

Armstrong, Terence and John 22–24

Ashworth, Dawn 179

Ashworth Hospital 100, 167, 273

Astin, Derek 231

Backhouse, Graham 24–7

Bamber, Jeremy and family 28–9

Bank of America, the 29–31

Banks, Shirley 68–71

Barlow, Kenneth and Elizabeth 31–4

Batstone, Cecily 291–3

Beck, Adolf 34–6

Beck, Richard and Elizabeth 55–6

Bedale-Taylor, Colyn 24–7

Bell, Mary Flora 46–9

Bennett, Keith 164–5

Bentley, Derek 126–7, 145, 168–9, 220–2, 261

Bible John 36–8

Bindon, John 39–40

Bingham, Veronica (Lady Lucan) 206–10

Black, Edgar 49–51

Black, Robert 51–3

Blake, George 53–5, 216, 251

Blakely, David 114–7

Birkett, Baron Norman 40–1, 45–6

Bowen, Graham 255–8

Bowyer, Linda 291

Bradley, Perry 173–4

Brady, Ian 164–7

Brett, Terry and George 75–8

Bridgewater, Carl 41–2

Bright, William 251

Brighton Trunk Murders, the 44–6

Brinkley, Richard 55–6

Brinks-Mat Robbery, the 56–7, 130

Broadmoor 191, 281, 286, 291–2, 309–11

Brown, Ernest 244–5

Brown, Martin 46–9

Brown, Robert 75–8

Browne, Derek 57–9

Browne, Frederick Guy 134–7

Bryant, Charlotte Frederick 59–62

Bulger, James Patrick 62–4

Burgess, David 297–8

Burnell, Freda 182–4

Camps, Professor Francis 12, 66–8,

Cannan, John 68-71

Cardy, Jennifer 51–3

Carruthers, Glenis 71–2

Castree, Ronald 189

Chapman, David 73–4

Chester, Peter 74–5

Childs, John 75–8

Cochrane, Kelso 78–80, 194

Coggle, Mary 143–4

Collier, Andrew 173, 175

Collins, Florence 294–7

Collinson, Harry 103–4

Confait, Maxwell 80–1

Connolly, Charles 64–6

Cook, Isabelle 211–3

Cook, Peter (Cambridge Rapist) 81–3

Cooper, John William 83–5

Cornell, George 190, 269

Coster, Herbert 251

Craig, Christopher 220–2

Crimewatch 85–7

Criminal Cases Review Commision, the (CCRC) 29, 66, 90, 181, 262, 280

Crippen, Hawley Harvey 87–90

Cummins, Gordon Frederick (Blackout Ripper) 90–2

Cunningham, Harold 287–90

Dando, Jill 92–4

Darby, Christine 228-31

Davey, James 239–41

Day, Alison 252, 254

Delaney, Robert Augustus 94–6

Denning, Baron Alfred Thompson 96–7, 211

Devlin, Lord Patrick 9–10, 12, 111

Dickens, Sir Henry 153, 308

Dickman, John 98–9

Dix, Glyn 99–101

Dixon, Peter and Gwenda 83–5

Dobkin, Rachel 101–3

Dobson, Gary 194

Donald, William 137–9

Dorn, Albert 236–9

Downey, Leslie Anne 164–7

Dryden, Albert 103–5

Duffy, John 252–5

Dunblane 105–6

Duncan, Amanda 107–8

Dunn, Christopher 173–6

Dunne, Sidney 211–4

Durrand-Deacon, Roberta
  137–9

Edmund-Davies, Baron Herbert
  109–12
Edmeades, Lilian 285–6
Ellis, Peter 112–3
Ellis, Ruth 113–7, 168–9, 261
Evans, Edward 164–7
Evans, Timothy 65, 145
Eve, Terry 75–8

Fabb, April 53, 117–8
Fairley, Malcolm 118–20
Flannelfoot 120–2
Fletcher, WPC Yvonne 123–4
Foster, Evelyn 244–5
Fraser, Frankie 161, 240, 271

Gadd, Paul Francis (Gary Glitter)
  124–6
Gardiner, William 151–4
Gardner, Margery 155–8
George, Barry 92–4
Gillbanks, Donna Marie 74–5
Goddard, Brenda 291–3
Goddard, Lord Rayner 9, 126–8
Goozee, Albert 128–9
Gray, Gilbert 129–31
Grayland, Sidney 231–5
Great Train Robbery, the 131–4
Gregsten, Michael 148–51
Gutteridge, PC George 134–7

Haigh, John George 137–9
Hall, Anthony 139–42

Hall, Archibald (Roy Fontaine)
  143–5
Hall, Donald 143–5
Hall, John and Charles 145–7
Hall, Victoria 108–9
Hamilton, Thomas 105–6
Hanratty, James 148-51
Harland, Alfred 74
Harper, Rose 263
Harper, Susan 51–3
Harsent, Rose 151–4
Hart, Michael 154–5
Heath, Neville 155–8
Henderson, Archibald and Rosalie
  137–9
Hewart, Viscount Gordon
  158–9
Hennessy, Peter 239–41
Hickey, Michael and Vincent
  41–4
Hill, William Charles (Billy)
  159–61, 162, 172
Hindley, Myra 164–7
Hogan, Terry 162–3
Hogg, Caroline 51–2
Holland, Richard (Dick) 188–9
Home Secretary 23, 27, 29, 116,
  125, 127, 188, 214, 249, 255,
  261–2, 292–3, 301, 310
Hoskins, Percival Killick 164–5
Howe, Brian 46–9
Humphries, Christmas 92, 115,
  168–9
Hungerford 169-73
Hutchison, Paul 16-19

Ireland, Colin 173–6

Ishmail, Mohammad   280–2

Jacoby, Henry   304–6
Jeffreys, Professor Sir Alec   176–9
Jenkins, Billie-Jo and Sion
   179–182
Jones, Harold   182–4
Johnson, Malcolm   285–6
Joyce, William Brooke (Lord Haw
   Haw)   185–7

Kaye, Violet   45
Kelly, George   64–6
Kennedy, William   134–7
Kerr, Isabella   273
Kilbride, John   164–7
Kiszko, Stefen   187–9, 261, 285
Kitto, Michael   143–5
Kneilands, Anna   211–4
Kray Twins, The   189–92

Lamplugh, Susannah   192–3
Lawrence, Geoffrey   10
Lawrence, Stephan   193–4
Leakey, Lydia and Norma
   128–9
Leeson, Nicholas William   195–6
Little, Florrie   183–4
Lloyds Bank, Baker Street
   Robbery, the   196–200
Lock, Anne   252–5
Lockerbie   200–4
Lord, Alan. Margaret   204–6
Lucan, Lord (Richard Bingham)
   206–10, 291

Manningham-Buller, Sir Reginald
   9, 23, 210–1
Mancini, Tony   44-6
Manuel, Peter   211–4
Mark, Sir Robert   214–5
Markov, Georgi   215–7
Marshall, Doreen   155–7
Marshall Hall, Sir Edward   41
Mattan, Mahmood Hussain   51
Maxwell, Susan   51–2
Mayes, Roderick, Sean and Joy
   217–9
McFarlane, Michael   280–2
McSwan, William and Amy
   137–8
McVitie, Jack (the Hat)   191
Miles, PC Sydney   220–2
Mitchell, Frank   190–1
Mnilk, Heidi   222–6
Molloy, Pat (DCI later DSupt)
   228–31, 256–7
Molloy, Patrick   41–4
Molseed, Leslie   187–9
Moore, Brian   236–9
Morris, George   280–2
Morris, Raymond   228–31
Morton, Frederick   244–5
Mulcahy, David   252–5

Neilson, Donald (the Black
   Panther)   231–5
Nelson, Rev James   234–6
Norris, David   194
Nuremberg Trials   40

Old Bailey, the   9–10, 35–6, 39,

115, 136, 155, 158, 168, 176, 200, 227, 270
Olive, Clive   236–9
O'Nions, Paddy (Paddy Onions) 239–41
Operation Eagle   241–2
Operation Julie   242–4
Otterburn   244–5
Overbury, Pia   99–100
Owen, Thomas   282–4

Packham, Peter   253–4
Paisnel, Edward (Beast of Jersey) 245–9
Pearman, Natalie   107–9
Peirrepoint, Albert   65, 92, 116, 137, 158
Pickering, Thomas   258–61
Poulson, John   129, 249–51
Pratt, Kelly   107–9
Prison Escapes   251–2
Profumo, John (Jack)   97, 203

Railway Rapists, the   252–5
Randall, Amanda   255–58
Read, Leonard (Nipper)   191
Reade, Pauline   164–7
Regan, Anthony and Florence (O'Rourke) 258–60
Reyn-Bardt, Peter and Malika 266–6
Reynolds, Margaret   228–31
Richardson Brothers, the   240, 268–70
Richardson, Supt Gerry GC 266–68
Rivett, Sandra   206–9

Robertson, Mary Jane   273–5
Robinson, James   41–4
Rosenthal, Daniel, Milton and Leah   270–3
Ruxton, Dr Buck   273–5
Ryan, Michael   169–73

Saunders, Dennis   306–8
Saunders, Ernest (Guinness) 275–6
Saville, Derek   275–79
Scott-Elliot, Walter and Dorothy 143–5
Seston, Jackie   279–80
Sewell, Frederick   266–68
Sheffield Pub Massacre, the 280–2
Sherwood, Frederick   75–8
Shipman, Frederick Harold 2824–3
Silverman, Sidney MP   283–5
Simpson, Professor Keith   22–3, 66, 101–2, 139, 156, 208–9
Sims, Edwin   285–6
Sims, James   254
Skepper, Donald   231–4
Smart, Peter, Doris and Michael 211–4
Smith, David   166
Smith, T Dan   252
Spilsbury Professor Sir Bernard 21, 44–6, 56, 66, 89–91, 286–7
Spiteri, Emmanuel   173–6
Spriggs, John   287–90
Stonehouse, John MP   290–2
Storie, Valerie   148–51
Straffen, John   291–3

Sutcliffe, Peter (Yorkshire Ripper) 293–4

Tamboezer, Maartje 252–5
Taylor, Albert 279–80
Taylor, Jane 228
Thirkettle, George 294–7
Thomas, Helen and Richard 83
Thomas, Jacqueline 139–42
Thompson, Robert 62–4
Tift, Diane 228–9

Venables, Jon 62–4

Waddington, David 188, 285
Waddington, Yolande 297–8
Wallace, Julia and William 159, 299–300

Walker, Peter 173–6
Ward, Stephen 300-2
Watt, Marian, Margaret and Vivienne 211-4
West, Rosemary and Fred 302–4
White, Lady Alice 304–6
Whitehouse, Sylvia 139–42
Whittle, Leslie 231–4
Whybrow, Christopher 306–7
Wigmore, Jeanette 299
Williams, Dr Ivy 307–08
Williams, Jacqueline 297
Wooliscroft, Angela 154
Wright, David 143

Young, Graham 309–12

Also available from Amberley Publishing

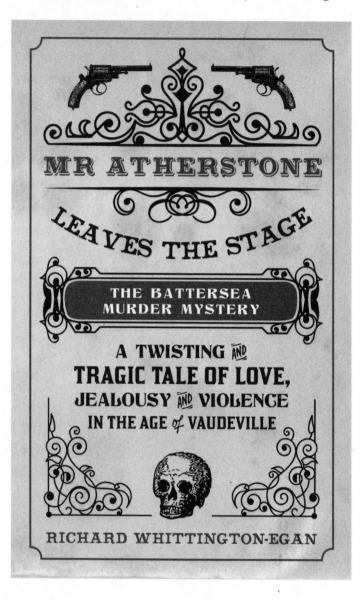

MR ATHERSTONE

LEAVES THE STAGE

THE BATTERSEA
MURDER MYSTERY

A TWISTING AND
TRAGIC TALE OF LOVE,
JEALOUSY AND VIOLENCE
IN THE AGE of VAUDEVILLE

RICHARD WHITTINGTON-EGAN